LOOKING INTO HELL

LOOKING INTO HELL

Experiences of the Bomber Command War

MEL ROLFE

RIGEL

Dedication
To everyone who served in RAF Bomber Command during the
Second World War - in the air and on the ground

Acknowledgements

My grateful thanks go to all Bomber Command aircrews who patiently helped
in the preparation of their stories. Thanks are due, also, to Des Richards, Roland
Hammersley, DFM; Bill McCrea, DFC; and Rob Owen; and to my dear wife
Jessie who provided such an outstanding and comprehensive sub-editing service.

Rigel Publications
A division of the Orion Publishing Group Ltd.
5 Upper St Martin's Lane
London WC2H 9EA

First published by Arms and Armour 1995
Cassell Military Paperbacks edition 2000
This edition published in 2004

British Library Cataloguing-in-Publication Data
A catalogue record for this book is available from the British Library

ISBN 1-898-79980-6

Printed and bound within the European Union

Contents

1

B-BASTARD'S
LAST OPERATION

On the night of 2 November 1944 a vast armada of 992 aeroplanes left England to hit the Krupp armament works at Düsseldorf in the Ruhr Valley, Germany's industrial heartland. They included 561 Lancasters and 400 Halifaxes, accompanied by thirty-one twin-engine Mosquito marker aircraft. A total of 946 four-engine heavy bombers attacked the massive factory on which they unleashed 4,484 tons of bombs.

Nineteen bombers were lost on the raid, including one from 467 (Royal Australian Air Force) Squadron, based at Waddington in Lincolnshire – Lancaster DV396, B-Baker, more commonly known as B-Bastard. This is the story of the last operation of B-Bastard, which had already logged over 400 flying hours at a time when the life expectancy of a Lancaster was reckoned to be no more than twelve trips, while that of an aircrew offered only a one in three chance of survival.

It was a clear dry night as B-Bastard's seven-man crew were driven to dispersal where the big Lancasters waited, grimly silent, the ground crews bustling around them carrying out last-minute checks. The aircrew were quieter than usual as they clambered aboard B-Bastard half-an-hour before take-off, for their target tonight was the big one – The Ruhr – known in the flippant black humour of young aircrews as 'Happy Valley'. The Ruhr was heavily defended by anti-aircraft guns and swift fighter aircraft which could cause havoc among the slow, heavy bombers. Added to the crew's worries was the result of tests which showed that B-Bastard was sluggish, particularly when flown on only three engines.

Yet there was some comfort. B-Bastard was one of nearly 1,000 aircraft heading for Düsseldorf that night, providing safety in numbers and lengthening the odds against anyone getting the chop. The aircrew briefings had reported a full moon, with some cloud cover en route, but little or no cloud over Düsseldorf. Ideal conditions for a raid. Ideal conditions, too, for German anti-aircraft gunners and night fighters seeking to destroy the intruders. This was the ninth operation for six of the crew. Behind them were relatively easy daylight trips across the Channel to hit German gun emplacements on the Dutch island of Walcheren.

The new bod in the crew was Australian rear gunner Flight Sergeant Bill Lemin, recently recovered from a motorcycle accident. He had replaced the old man of the crew, short, round-faced Welshman Bert Davis, thirty-three, who had reported sick. The pilot, a quiet and thoughtful flying officer, Leslie Landridge and his flight engineer, Sergeant Jack Halstead, scrambled through the narrow fuselage which was packed with equipment.

Not built for the comfort or even the safety of its crew, the Lancaster's only piece of armour-plating was behind the pilot's head. The aircraft's role as Britain's premier battleship of the skies was death and destruction on an awesome scale, with its ability to deliver up to 18,000lb of high explosives on the enemy or, with special modifications, one of Barnes Wallis's awesome 22,000lb deep penetration Grand Slam bombs.

First used operationally in March 1942, almost 7,400 Lancasters were eventually built. It had six fuel tanks in the wings, which could hold a maximum 2,154gals of high octane fuel. By taking less petrol, the bomber could carry more bombs. The further away the target, the more fuel was needed, and fewer bombs carried, unless auxiliary fuel tanks were fitted in the fuselage. Some Lancasters were fitted with one or two 400gal tanks in the bomb bays.

In common with most large aircraft, the worst obstruction inside the Lancaster was the huge main spar which held the wings to the fuselage. It was difficult enough to climb over it wearing a flying suit and carrying a parachute, when the aircraft was stationary at dispersal, but when a Lancaster was seriously damaged and diving – possibly in flames, and awash with hydraulic fluid – negotiating the main spar in the dark, wearing a parachute, was like climbing an ice-capped mountain in carpet slippers.

Only one of the crew was older than twenty-one. Had they been born fifty years later, few of them would have been entrusted with taking out the family car. Halstead was the youngest at eighteen and was one of two Englishmen in an otherwise Australian crew. A six-foot well-built Yorkshireman he had worked as a butcher, then in a Wakefield tank factory, in 'Civvy Street'.

As the pilot strapped himself into his seat, the second Englishman, Derrick Allen, placed his parachute beside the step leading to his mid-upper turret. Neither gunner had room to wear a chest-type parachute in the cramped turrets while operating their Browning machine-guns. After tipping down his seat and getting comfortable, Allen adjusted around his neck a white silk scarf, the lucky mascot from his girlfriend which he wore on all flights. He had left his trade of carpenter and joiner two years ago at eighteen to be a flier – and escape the waspish tongue of his unpleasant stepmother. Before take-off he would murmur a short prayer to himself and, probably like the others, privately wish he was anywhere but in a bomber on its way to Germany and possible death. But that was something none of them ever talked about.

Halstead sat on the right of the pilot. He only sat down before and towards the end of an operation. The engineer's seat was in an impossible position for keeping an eye on the banks of gauges and instruments. A Lancaster flight engineer usually spent every trip standing. Halstead was no exception.

Behind them, in a small curtained-off cubicle, was the navigator, Flight Sergeant Doug Beverley, prematurely grey and, at twenty-three, the oldest member of the crew, who had already survived an escape from a crippled aircraft. Beverley was assisted in his task by the navigational and blind-bombing aids H2S and Gee. With his Gee box, the navigator could fix the bomber's position to between about one and five miles.

The lanky wireless operator was Flight Sergeant Bill Denny, later to marry a Scots girl. A devout Christian, he had already wiped from his mind the recent lively but good-natured arguments in the sergeants' mess about God, with Beverley, an atheist. Denny sat in front of his T1154/R1155 transmitter/receiver sets and switched on the intercom.

In the nose of the Lancaster, the Australian bomb-aimer, thick-set Flight Sergeant Keith Woollams, settled at his position.

As the time drew near for take-off, ground crew removed the covers which protected the tyres from engine oil. The trolley accumulator was wheeled into position and plugged in beneath the bomber to conserve its batteries during start-up. Then the four cold 1,640hp Rolls-Royce Merlin engines were started in sequence. One by one they coughed into life, building up to a roaring crescendo. Pilot and engineer then began to go through their interminable list of pre-flight checks: altimeter, pressures and temperatures, oxygen regulator, DR compass – set to magnetic, bomb doors – closed – and dozens more.

The checks continued as the Lancaster lumbered forward on the perimeter track, its four bellowing engines gulping down fuel so greedily that by the time it reached the end of the runway the bomber had already consumed 50gals of precious fuel. Occasionally a bowser waited to replenish the Lancasters' fuel tanks, but not tonight. Noise and fumes from Lancaster engines drifted across the airfield where knots of ground crews and others gathered to see the aircraft leave.

B-Bastard's crew waited impatiently for a green light to flash the take-off signal from the top of the controller's caravan, situated at the end of the Waddington runway. The Lancaster in front of them, weighing nearly thirty tons, completed its take-off run and lifted into the night sky, while the bombers that followed in its wake took off approximately every two minutes. Any delays in this sequence built up layers of nervousness in the aircrews, but these were soon dispelled when they left the ground and slipped into a busy routine.

Twenty feet above ground, the pilot sat tensely in the cramped cockpit running-up the engines against the brakes, building up the power, observing strict radio silence. The green light beamed out, Landridge released the wheelbrakes to send the Lancaster, carrying fourteen 1,000lb bombs, surging forward down the runway. Full power, take-off boost, 3,000rpm, the superchargers gave manifold pressures of 14lb/sq in.

Halstead, anxious not to be sick as he had been on earlier flights, called out the air speed as Landridge concentrated on keeping B-Bastard straight – 90, 95, 100, 105, 110... As the Merlin engines roared almost to their limit, the engineer took over the throttles because the pilot needed all his strength to pull on the control column for take-off. Halstead held the throttles wide open against the stops and the end of the runway flashed by below.

Undercarriage up. Engine failure now would be disastrous. Air speed was 130kts. B-Bastard climbed slowly to 300ft. Flaps up. Each of the crew spared a moment to glance fondly at the countryside dropping away into the darkness, already looking forward to their return in the morning.

That night thirty Lancasters left Waddington, the total shared equally between resident 463 and 467 Squadrons. Their navigation lights were turned off as they cleared the circuit. Each movement was plotted fastidiously in Waddington's control tower. The bombers gained height over crouching, blacked-out Lincolnshire, and headed for the rendezvous above Reading before pouring into a long thundering predatory stream over the Channel, at which point B-Bastard levelled off at 17,000ft.

The well-disciplined crew got on with their jobs. Woollams, lying on his stomach in the nose, calmly called out landmarks to the navigator – a church here, a railway line there, information which helped Beverley provide his pilot with an up-to-date fix. Halstead anxiously watched the numerous dials and warning lights for falling oil pressure, fuel consumption, overheating, or any fault in the electrical system, while snatching glances into the night sky for signs of marauding German fighters. Landridge concentrated on maintaining course and height. The wireless operator checked wind pressures and got fixes from base to pass on to the navigator, who checked they were on the right course, and gave the pilot regular compass readings.

Both gunners watched for beacons, other bombers converging on them and later, flak and fighters. Allen spent a little time calculating the weight of the Lancaster and the fuel, to keep his mind active. The cold might easily retard reactions to a crisis. Despite electrically-heated suits and gloves, bitter cold infiltrated both gun turrets. Allen experienced six-inch long icicles hanging from his oxygen mask on this trip, with frost clinging to his eyebrows. Occasionally, ice which had formed on the propellers rattled disconcertingly against the fuselage like bullets.

There was no gun turret in a Lancaster's underbelly, which made it vulnerable to night fighters attacking from beneath. It was not easy for the crew to detect fighters attacking from below, but continual side-to-side banking of the aircraft widened their range of vision.

The bomber stream flowed over the French city of Strasbourg, then turned in a dog-leg north into Germany, hopefully having deceived the enemy of their intended target. The tension increased. Woollams set his bomb-sight with the wind speed direction given him by the navigator, then checked the bomb selector switches. The bombs would drop in sequence, thereby maintaining the trim of the Lancaster. Allen gave his scarf a stroke. So far so good.

Medium to heavy flak was exploding all round them now. Shrapnel slapped harmlessly against B-Bastard. Shells needed to explode within about 30ft of an aircraft to have any damaging effect. They also saw what were either bombers being shot down or 'scarecrow' shells, believed to be a German invention which simulated exploding aircraft. In fact, 'scarecrow' shells were a myth which softened the horror experienced by aircrews seeing their own bombers explode while sharpening their alertness.

The burning city of Düsseldorf was visible from many miles away. The flak became more intense and they heard the 'kerumph' of exploding flak shells. The Mosquitoes had flitted low over the city, identifying the target, putting down green and yellow markers, before calling in Lancaster pathfinders to drop more coloured flares round it. The flares were all timed to be in position before the first bombers loomed into view.

As B-Bastard approached the target area at 17,000ft they saw diversionary targets being marked by the Mosquitoes. Every enemy fighter lured away meant fewer problems for the bombers. Halstead recalled the moment: 'This was when you had to have eyes in the back of your head. Hundreds of bombers were passing over the target in limited time. Beforehand, we could bank and search. On the bombing run we had to maintain our height, course and speed, making us a sitting duck for flak and German fighters. On this occasion there was little or no flak over the target which suggested there were fighters about.'

Allen had a clear view over the side of the Lancaster from his perspex bubble. 'It was like looking into Hell. I could have read a newspaper from the night fighter flares.'

The bomb doors were opened. The bomb-aimer, still on his stomach, watched eagerly for the target markers. The whole crew was taut and apprehensive. Waiting. Waiting. Then 'left... left... steady... steady...' and six-and-a-quarter tons of bombs dropped on to a target already ablaze, and onto an unknown number of Germans lying dead and maimed.

B-Bastard reared up as it was relieved of the bomb load, while the pilot struggled to maintain the same level course for the photo flares to drop and the aircraft's automatic camera to take their aiming point photographs of the target, thus ensuring a crew did not dump their bombs just anywhere. Woollams checked the selector switches and reported no hung-up bombs.

The Lancaster banked away from the inferno and a direct course was set for home. It was a little after 00.30 on the morning of 3 November 1944. There were sighs of relief. The worst part was over, but they must remain alert for the long flight back to Waddington.

Minutes later the Lancaster was pinned against the velvet sky by a radar-controlled searchlight. It was a desperate moment. If they were unlucky, other searchlights would lock on to them, passing the Lancaster from one light to another, while the gunners below had a field day and the fighters above homed in eagerly on the illuminated bomber.

Landridge threw the bomber into a diving corkscrew. Halstead recalls vividly his own feelings: 'Your heart is beating faster and your mind takes off during a corkscrew. One minute you feel as if you are going through the roof, and the next it feels as if your feet are going through the floor.'

As B-Bastard escaped the searchlight's glare, plunging into the murky cosiness of night, they all risked a fleeting thought of Waddington and a warm bed. Then a cry of alarm from Bill Lemin in the rear gun turret: 'Do something, skipper! Do something! Dive to port!'

The pilot flung the aircraft into another thundering dive, but it was too late. Lemin had seen the shadowy streak of a German fighter hurtling towards them below after its pilot had glimpsed the bomber's tell-tale exhausts. A rapid burst of cannon fire from the Focke-Wulf FW190 raked the Lancaster's unprotected belly. Lemin heard and felt the explosion beneath him as the bomber shuddered. Puffs of dark smoke erupted from the port outer engine, which burst into flames.

Halstead, standing beside the pilot, feathered the damaged engine, but flames continued to pour out of it. An FW190, probably the same fighter, appeared like an executioner over the port quarter to finish them off. The scream of the fighter's single engine rose above the Lancaster's remaining three throbbing Merlins.   Lemin and Allen answered the German's more powerful cannon fire with their own .303in Browning machine-guns. There were four in the rear turret. Allen had two. Their range was 600yds. A fighter shell struck the port tail fin. Allen watched the 12ft-high fin go spinning into space as the FW190 disappeared, satisfied with a good night's work. Lemin thought they had scored a hit on the fighter, but could not be sure. The Lancaster began wallowing.

Halstead again: 'Over the target we had been keyed-up and excited. Fear crept in when we were attacked by the fighter. When the aircraft caught fire it was almost panic stations. Then, suddenly, the panic was gone and we were fighting the blaze. We were unable to get the fire under control, either by feathering the prop or using the built-in extinguisher.' The pilot tried to put out the flames by diving, but instead of being snuffed out they spread more rapidly and became a raging inferno.

'Captain to crew. Captain to crew.' Cool as a cucumber and according to the book, 'Prepare to abandon aircraft.' The navigator gave the skipper a fix 60 miles south-west of Aachen, in Belgium. The intercom became alive with chatter: the pilot ordering the crew to bale out and the rear gunner, a bit panicky, reporting he was trapped in his turret. The hydraulic system had been damaged and Lemin could not operate the turret's traversing mechanism by hand. As the bomb-aimer, flight engineer, wireless operator and navigator left in that order from the nose, the pilot told Allen to get the rear gunner out and report back on intercom when Lemin was free.

When Landridge had given the order to abandon aircraft, Halstead turned around to feel for his parachute, but someone else had claimed it. There was a moment bordering on outrage and fiasco before the flight engineer finally found his 'chute and clipped it on. Halstead made sure he wore a parachute on his next twenty operations, from the moment they crossed the enemy coast to the moment they left it again to return home. Before now it had been an encumbrance, never worn, never needed. Now he realised it really was the difference between life and death.

As Halstead left the flight deck, the pilot asked the navigator for a fix. The bomb-aimer had already made his escape when the engineer hurried into the nose cone. Halstead recalls: 'There was no time for thought when I launched myself into space. Then, as I floated down, I thanked God for being alive. As I continued to float, I wondered if I'd be hanging about up there for ever. I couldn't see the ground. I couldn't see my feet. I also remembered the navigator, Doug Beverley, owed me for a film I'd had developed. I never did get the money for that film.'

Halstead landed safely in a field. A thin layer of snow covered the ground. A dog was barking. Self-preservation suddenly became more important than hiding the parachute. He left it lying in the snow and fled into a pine forest. The barking faded, but he continued to walk quickly and stumbled across a massive stockpile of fuel cans, thousands of them. It was impossible to move silently among dead leaves, which crunched noisily underfoot, so he decided that rather than risk being surprised by the enemy, he would settle under a tree for the rest of the night, dragging dead branches and twigs over himself for concealment.

A frosty dawn found Halstead on a hill at the edge of the forest, overlooking a deep attractive valley. Parked on a distant road was a German staff car. He later learned it had been captured by the Allies. He needed to find out where he was and searched in vain through his clothes for the escape kit of silk map, compass and paper money. It had probably been lost when he baled out.

He wondered which way to go then heard the sound of engines overhead. He saw dozens of Doodlebugs (V1 flying bombs) and, assuming they were heading towards Britain, Halstead followed their direction of flight. He breakfasted on swedes taken from a field and walked all morning, keeping to hedgerows, until early that afternoon he heard farmers speaking French. One of them took Halstead to an old stone farmhouse and gave him a plateful of warmed-up potatoes and a fried egg, which he wolfed down hungrily with a glass of milk, before falling asleep, exhausted, in front of a woodburning stove.

Satisfied his visitor was dead to the world, the farmer sent a girl to a nearby American unit with the message that he had captured a German spy. The engineer might have been anyone. He had deliberately removed his stripes and RAF badges during his long walk across the fields.

Halstead awoke, alarmed to find himself covered by a grim-faced soldier pointing a rifle through a window. Another was levelled at him from the door. Then he noticed the distinctive American helmets and bluntly told the GIs what to do with their rifles. Halstead was fed before being passed on to a Canadian unit, which put him in touch with the British Royal Engineers, who had a whip round for him to have several nights out in the Belgian town of Spa. He was flown back to England in a Dakota a few days later and given a month's leave, before resuming operations at Waddington.

It was only when mid-upper gunner Derrick Allen left his turret that he realised the extent of the damage to the Lancaster. A massive hole had been torn in the floor of the fuselage. Allen suddenly realised his luck was in. His legs had not been smashed to pulp by the fighter's cannon shell, and his parachute had not disappeared through the hole. He quickly clipped on the 'chute, sparing a second to touch his lucky scarf before plunging, stooped and anxious, towards the tail, unlatching the rear door on the way before grabbing the axe stowed at the side of the fuselage. He used it to lever open the rear gunner's sliding doors as the pilot, wrestling with the controls of the burning aircraft, waited for the word over the intercom. It never came.

Lemin, trembling with relief, dropped from his turret and went back along the fuselage, his parachute clipped on. He followed Allen who was hurrying to plug into an intercom point and tell his skipper he could leave the aircraft, but time had run out. It is often precious seconds and lady luck that determine who lives and who dies in war.

The stricken Lancaster, both port engines now blazing, began spiralling to earth, flinging Allen and Lemin to the sides of the fuselage where they were pinned by the G-force, unable to scramble three feet to the open rear door, through which an icy wind was whistling. Allen wanted to scream out that they must drag themselves to the door, but the words stuck in his throat. Terror-stricken, helpless as flies stuck in a pot of glue, they stared at each other and waited for oblivion.

Then, with a hideous screech of tearing metal, the aircraft broke in two, emptying the men into the cold night air less than 1,000ft from the ground. Allen recalls: 'The last thing I remember is floating face-down, as if in a tunnel, watching a large dark mass of earth and trees coming up at me. I know my parachute opened because I got a black eye when the chest harness came up and hit me.'

Allen was semi-conscious when the parachute caught in the branches of a tree. His ears had been blocked up by the roar of the Lancaster's engines and the sudden descent. Now all was quiet. He dangled from the tree and thought he was in Heaven. It was a sort of heaven, although it was some time before Allen knew he had landed near Spa, behind the American lines.

When Allen came to his senses, his ears popped and unblocked. He worked his way to the trunk of the tree, released the parachute and shinned to the ground. His luck had held. He had landed in the last tree on the edge of a forest. The tree had broken his fall. If his parachute had carried him another yard, he would have been killed. Instead, he had only sustained a few bruises.

Bill Lemin missed the forest by a few yards and was killed. The sensitive Belgians later erected a rectangular memorial around the deep indentation made by the rear gunner's body when it struck the ground. The dead pilot was found nearby.

Allen heard the roar of the burning Lancaster in the next field. Bullets inside it were going off and he remembered the drill: get away from a crashed aircraft as quickly as possible. He looked at his watch. It was about 2.00am and bright moonlight. Allen was suddenly surrounded by a herd of inquisitive cattle. They jostled and scared him, and he thought of the ignominy of escaping a burning bomber only to be trampled to death by panicking cattle.

A farmer saw B–Bastard crash. He watched from the farmhouse as the mid-upper gunner scrambled down the tree and ran across a field, followed by the cattle, only just managing to leap over a gate ahead of them. Allen found a potting shed next to a bungalow and sat in the back of it, drained and frightened, trying to pull himself together. He heard shouting and barking dogs and from the euphoria of escape he was plunged into deep gloom. He did not expect to see his father again and steeled himself for a squad of vengeful Germans bursting into the shed with guns or knives.

Then he plucked up courage to see if he might escape across the fields. It was in the shadows of the garden where he heard loud American voices. He found a big American soldier leaning placidly over a gate watching the fiercely burning Lancaster. A Jeep stood nearby. Allen was taken to an American medical centre in Spa and reunited with Beverley, Denny and Woollams. They were flown back to England and soon after, the Australians were returned home to their own country.

Allen was awarded the Conspicuous Gallantry Medal (CGM) for 'outstanding gallantry in the face of extreme danger' in recognition of his night's work. He went on to complete another ten ops.

Although they both joined new crews at Waddington, Allen and Halstead did not meet again after B–Bastard's last op for another forty years. Allen returned to his job as a carpenter and joiner in Civvy Street. Halstead became a detective at Scotland Yard.

2

DICING WITH DEATH
OVER PEENEMÜNDE

On the moonlit night of 17/18 August 1943, 596 RAF bombers poured across the North Sea and headed over Denmark for the Baltic coast to attack a small, remote fishing village in eastern Germany. The village was Peenemünde where, since 1937, the Germans had been secretly developing their V2 rocket weapons. Hitler had lavished money on the experimental establishment, for it was his belief that rockets armed with warheads of high explosives could destroy London and bring Britain to her knees.

Although the 400mph V1 flying bomb was vulnerable to attack by fighters and anti-aircraft guns, there was no defence against the V2. With a range of about 200 miles it travelled at a maximum speed of 3,600mph before dropping out of the sky without warning, bringing terror and destruction. Both the V1 and V2 were Hitler's *Vergeltungswaffen* ('Revenge Weapons').

When British intelligence confirmed that rockets were being developed at Peenemünde, their threat became chillingly clear. The War Cabinet ordered that the site must be attacked. It was the only time in the latter half of the war when all of Bomber Command's might was concentrated on the precision bombing of one small target.

Lancaster ED545, F-Freddie, of 467 (RAAF) Squadron, based at Bottesford, Leicestershire, was among the 560 bombers which eventually reached Peenemünde to drop nearly 1,800 tons of bombs on the target. Ten Lancasters from 467 Squadron flew on this operation: nine bombed the target, two aircraft did not return to base. Ten aircrew were killed, five became prisoners of war.

Although the aircrew belonged to an Australian squadron, only two of them came from the Antipodes. One was the pilot, Warrant Officer Warren 'Pluto' Wilson, from New South Wales, who received his nickname during a long, wearisome sea journey to Britain, when he gleefully won most of his opponents' money at cards. He became known as 'the filthy plutocrat', later shortened to Pluto. Slightly built, he was an endearingly friendly character, usually dishevelled in appearance, a typically irreverent Aussie, with an acute sense of humour. Beer sharpened rather than blunted his flying skills. His crew believed he flew like an angel when he had a pint or two inside him. Aircrews were supposed to stay on station before an op, but there were opportunities for sneaking off. Stone cold sober, Wilson occasionally bounced the bomber on the runway when returning from an operation or training flight.

The other Australian was Flight Lieutenant 'Swill' Campbell, the bomb-aimer. Campbell was one of several substitute bomb-aimers – 'spare bods' – to fly with the crew after their regular, Sergeant Adam Harbottle, sustained back injuries, in an unfortunate accident on the perimeter track at Bottesford, which brought a temporary halt to his flying career. The crew were being given a lift from dispersal to the crewroom by a pretty WAAF driver after a training flight when the small Hillman van, in which they were crammed, suddenly overturned. It was popularly believed the WAAF's driving had gone to pieces after being startled by a hand making a perfect three-point landing on her knee and taxiing purposefully towards the hangar.

The navigator was West Countryman Pilot Officer Harry Crumplin, a broad, handsome six-footer, shy and reticent, but thorough and competent, the oldest member of the crew.

The flight engineer was a lively, cheerful lad from Dalston, East London, Sergeant Charlie Cawthorne aged nineteen, whose RAF career began in 1939 as a Halton apprentice. Pluto Wilson occasionally joined Cawthorne, a builder's son, at his London home, promptly nicknaming the engineer's mother 'Queen Victoria' because she was staid in her ways, didn't like drinking, smoking and swearing, while the pilot was a master of all three. Cawthorne recalls: 'Despite their different views on life, mother loved him and for many years spoke so affectionately about the Australian who liked to have all his meals as a sandwich.'

Wireless operator Dave 'Bing' Booth, an outgoing young man from Manchester who thought he could sing a bit, enjoyed wisecracking and clowning around during training flights, but respected the need for sobriety during a bombing trip when there was no place for flippant smart-arse remarks.

The mid-upper gunner was Sergeant George Oliver. The rest of the crew saw little of the suave, smartly dressed gunner during their spare time because he went home to his wife in Nottingham.

Sergeant Patrick Barry, the jovial rear gunner, could easily have avoided being involved in the war. Born in the city of Cork in the Irish Republic, he had moved at the age of seventeen to work with his foreman joiner father in South Wales, building munitions factories. He could have remained in South Wales or returned to Ireland, but he joined the RAF in 1941 at the age of twenty-two because he believed it was time to knuckle down with other young men in fighting Nazi Germany.

Stockily built at 5ft 5in, the pilot called him 'Five-By-Five', after a popular song of the day. Strictly teetotal throughout the war, he didn't go out with the others much, preferring instead to visit a theatre or chase girls. There was little to do at Bottesford, apart from the camp cinema and most aircrews drifted into Nottingham for a good night out.

It seemed extraordinary to Barry that he faced death nightly with a bunch of fine fellows who were all pals together, yet they knew so little about each other's background:

'At Bottesford, we lived in the quiet heart of the countryside. One day you'd be ambling through the fields with a WAAF on your arm and the next night you'd be dicing with death over Germany. We bombed a few easy targets, but a single successful trip to anywhere like the Ruhr Valley was an achievement for any aircrew. We went several times to the Ruhr, which was very heavily defended. This was the situation. This was why we got leave every six weeks. And then, of course, we went to Peenemünde.'

As a rear gunner, Barry always considered himself in a privileged position. 'My fellow crew members had to fly into the target. They flew into the gunfire and searchlights, whereas when I saw the target, we were on our way home. I suppose I felt safe there at the back of the aeroplane.' He flew once in the mid-upper position during a training flight and felt naked and exposed. 'I was more a part of the plane in the tail, as much as I was separated from the others.'

The crew were plunged into weeks of intense flying, particularly to the Ruhr. Flight engineer Charlie Cawthorne remembers:

'In one 48 hour period, we flew a test flight in the morning, did a bombing sortie that night of over nine hours, had a quick sleep, carried out another test flight next morning, then went on another seven hour-plus bombing trip that same night. As we progressed through our tour, we became very proud of the number of kangaroos we had painted on the side of our aircraft. Each kangaroo represented one bombing trip.'

In the days leading up to the Peenemünde raid, the crews of 467 Squadron received special training, but were not given any information about the target. Training included low-level bombing and what was referred to as time and distance bombing. This involved reaching a series of clearly identifiable landmarks during a straight run to the target. Cawthorne again:

'Rumours abounded. Little did we know that we were to undertake the first major low-level bombing raid in full moon conditions, involving over 500 aircraft.

'At briefing, the target was revealed as being Peenemünde in the Baltic. Nobody had heard of it and we all thought it strange because all our other targets had been major ones in Germany and Italy. We soon realised the importance of bombing the rocket research establishment and were told in no uncertain terms at briefing that the target had to be destroyed. That is why we were going during the full moon period and bombing at comparatively low level.'

After briefing, the two gunners made sure their Browning machine guns were in good order and properly aligned. Barry was always particular about gun alignment after Oliver shot the top off the rear turret during a flight. Barry recalls: 'There was a fairing and arrangements that were supposed to prevent this sort of thing. But on this occasion

George shot the top off and ruffled my helmet. If it had been half an inch or so lower, it would have ripped into my skull.'

The Lancasters stood at dispersal, their engines silent, when the pilot's anxious voice was heard over the intercom. 'Are you bombed up, Pat?' The rear gunner's reply never varied. 'Bombed-up, skipper.' Barry grinned to himself. He took a small missile on every trip to fling through the clear vision slit in the perspex after the bomber had left the target. It might be a big stone or half a brick. Once he found a long metal cylinder on the airfield. It was about 2in in diameter and 15in long, perforated with holes. He filled it with pebbles and crushed the ends. He often wondered later what effect his secret weapon had made on the cowering enemy population as it went whistling down towards them.

Barry and Oliver briskly tested their guns over the North Sea then settled down to rotating their turrets, continually searching the sky for fighters. Barry comments:

'You had to be alert, completely occupied with the job in hand, continuously interpreting everything you saw. If you let your mind wander, you could easily have dozed off. That could have been fatal.

'We didn't think Peenemünde would be heavily defended. It was an isolated and little-known target, even though we knew later the work going on there was vital for Germany. As far as we knew, it was important enough for us to be sent there to destroy it. We were not aware of the exact nature of the target until the publicity afterwards. For us that night, it was just another target.'

Cawthorne remembers: 'Our outward journey was completely uneventful with what appeared to be hordes of aircraft wending their way across the North Sea. The sky was very light and that was why we thought there were so many aircraft. Normally only the occasional aircraft was seen through the darkness in which we operated. I saw the moon reflected on the waters of the Baltic. The numerous islands scattered around the area of Peenemünde were most clearly outlined against the silver water of the Baltic. Quite soon, Harry Crumplin, the navigator, said we should be coming up to a specific island which the bomb-aimer should identify. From there we would carry out a time and distance run in order to drop our fourteen 1,000lb high explosive bombs on the target, which was becoming obliterated by smoke.'

Barry again: 'I saw tracer fire. Everything is happening so quickly, and there is so much of it. You are speeding in and out of the target. You don't have enough time to dwell on and absorb all those fleeting images. If you eventually get a picture of it in your mind, it becomes muddled. You are occupied with the events of the moment. You don't enter into conjecture about the future or the past. There's so much happening, so much going on around you. You don't relate to anything else. In a normal situation, you plan your future. You know where you are going to go next week, next month. You can arrange holidays and trips to a theatre. We weren't in that situation at all.'

The German gunners were getting the range of the invading bombers when Pluto Wilson's Lancaster appeared in a late wave at 6,000ft. They experienced only light flak around the target. Several German fighters had been lured to a diversionary raid on Berlin by eight Mosquitoes.

Cawthorne looked through the perspex blister on the starboard side of the cockpit and saw the target area covered by fire, smoke, exploding bombs and masses of incendiaries. They released their own bombs and incendiaries on to the experimental works at Peenemünde. Other bombers hit the V2 rocket factory and workers' living quarters. Barry flipped his own small bomb, a brick, out into the night, and enjoyed the brief satisfaction of imagining the damage it might cause below. Everyone aboard was convinced the target had been obliterated and Pluto Wilson set course for home.

A pack of German night fighters pounced within minutes of them leaving the target area. Measured withdrawal became pandemonium as the fighters ran amok. Cawthorne saw a barrage of tracer tear open the sky as British and German aircraft fought to the death. Several bombers went down in flames.

Suddenly machine-gun bullets clattered into their own aircraft, and cannon shells ripped into the Lancaster's underbelly. Barry gasped as pain tore savagely through his legs. He shot instinctively at the dark shadow of a fleeing Messerschmitt Bf109. Oliver, in the mid-upper turret, who also fired off a burst at the 109, saw flames licking through the fighter, which fell out of sight in a twisting, blazing wreckage. Barry remembers the event vividly:

'We had just turned from the target at 1.00am when the fighter came up underneath and from behind. It was an explosive and confused situation. It happened so quickly and so drastically. Cannon fire ripped in from the 109. There was an explosion inside the bomber. The fighter came up, exposing his belly and I got a burst in before my hydraulics were destroyed and the turret was immobilised. Everything went haywire. The ammunition started exploding in the ducts, the damned aircraft was on fire and in a mad, screaming dive at a sharp angle. It was, I thought, a death dive.'

The pilot had not deliberately put the bomber into a dive to flee the fighters. In fact the flying control trimming tabs had been damaged, sending the Lancaster plunging out of the sky. Cawthorne, the engineer, helped him pull back the stick and they managed to get the aircraft level again.

The perspex was shattered in the rear turret, which hung askew, open to the sky, and the injured gunner was unable to manually open the doors. He later discovered that his parachute had been shot to ribbons and burned. Barry was in agony. Shrapnel and shards of perspex had peppered and perforated his face and forehead, even sneaking under the flying helmet to do more damage, while blood poured from a terrible wound in his right ankle. A fire raged in the fuselage, immediately behind his turret, but the smashed perspex had at least given him air to breathe. 'I had a feeling of rebellion and revulsion of what seemed inevitable. Then a feeling of calm acceptance washed over me. It was extraordinary. I have never since experienced anything like it. But it was a unique situation. I sat there, completely relaxed, waiting to die.'

He had not reckoned on the skills of the pilot who, with Cawthorne, had hauled the aircraft out of its plunge. Oliver scrambled from his mid-upper turret, took one look at the wall of fire raging in the rear of the fuselage and decided it was time to bale out. He snatched up his parachute, clambered through the smoke forward to the cockpit, reached wireless operator Bing Booth and gestured behind him at the fire. Oliver, on his twenty-third operation, suddenly wanted very much to be spared for his twenty-fourth. Booth grabbed his parachute and began leading the way to the escape hatch in the nose. Navigator Harry Crumplin followed them and the three appeared like a worried deputation behind the pilot who, having just prevented the Lancaster from diving into the ground, was understandably feeling pretty pleased with himself.

'We're on fire skipper,' Oliver said anxiously, pointing back down the fuselage. He made no secret of his belief that they must quickly bale out or be blown to pieces in the inevitable explosion. Wilson frowned, as if the decision to abandon the aircraft was one which had never occurred to him. Barry had already explained over the intercom that he was wounded, the turret was useless, there were explosions in the ducts, and he needed assistance. Wilson had assured the gunner that he would send the others to dig him out. The young Irishman was still keeping a look-out for enemy aircraft, despite extreme pain. Flight engineer Charlie Cawthorne had already reported the fire to Wilson and explained the gravity of the situation. Wilson, now back in control of the Lancaster which he claimed was behaving normally, said, sharply: 'Well, go and put the bloody fire out!'

Barry, sinking into and out of consciousness does not remember struggling to stay awake and reporting the sightings of fighters in a hoarse, halting voice to his skipper. He did not even know at this time if the intercom was still working.

Cawthorne and Oliver, armed with fire extinguishers, forced their way into the choking black smoke erupting from the burning hydraulic fluid at the rear of the Lancaster, where .303in bullets were still exploding, causing a raging fire. They were quickly joined by Booth. There was no time to think of the extreme danger they were in. They no longer even thought of baling out. Their skipper had told them the bomber could be flown back to England, and they trusted his judgement, but first they had to put out the fire. Coughing and spluttering, the men worked hurriedly and in relays because of the thick smoke and confined space.

Cawthorne describes their desperate task: 'We used fire extinguishers and damped down the flames with our gloved hands. We soon extinguished the blaze, but it was difficult to stand in the fuselage due to the amount of oil sprayed in the area after a cannon shell had hit the "dead man's handle". This is a device which enabled the rear turret to be rotated if the gunner was disabled.'

It seemed very likely to the tired fire-fighters that the turret had become a tomb for a dead rear gunner, but Oliver hacked open the jammed doors with an axe and they eased Barry, still alive, but semi-conscious, into the murky fuselage. Barry was not aware the others were coming to get him until he heard the axe crashing into the turret doors. 'I couldn't smell the smoke,' he recalls. 'I haven't got a sense of smell. The fumes were bad, if they had not arrived when they did, I would have been burned to a crisp. They chopped me out, carried me through the fuselage, laid me on the rest bed and patched me up as best as they could. I was in dire agony with a big hole in my right foot, and low in spirits.'

The bomb-aimer, Swill Campbell, and Cawthorne cut away Barry's clothing and blood-soaked flying boots, inadvertently cutting into the gunner's flesh in the initial panic, but in time morphine was injected into him and he settled down for the journey home.

They had lost a lot of fuel from a leaking tank and a diversion to Sweden was contemplated until they realised they had enough to get home. The aircraft made life difficult for the pilot, wanting to climb because of trim tab failure. Wilson wedged himself against the back of his seat and with outstretched arms managed to prevent the control column easing back. He could not maintain this position indefinitely, so his Mae West, and Cawthorne's, were inflated and jammed between the control column and Wilson's seat to ease the strain on his arms. Once they had crossed the enemy coast Cawthorne gave the pilot a rest by flying part of the way across the North Sea.

Barry again: 'The boys wanted to flop into the first airfield. I wanted to get home to Bottesford. They felt we should make an emergency landing as soon as we crossed the British coast. I didn't think it was necessary, although I wasn't in any position to judge. I travelled home in a haze.'

Everyone came to see Barry with words of encouragement, patting him on the shoulder, reporting that they had just crossed the coast and would soon be safely home. 'We seemed to cross an awful lot of coasts on the way back that night, but of course we did cross the east and west coasts of Denmark and England's east coast.'

The Lancaster limped across Germany, the Danish coasts and the North Sea to England, just maintaining its height, luckily not pestered by flak or more fighters. When they approached Bottesford, Oliver, Booth and Crumplin sat tight in the rear of the fire-scarred fuselage as ballast. With the tail unit damaged, the tailplane tended to lift.

All pilots based at Bottesford looked hopefully for the slim spire of St Mary the Virgin parish church, which topped 210ft and was directly in line with the main runway. Wilson sighed with unconcealed relief as he saw the welcoming red light on top of the tallest village spire in the country. They were given priority landing. Cawthorne relates:

22

'On the final approach it is normal for the flaps to be selected fully extended, which I was quite prepared to do but Pluto quickly reminded me of an Australian pilot who had sustained damage to the rear of his aircraft a few nights previously. The pilot had selected full flap and his tail immediately broke off. The aircraft crashed and burned. There were no survivors. Pluto's decision probably saved us from serious trouble because our rear fuselage, together with the tail unit, elevators and trim tabs, had been severely damaged.'

Their Lancaster landed safely on the main runway but was so badly damaged that it was later dismantled and returned to Avro for rebuilding. One reason for celebration was the crew's discovery later that the aircraft's flash photograph had given them an aiming point – they had hit the target.

It was difficult to manoeuvre Barry on his stretcher out of the Lancaster. Excruciating pain flared as the stretcher was wriggled through the fuselage door, down steps and into a waiting ambulance. It had been Barry's twenty-first and last operation.

Bomber Command lost forty aircraft that night: twenty-three Lancasters, fifteen Halifaxes and two Stirlings. On the credit side was the official estimate that the severe damage caused by nearly 1,795 tons of bombs and incendiaries which were dropped on the experimental site, set back the Germans' V2 programme by two months, reducing the number of rockets which would eventually be fired at Britain.

Thanks to the skills of Pluto Wilson, his decision to fight the fire and the courage combined with spirit of his crew, a twenty-fourth Lancaster was not lost that night.

An immediate Conspicuous Gallantry Medal was awarded to Oliver, the mid-upper gunner, and a Distinguished Flying Cross (DFC) to Wilson. The rest of the crew were all decorated at the end of their tour, including the convalescing Barry, who received a Distinguished Flying Medal (DFM).

Barry's citation for a DFM reads: '...although almost suffocated by smoke and fumes from a fire in the fuselage, he kept his captain informed of approaching fighters and while suffering great pain displayed the greatest fortitude.'

DFMs also went to navigator Harry Crumplin, flight engineer Charlie Cawthorne and wireless operator Bing Booth. The bomb-aimer that night, Swill Campbell, received a DFC.

Barry was given emergency treatment at Bottesford's sick quarters. The priest who was summoned believed the badly wounded gunner was at death's door. Barry says: 'He asked for my confessions and I said I didn't have any. I can still see the stunned expression on his face. He thought I was dying. I was young and naive, and must have looked absolutely appalling.'

He was taken to Rauceby Hospital for an operation to repair the hole in his right foot. While he was waiting outside the operating room, he was attacked by a very small flying machine when a wasp stung him on the chest. A few days later Barry lay in bed, his feet on a pillow, head hanging over the end of the bed as a nurse armed with a needle and a pad of cotton wool, picked pieces of metal and perspex out of his scalp and forehead. Barry was later transferred to the hospital at East Grinstead where pioneering plastic surgeon Archie McIndoe and his team saved his leg. He still has a piece of shrapnel lodged in his skull.

Counselling was not available then for the young aircrews who faced death night after long night in aircraft packed with high explosives, incendiaries and petrol. Barry said they were left to cope with stress as well as they were able. Signs of weakness were not tolerated, often leading to accusations of cowardice, officially known as 'Lack of Moral Fibre', or LMF. Counselling would have been useful, but that was something about which they were unaware. Counselling belonged to the future. Barry suffered from nightmares for many years after his flying career had ended. 'In these nightmares I was always confined to a room in which the ceiling was coming down and the walls were floating in on me. I was sometimes afraid of going away and sleeping on my own in strange bedrooms in case I might be tempted to climb out of the windows. I suppose I was still trying to escape from the rear turret of that Lancaster.'

3

BATTLE ORDERS

The briefing room near the main gate at Scampton was a large Nissen hut full of tables and chairs with a platform at the far end. Posters were stuck on the walls, and a large map of Europe was pinned at the back of the platform. On the afternoon of 31 October 1944, sixteen navigators sat at sixteen wooden tables which were covered in charts and logs for recording details of the flight.

These young men, few older than twenty-four, were responsible for getting the Lancasters of 153 Squadron to their targets and safely home again. They took their job seriously. They had to, the lives of their crewmates depended on them. Their training had been long and thorough, although there was a certain amount of hanging about between courses. It could take up to two-and-a-half years from joining the RAF for navigators and pilots to be ready for operations. This represented a big investment for the British taxpayer, particularly as so many aircrew died within six months of qualifying.

Earlier that month the squadron had moved to Scampton from Kirmington (now Humberside Airport). Facilities at the new base were good: officers had comfortable rooms, while NCO aircrews were billeted in former married quarters, small houses with two bedrooms, kitchen and indoor bathroom. This was luxury after the spartan Nissen huts and mud at Kirmington, and morale was high. Three long concrete runways had been laid at Scampton since the end of August 1943 when the Dambusters' 617 Squadron had left for Coningsby, and 57 Squadron took up residence at East Kirkby. Scampton had been transferred from 5 Group to 1 Group, with its headquarters at Bawtry, near Doncaster. Now, only 153 Squadron was based at Scampton.

The young men were joined by their navigation leader Flight Lieutenant E. O. Wheelwright, DFC, who gave them details of the route to that night's target, Cologne. Base to Reading, on to Beachy Head, across the Channel to a point near Cap Gris Nez, then a long leg to point E, about thirty miles south of Aachen on the German border. Here they would turn north-east straight to Cologne. Their return route was west over Belgium, then north-west to the English coast and back to Scampton. Wheelwright, slim, over 6ft tall, was down to earth and jolly, just the right man to get the navigators in good humour for their night's work. He also gave them times, speeds, heights and the strength of winds they would encounter. The navigators then set about working out their flight plans, including track and distance of each leg, course required, time taken, and the ETA (estimated time of arrival) at each turning point and the target.

As the navigators struggled with their calculations, aware that a simple error could prove fatal, the rest of the crews noisily piled into the hut for the full briefing, grumbling a bit when they saw the map. A red tape led from north of Lincoln across the North Sea to Cologne. The squadron had bombed the west German city three days ago, then again the previous night. Only three Lancasters and four Halifaxes had been lost out of a total 1,638 aircraft, but aircrews were a suspicious breed. Would they get away with it so easily a third time?

Their chatter and good humoured banter was brought to a sudden halt as someone bellowed: 'Atten-shun!' They clattered to their feet as the plumpish, serious figure of the station commander, Group Captain Peter Lloyd, marched briskly through the crews on to the platform, leading his entourage who included the squadron commander Wing Commander Francis Powley DFC, AFC (a Canadian), various section leaders and intelligence and met officers. Powley, a robust six-footer, was a good leader, well liked and respected. Very thoughtful before a raid he enjoyed the high jinks that went on in the mess.

Lloyd entreated: 'Please be seated, gentlemen.' An intelligence officer showed them target maps and said they would be bombing industrial centres. Out of a total of 493 aircraft – 331 Lancasters, 144 Halifaxes and eighteen Mosquitoes, from 1, 3, 4 and 8 Groups – 153 Squadron would send sixteen Lancasters.

Navigation, signals, bombing, gunnery and flight engineer leaders gave technical information, reminding crews of flak areas, the need to keep on track, enemy fighter tactics, petrol consumption, speeds, heights, the PFF (Pathfinder Force) marking and master bomber instructions. Each Lancaster would carry one 4,000lb Cookie, plus six at 1,000lb and four at 500lb, making a total of 12,000lb – nearly five-and-a-half tons of high explosives. The met officer reported probable thick cloud over the target, hence the Wanganui marking. Wanganui was the codeword for sky markers dropped by Mosquitoes equipped with Oboe, a radio-based navigation aid.

Powley made some final remarks, mainly for the benefit of the pilots, then watches were synchronised. The station commander wished them good luck and the crews filed out, walking the quarter-mile to the crew room to get into their flying clothes, while the navigators finished their calculations.

One of the navigators was Sergeant Freddy Fish who, six days before as they had finished a daylight raid on Essen, remembered it was his twenty-second birthday. He says of the Cologne raid:

'We carefully plotted the points in latitude and longitude on our charts, writing in our expected times at each turning point. We knew heights and air speeds, and a comprehensive weather forecast showed wind speeds and direction for various areas and temperatures at different heights, such as minus 30 degrees centigrade at 30,000ft. With our hand-held calculators we took our rectified air speeds, adjusted for height and temperature and arrived at the true air speed. Taking the forecast winds, we calculated the course required to make good the actual track, actual ground speed, distance on each leg, time taken and ETA at each point. All this had to be carefully filled in on our flight plan. H-hour (when attack was due to start) was to be 9pm and my time over the target was 9.09pm at 17,000ft.

'We had to bomb on a heading of 039 degrees. We would be allowed to switch on our navigation aid, H2S, when we arrived at 5 degrees east, and not before. We had this restriction because the Germans could plot H2S transmissions and the route and progress of the bomber stream. They also had a radar detection device called "Naxos", by which a night fighter could home on to the bomber's H2S transmission. "Window", thousands of metallic strips which confused the enemy radar, had to be dropped continuously 50.15 degrees north, 6 degrees east, before the target, and then on until we returned to 4 degrees east. I also took a card on which I had to make a report on the weather found between 5 and 6 degrees east. A tremendous amount of arithmetic and paper work was required even before you took off.'

The crews had already eaten their pre-flight meal of egg and bacon, but not baked beans because the latter caused intense indigestion problems at altitude. There were the usual flippant remarks: 'Can I have your egg if you don't get back?' The trip would be a short run of about five-and-a-half hours.

Lockers were opened in the crew room and they dressed slowly, carefully and sometimes, because there were so many layers, with difficulty. Under their normal battledress of tunic and trousers, gunners usually wore long silk underwear. They had an outer electrically-heated flying suit, plus flying boots, Mae West and parachute harness. They needed it all. At 20,000ft the outside temperature could be minus 20 degrees centigrade. Often the rear gunner came back with his eyelashes frozen together and his cheeks covered by ice. A strip of perspex had been removed in the turret for clear vision and to prevent oil smears being mistaken for the shadowy outline of a night fighter. Gloves were essential, silk inners, a pair of wool, then leather gauntlets. Touching metal at extreme heights might strip off the flesh. Those near the front of the bomber, less exposed, would just wear a thick pullover under their tunics, scarves and gloves and hope the heating system worked.

Fish found it impossible to use gloves while drawing pencil lines, operating calculator and protractor, or writing. When his fingers froze, he rubbed his hands vigorously and put them in his flying boots until the feeling had returned.

Clip-on type parachutes were collected from the building next door, then crews were driven out to dispersal by WAAF drivers. They climbed into the aircraft, started the engines and carried out the usual pre-flight checks. The navigators followed thirty minutes later and checked all their equipment. About forty minutes before take-off the aircrew went into the dispersal hut with the ground crew to sit round the hot stove for a warm-up, chat and a few cigarettes. Then Fish checked his watch and said: 'Time to go!' They had a final bladder emptying ritual on the grass or against the rear wheel and climbed aboard.

The men had taken their Benzedrine 'wakey-wakey' tablets which kept them mentally alert, especially for the first two or three hours of an op. Problems arose when a trip was cancelled after swallowing the stimulants and they couldn't sleep.

As the heavily laden Lancasters negotiated the perimeter, as many as 1,000 ground crews and administration staff gathered outside the control tower to wave as they taxied by. Belting down the runway at 100mph, the aircrew prayed they would keep straight and not have an engine failure. At the point they lifted off, there as usual were the station commander and his wife giving them a final wave. Aircrew not flying that night were also there with thumbs up and two-fingered salutes. It was 6.03pm. Two of the sixteen bombers did not take off. One became bogged down after leaving dispersal, preventing another from getting through.

On Lancaster NG185, A-Able, pilot Flying Officer Lionel 'Whizz' Wheeler, twenty-two, and flight engineer Sergeant Vic Morandi, twenty, retracted the undercarriage and flaps and adjusted for climbing revs. They climbed steadily to 16,000ft. At Reading the bombers formed a compact stream ten miles wide, becoming denser as they headed for Beachy Head. Navigator Freddy Fish was getting Gee fixes every six minutes to check he was on track, also to establish wind direction and speed, and actual ground speed to ensure adjustments in order to arrive exactly on time at the turning points. The latest wind finds were then used to plot the new courses. They had been on oxygen since 10,000ft and would stay on it for the next four hours, until descending below that height on the way home.

All was going well. They were keeping on track. Bombs had been fused and the gunners had tested their guns. Wheeler and Morandi watched controls and instruments. Bomb-aimer Flying Officer Ted Durman, a New Zealander, lay in the nose looking for pinpoints and other aircraft. Wireless operator Flight Sergeant Bill Turner, an Australian, was hunched over his radio and the two gunners quartered the sky, keeping a sharp lookout.

At 7.48pm they reached the point near the French coast and altered course to point E, at 06.10 degrees east, just on the German border about thirty miles from Aachen. This was a leg of 186 miles. At 8.52pm they swung north-east to Cologne and Morandi was in the nose throwing bundles of Window down the chute at regular intervals. He would keep this up until they had left Cologne 80 miles behind them after the raid.

It was at this point in the trip that they saw a light on the starboard side, which some of them thought was a Messerschmitt Me262, the world's first operational jet fighter.

Tension increased as they braced themselves for the inevitable flak. Then the way ahead was filled with red flashes. Small pieces of shrapnel rattled against the fuselage. The first marker went down at 9pm and they settled into their bombing run. Fish recalls: 'The bomb doors opened. To me, this was the most frightening part of the whole trip. The vast bay, some 33ft long and 5ft wide, holding 12,000lb of high explosives, was fully exposed a few inches beneath my feet. It would take one very small piece of red hot flak out of thousands being pumped up into the sky to hit us and blow us to kingdom come. Through the cracks in the floor I could see fires and lights creeping slowly backwards.'

Suddenly, the Lancaster gave a sickening lurch to the right and heeled right over. The pilot quickly righted it. They were used to that, usually turbulence from other aircraft's slipstreams or, more likely, a flak burst under the port wing. Fish gave Durman the wind reading to feed into his Mark XIV bomb-sight and the bomb-aimer took over. 'Steady, steady, a bit right, hold it, steady.' Wheeler held the bucking Lancaster as well as he could, then came the call 'Bombs gone!'

Fish logged the time at 9.08pm, one minute before their target time. They had released at 17,500ft on a heading of 040 degrees. Marking was very concentrated and a large red glow could be seen through the cloud. Fish again:

'There was a small measure of relief when bomb doors were closed. Somehow you felt safer, but this was an illusion. Fighters were usually encountered after the target because often they had been lured elsewhere by diversionary raids. You still had to maintain 100 per cent effort all the way back until you crossed the English coast. Even then you could not fully relax. When the V1 Doodlebugs were being fired, there was a special corridor across the Channel where our own fighters had been instructed to shoot down anything that moved. German fighters sometimes lurked around our airfields, waiting to shoot down unsuspecting bombers as they prepared to land.'

Shortly after leaving Cologne someone noticed a huge hole in the starboard wing. It was Turner's job, over the target, to leave his radio and watch from the astrodome for aircraft and bombs from above. When asked, not too politely, why he had not called out a warning, he said he had seen a 1,000lb bomb hurtling down towards them, adding, sheepishly, 'I was too paralysed to speak'. Had Turner yelled for the pilot to take swift avoiding action, they would probably have been killed.

The aircraft flew almost normally back to Scampton, where they touched down at 11.18pm after covering 1,150 air miles in 5hr 15min. They were debriefed, had a meal and inspected the Lancaster in the hangar next morning. The bomb which had hit them had not completed its arming cycle, so was not 'live' and had not exploded on impact. There was a hole the size of a kitchen table in the outer wing. About two inches inside the jagged edge was the outer petrol tank, missed by a whisker. If they had moved a few feet to port in the fraction of a second between Turner seeing the bomb and taking evasive action, they believed the 1,000-pounder would have sheared off the end of the wing. A slight move to starboard would have allowed the bomb to crash through the petrol tanks, the wing root, or the fuselage, with fatal results. Fish comments:

'We were saved by a million-to-one chance. You could not have done better if you had sat down at a drawing board and calculated it to the nearest inch. I have thought since, that in addition to some recorded cases of aircraft returning after being hit by bombs, there must have been more which simply exploded or crashed over the target, perhaps wrongly attributed to flak. When you think that we used to pass up to 1,000 aircraft over the target area in twenty minutes, such accidents must have been almost inevitable. Needless to say, our vigilance after that increased considerably.'

Two Lancasters had been lost on the operation to Cologne, but none from 153 Squadron. It had been the sixth sortie for Whizz Wheeler, the fifth for his crew. Wheeler, was a Londoner, who had left elementary school at fourteen without qualifications and had become an apprentice billiard table maker. He drove his crew hard, but they responded and appreciated his sense of humour. He was recommended for a DFC after his twenty-first trip. Wheeler's extra trip had been as second pilot with a veteran crew to gain operational experience.

Fish, the navigator, a slim six-footer, had been brought up in Sydenham, south London. He had left his job as an audit clerk with a firm of accountants to join the RAF. Quiet and serious, he always went on an op clean and tidy, believing that if he felt smart and fresh, his work aboard the Lancaster would benefit. If he was sloppy, then he thought his work might also become sloppy.

Turner, twenty-eight, the wireless operator, was tall with weatherbeaten features, mild mannered and inclined to be absent-minded. The rest of the crew always checked him over before a flight in case he had forgotten a piece of his equipment. He would shortly be promoted to warrant officer.

Durman, the bomb-aimer, thirty-two, of the Royal New Zealand Air Force, was tall, well-built, with a pencil moustache and a sense of humour that propelled him into gales of laughter at any joke. Completely unflappable, he sometimes settled in the nose with a Western paperback after leaving Scampton. As they crossed the English coast, he marked the page, and got on with his job.

The flight engineer, Morandi, of Italian parentage, was born in Brixton. The joker of the crew, his bubbly and carefree personality kept the others amused with extravagant comments and flights of fancy.

Mid-upper gunner was Sergeant Alec Hodges, twenty, a north Londoner. He was cocky and self-assured, his forage cap perched perkily at an acute angle over his blond hair. Rear gunner Sergeant 'Scotty' Scott, nineteen, from Stockport, Lancashire, was small and thin, but aggressive and eager in the turret. His keen eyesight saved them many times by spotting enemy fighters.

At the time British ground forces were crossing the river Rhine in the spring of 1945, a small force of 173 Lancasters and twelve Mosquitoes from 1, 6 and 8 Groups were briefed on 24 March for a daylight attack on the Benzol plants at Harpenerweg, near Dortmund, and the Mathias Stinnes plant at Bottrop. Germany was already suffering from severe oil shortages after earlier bombing. Damage to their synthetic oil plants was vital, therefore, to hasten their ruin.

Wheeler, recently promoted to the rank of flight lieutenant, took off with nine other Lancasters from 153 Squadron at 1.02pm in Lancaster ME541, A-Able, a brand new aircraft. One Lancaster returned to Scampton with engine trouble. A-Able set course for Reading, then on to Beachy Head, across the Channel to a point ten miles into France, turning east for a leg of 389 miles almost to Cologne, then north-east across the Ruhr straight to Harpenerweg. They were to return south-east towards Cologne, then a long leg to the Dutch coast, over the North Sea and home. They carried one 4,000lb Cookie, twelve 500lb bombs and four 250-pounders. A-Able was due to be over the target at 4.30pm, four minutes after the Pathfinders had dropped red target indicators, followed by greens and further reds. The raid would be controlled by the master bomber, code-named 'Boxkite', while the Main Force would be 'Thunder'. They were to bomb from 19,000ft and listen out for Boxkite's instructions on VHF, channel C.

Fish, now a flight sergeant, got regular Gee fixes every six minutes to keep on track. As they approached 4 degrees east, they started climbing from 7,500 to 15,000ft, putting on their oxygen masks. The last fix at 4.09pm put them just north of Aachen, at 6 degrees east, before Gee was jammed by German counter-radar, which flooded the cathode ray tube with long spiky 'grass' and blotted out the correct blips, which Fish had to measure to get a position. He still had his H2S, which gave a very rough picture of the ground over which they were travelling, but was virtually useless over built-up areas like the Ruhr. At 4.19pm they reached turning point D and set a course straight for the target. Fish's calculations showed they would reach Harpenerweg at 4.30pm. Fish remembers:

'We checked switches, opened bomb doors and the R/T was put on to hear the master bomber's instructions, which came over loud and clear. I gave the bomb-aimer the wind to set into his bomb-sight and noted in my log that at 4.25pm an aircraft was shot down on the starboard quarter. This was done so that at debriefing, confirmation of losses could be cross-checked. At 4.27pm I got an H2S fix which placed us at 220 degrees, 15 miles and three-and-a-half minutes from the target.'

The flak was concentrated and they heard shrapnel clattering along the fuselage. Fish logged 'bombs gone' just after 4.30pm, 27 seconds later than the time they had been given at Scampton. Not bad. Fish again:

'On a heavy raid at night, it was an awesome sight. Below, a carpet of red where thousands of incendiaries had fallen, with big yellow bubbles of light as bombs hit the deck, especially the 4,000lb Cookies. It was like looking at a pile of red hot ashes, with violent eruptions of sudden light from explosions. Drifting down in the sky would be the Pathfinders' red and green flares, dripping clusters of light, whilst all around was the crack, red flashes and puffs of black smoke from the flak. Searchlights in their hundreds sometimes illuminated the target, fingers of light waving backwards and forwards, occasionally trapping an aircraft in their beam. It looked like some sort of hellish inferno. On one trip, to Nuremberg, I recall the light from the fires below illuminated the sky so much it was like daylight and I was able to read my log at 18,000ft.

'I was fascinated by tracer fired from the ground. It came up slowly in lazy curls, usually yellow, then accelerated rapidly as it whistled past you. Sometimes the fires could be seen for up to 150 miles on the way back. On some raids you could still see fires burning at targets 50 miles away that you had bombed a night or two before.'

They left the target area over Harpenerweg and set a course for a short leg south-west over Hagen. Wheeler said suddenly: 'Fred, some of the others are going over to port, are we OK?' Fish looked out and saw several aircraft to the south, presumably to avoid flak from Hagen. 'They're off track,' he said, 'but we're dead on track.'

At that moment a tremendous bang rocked the Lancaster. Fish recalls the moment: 'We had obviously been hit by predicted flak from Hagen. Being out on our own, we had been a nice easily plottable target. The predictors had caught us fair and square. I think our stiff upper lips quivered slightly as we looked at the damage.'

The port inner engine was on fire and the starboard inner showed some flames where the constant speed unit for the propeller had been shot away. A starboard petrol tank had been holed and a stream of petrol flowed back over the wing. If the flames from the starboard inner had reached the petrol, the aircraft would have disappeared in a ball of flames. Both engines were switched off and fire extinguishers operated. The port inner propeller was feathered (blades turned edge-on to minimise drag), but the starboard inner propeller could not be feathered because of damage to the constant speed unit, and it continued to windmill (blades turned full on to the oncoming air stream), causing a certain amount of drag.

Wheeler dived the bomber from 20,000ft, hoping to put out the fires. It worked and he levelled out at 12,000ft. The aircraft had also lost hydraulic power which was needed to put the wheels down, and the instruments and throttle controls were damaged. Fish told the pilot that Brussels, about 100 miles away, was the nearest known airfield, then Morandi cut in and said they didn't have enough fuel to make it. There was a moment's silence. Then Fish suddenly remembered his information sheets:

'As navigators, we were bombarded with information, including emergency landing fields for the continent. Some regarded it as bumph. For twenty-nine trips I had never even looked at them, but being a conscientious type, I always kept the information sheets in my navigator's bag. I dug them out. There were six airfields, the nearest was Eindhoven, Holland, about 60 miles away. I quickly worked out a course and we swung north-west. Luckily, the Gee set was still operational and I was able to plot our track quite easily. We were hit at 4.35pm and arrived over Eindhoven at 5.02pm. From my sheet I could tell Whizz that it had a 24-hour "Darky" (emergency) system on the radio frequency of 6440Kcs and there were three adequate length runways. Whizz called control and got immediate permission to land.'

The pilot was told that he had only 500yds of runway available as it had been badly cratered by German attacks. He had to put down right on the edge of the runway, since excessive braking might burst a tyre. Landing a Lancaster on a short runway was not easy. Putting down one that was badly damaged would be a severe test for its pilot. Wheeler and Morandi stayed at the controls while the others went to crash positions. Wheeler started his landing orbit and everyone held their breath as the flight engineer operated the emergency compressed air system to lower the undercarriage and flaps. The wheels came down with a loud hiss. The flaps were also lowered, but there was insufficient pressure to raise them again. Wheeler gently eased the aircraft round and headed for what seemed to be the runway. Visibility was poor and Morandi suddenly shouted: 'Look out, Whizz! It's the main road!' Wheeler pulled up just in time and coaxed the bomber round for another circuit, making a skidding turn, afraid to bank with two engines out as there was danger of loss of lift and stalling straight into the ground.

Turner, the wireless operator, unable to see what was going on, jettisoned an escape hatch and stuck his head out. The powerful slipstream caught under his helmet and started yanking him out. Fish recalls the moment: 'With a tortured cry of "Bill!" I dived, caught him round the waist and dragged him inside. We all laughed and Whizz, hearing this over the intercom thought: "Here we are struggling with the controls in a tight situation and those buggers are laughing. What the hell are they doing?"'

Wheeler approached the runway, needing to make a very fine judgement on distance to ensure they landed in the right place. Gradually losing height and wrestling with the controls, the approach was excellent. The Lancaster's wheels scraped over the control wagon at the edge of the runway and Wheeler saw the startled face of the airman inside. They landed with a bump, just avoiding the craters. A Jeep shrieked to a halt beside them indicating they should park on the grass beside the runway. They stopped, switched off, and climbed out, weary but elated, and inspected the damage. Large holes had been torn in the aircraft. Petrol still oozed from the tank, a total of 360gals had been lost. The header tank had been smashed, which caused the loss of instruments. The brand new Lancaster was later declared to be a write-off.

Looking around, they were amazed to see the airfield littered with German fighters, mainly Focke-Wulf FW190s. Closer inspection showed they were inflated rubber dummies.

This had been the thirtieth operation for the crew of A-Able. Ordinarily it would have meant they had completed their tour but since January, Bomber Command had increased the first tour from thirty to thirty-six sorties. The last few were always the hardest. Everyone was desperate to survive.

Not long after they had returned to Scampton, Whizz Wheeler burst into Fish's bedroom in the officers' mess and cried: 'The tour has been reduced back to thirty trips!' Their fighting war was over. To celebrate, they took their loyal ground crew out for the customary celebratory booze-up, followed by a fish and chip supper in Lincoln.

In July 1945, Freddy Fish, now a flying officer, received a small packet in the post. Much to his surprise, it contained a DFM, with a short printed message from the King. Fish had never been told that he had been recommended for the award.

4

ADRIFT ON THE NORTH SEA

The last entry in the logbook of Flight Lieutenant Chan Chandler, on 22 June 1945, reads starkly: 'Thank God, no more bloody aeroplanes for me.' The war had ended. He no longer had to go out in the middle of a cold night riding his luck through German flak, nor peer into the inky blackness for the first faint sign of an approaching night fighter. A veteran of 106 operations, 96 of them as a wireless operator/rear gunner in bombers, the rest as a cameraman with an RAF film unit, Chandler had good cause to rejoice. Aged only eighteen when he joined the RAF in December 1939, he had lived through hell a thousand times by the time he was twenty-four.

Wounded five times, Chandler had flown in six bombers which were shot down or had crash-landed. He had returned eleven times from ops in badly damaged aircraft, seven of them in a Hampden which had been reduced to one engine. His luck was phenomenal. He had flown with thirty pilots, but they had not been so lucky: over half of them had been killed during the war.

Always nervous and fearing the worst before the start of each operation he had, at first, enjoyed the excitement of war, especially when the Germans were building up the Kammhuber line, a belt of guns and searchlights which had to be negotiated to get to the Ruhr. On three occasions Chandler's crew were among those briefed to fly at 50ft to shoot up gun emplacements and searchlights before climbing to drop their two 250lb bombs on anything they fancied, while high above other bombers flew on to their target.

He finally decided he had had enough on his 90th operation, in a Lancaster of 617 Squadron, on 14 June 1944. While bombing U-boat and E-boat pens at Le Havre with a 12,000lb Tallboy, most of his rear turret was shot away and his right leg paralysed for a time. Chandler's nerves had been ground down over three difficult years. He flew six more sorties before he was transferred as a cameraman to No 1 Photographic Film Unit (PFU), RAF Iver Heath, based at Pinewood Studios. By then he was the holder of two DFCs and the Soviet Medal of Valour, the latter rarely awarded to RAF aircrew.

Christened Edmund Basil, he had been known as 'Chan' since early in the war. Living in Sussex as a youngster, he had loved the sea, owned a boat since the age of five, and desperately wanted to join the Royal Navy. The Navy's recruiting sergeant in Brighton took one look at the slim, quietly spoken, thoughtful youth with a mane of fair, wavy hair, scowled and bellowed: 'Don't waste my bloody time. Go home to your mother and come back in a couple of years.' Chandler's mother Hilda was a widow. Her husband, also Edmund, had died from the effects of gassing in the First World War when Chan was eleven years old.

Fuming, Chandler, then employed as a laboratory assistant, went to the RAF recruiting office next door where he signed on as a trainee pilot. Later he would be persuaded to change from pilot to wireless operator/air gunner (WOp/AG) as there was a current shortage, having been assured that he would eventually be accepted on a pilot's course. He never did train as a pilot, although he was given the opportunity several times, including on the day of his demob in January 1946.

Of all Chandler's brushes with death the one remembered most for its abject misery and fading hope began on a warm summer's night in 1941. At this time Chandler was a sergeant with 49 Squadron stationed at Scampton. He shared the rear of a Hampden twin-engine bomber with Sergeant Jack 'Jock' Wood, a thin, jovial Scot. They were regular drinking partners in Lincoln, or Dunholme where, at the Black Bull, they competed enthusiastically in schooner races with 83 Squadron, which was also based at Scampton. The schooners contained sherry and contests usually ended in a drunken draw.

The Handley Page Hampden had a crew of four. There was a pilot, and a second pilot, whose duties included navigating and releasing the bombs. Twin Browning machine guns in the wings were operated by the pilot. With its twin 980hp Bristol Pegasus XVIII engines, the Hampden cruised at 167mph, with a maximum 265mph at 15,500ft. The aircraft was known as 'the flying suitcase' because inside there was only enough space for the crew to sit down. To reach the cockpit the pilots climbed onto the port wing and opened a sliding hatch. The gunners wriggled through a door 18 inches wide on the starboard side to get to their positions. Chandler recalls:

'The rear gunner was underneath in what we called "the tin", which was very cramped, with a pair of Vickers gas-operated guns. There was a little more room upstairs where there was another pair of identical guns and the radio. We didn't have a belt feed like the Brownings. We used to slam a pan of ammunition on top. Each pan contained a couple of hundred rounds. They fired about 1,200 rounds a minute so you had to change rather rapidly if you were in trouble. In the tin, or ventral position, you sat on the floor with the two guns between your knees. If you weren't careful you'd catch the wire on the side of the door. It was a quick-release mechanism, which meant the door flew off and you froze to death all the way out and all the way home.

'Both gunners had perspex panels in front of them. These were hinged with slots for the guns, but to fire the guns you had to throw the whole thing upwards in the downstairs position. Above, the perspex went right over you and finished behind your back. In the wireless operator's dorsal position you stood up in fresh air to fire the guns, sitting to operate the radio. The gunner below sat in fresh air. In the Hampden you had to be careful you didn't shoot your own tail off with the top guns. There was a piece of wire around the gun position that in theory prevented you from hitting your tailplane. It pushed the gun barrel out of the way as you traversed it, but the wire often got a bit bent and a lot of chaps came back with their own bullets through their tails.'

After a few sorties, the junior WOp/AG went on a trip as a wireless operator, with the senior man in the tin to look after him. Similarly, after one or two trips, the second pilot actually flew the aircraft, supervised by the captain.

The 30 June 1941 was a warm night when they took off from Scampton at 11.15pm in Hampden 3134 – official call-sign D-Dog, but re-christened D-Donald Duck by the crew. A huge Walt Disney duck, wearing an expression of fierce aggression while wielding a lasso, had been painted on the nose by the squadron artist Danny Mercer, an armourer. The target that night was Düsseldorf, which represented the crew's second sortie to the Ruhr. They wouldn't make it. It was Chandler's sixteenth operation, his twelfth with pilot Brian 'Woolly' Woolston, a big man with a small moustache. Second pilot was 'Mac' McKay on his first trip with them. Both pilots were sergeants.

This trip was in the heady days before bombers flew in streams. Crews were given the target details and all available flak information, then it was left up to each individual pilot to work out his own route. There was no fixed time at which to reach the target as there would be soon, when several hundred aircraft headed towards the target on a set course with strict waypoints along the route.

The crew of Donald Duck were taken unawares by a burst of flak at 10,000ft near the Zuider Zee shortly after crossing the Dutch coast. Shrapnel hit the port engine which immediately cut out. They had flown this way before into Germany between two known flak batteries without encountering any hostility. The Germans, it seemed, were plugging their defences. Normally a Hampden flew quite well on one engine, although the aircraft tended to crab and needed full trim and rudder to persuade it to maintain a reasonably straight course, but it would have been stupid to continue towards Germany. Woolston put more throttle into the starboard engine and turned for home. They carried a mixed load of bombs totalling 4,000lb. These were jettisoned into the North Sea, and to further lighten the aircraft they threw out the two batteries, four rear guns, the radio and ammunition. There was some danger of hitting the tail, but it was a question of heaving everything out as quickly as possible and hoping for the best.

The two batteries were charged by the port engine generator and Jock Wood had not managed to get off an SOS before they went dead, so when the starboard engine began spitting and coughing they knew they had a real problem. They were at between 3,000 and 4,000ft, forty miles from the Dutch coast when the second engine stopped. Chandler remembers:

'Once we'd lost the starboard engine we went straight into a spin, losing height very rapidly. The only way to get out of it is to stick your nose down to get your speed up.

We did a fairly flat, quite good landing actually, but we discovered that coming down on water is quite different to crash-landing in a field. The previous month, after bombing Hamburg, we were forced down into a Suffolk field after losing the port engine. Then we just ploughed up the earth; landing on water was like hitting a brick wall.'

Going down the aircraft spun twice, while Woolston, fighting the controls, tried gallantly to turn the sea into a runway. Their chances of getting out alive would have plummeted if the Hampden had plunged nose first into the sea. Preparing to ditch, Chandler scrambled up into Jock Wood's compartment to avoid being drowned. They crouched together like a pair of nervous sardines.

When it came, at 2.15am, the thunderous crash knocked the breath out of everyone. Wood thought they must have got their navigation wrong and had hit the ground, such was the ferocity of the landing. Chandler, up to his waist in cold water, scrambled out to find Woolston struggling with the emergency dinghy which had inflated itself automatically, but which was wedged in the port engine nacelle. McKay helped the skipper release it but Woolston slipped off the wing into the water, dragging the H-Type dinghy, upside-down, on top of him. By the time they rescued him the Hampden was sinking. Wood wanted to go back to rescue the two carrier pigeons, but was restrained by Chandler who said he wouldn't make it back to the dinghy.

All bombers carried pigeons during the war. In the Hampden they were kept in a small cage on the D-spar, the main spar which went through the wings. Pigeons rarely served any useful purpose. A crew going down in a crippled aircraft could hardly spare the time to write a message to put in the tube on the leg of a terrified pigeon. Chandler recalls: 'In Hampdens you had to wrap the poor things up in newspapers otherwise they lost all their feathers when thrown out. Some laid eggs during the flight. God only knows what use they were. You know what they say, "only birds and fools fly, and birds don't fly at night", but that's when they were being chucked out.'

The four men soon realised that D-Donald Duck had been inappropriately named as their aircraft sank out of sight, taking with it the unfortunate pigeons, the big main dinghy, and their emergency supplies which were carried in a huge valise. They feared being sucked under, but the bomber disappeared quietly, only a few pieces of aileron and splashes of oil marking its grave. The skipper and Wood were both sick after swallowing sea water and Woolston had a nasty gash on his head, sustained during the crash. The yellow dinghy was small, about the size of a tractor tyre, the sea was running and water kept slopping in over the side. Chandler regretted losing his flying boots in the sea and his biggest problem was keeping his feet out of the water. They soon became numb and he eventually gave up trying to keep them dry. Chandler had remembered his cigarettes, but his lighter wouldn't work. Woolston found three matches and they shared the cigarettes.

Had he retained his boots, although saturated Chandler would have been reasonably comfortable wearing a warm Irvine jacket and trousers. Jock Wood had on an old-fashioned one-piece Sidcot flying suit, made of canvas, plus an Irvine jacket. Both pilots had Irvine jackets. All four wore battledress. Chandler comments:

'There was quite a bit of wind and being so wet we were all freezing cold. I had never felt so miserable in all my life. We felt very alone and small sitting there in the middle of the sea. For the first hour or two we did not say much, just sat there, in shock, I suppose. I noticed that every time the dinghy dipped into a wave there was a stream of phosphorescent bubbles. It was strangely beautiful and I looked for it on other nights, but it only happened a couple of times. Eventually we came round a bit and took stock of ourselves and the dinghy. We found we had two pyrotechnic distress flares, a small tin of Horlicks tablets, a tiny piece of chocolate and a rubber hot water bottle containing a pint of water. There was a minute bottle of rum too, and a sea anchor.

'We had not managed to send an SOS so decided we should ration the water from the start. It was too rough to try to sleep so we all sat round on the edge of the dinghy, waiting. Some hours later we heard the boys coming back and when we saw a Wimpy (Wellington) fairly near to us we tried to fire one of the distress signals but it wouldn't work. This rather cast us down, but we decided to try to dry out the rockets in the sun next day.'

Two Hampdens, including Donald Duck, and two twin-engine Whitleys were lost on three separate bombing raids over Germany that night.

All they heard in the dark was the splash of the North Sea as they bobbed upon it, vulnerable and uneasy in the tiny wet and dismal dinghy. They had thought it would be a piece of cake firing off flares as the bombers returned triumphantly to England. Somebody would see them and radio their position. What, they thought bitterly, was the point of being issued with emergency flares which would not work when they got damp? Unable to sleep, they told themselves they would not be there for more than a few hours. Through the night they all experienced glorious visions of being rescued and downing the first pint.

At dawn they anxiously scanned the horizon, but only saw water. They had not really expected to see anyone looking for them right away, but the awareness that they were still alone in the middle of a heaving sea was very disappointing. Somehow daylight emphasised their total isolation. The sun came up, warm and encouraging and the wind, which had gnawed at them ceaselessly overnight was less hostile. They tried, without success, to use it to dry out the flares on which their survival seemed to depend.

Breakfast was swiftly despatched: one Horlicks tablet each and a tin lid-full of water. They agreed to take it in turns to sleep without realising how hazardous and uncomfortable that would be. The sea was rough and they cut up Jock Wood's flying overall with a penknife to create a shelter against the spray and wind. It was impossible for the four of them to get into it without developing terrible cramp. The only way they could all get under cover was for their feet to meet in the middle of the dinghy, knees wedged under chins and unable to move. They could only lie down with two in the dinghy facing each other, their feet up on the other side. They rested or slept fitfully. The pair on a two-hour watch lay curled round the top edge of the dinghy. It was a miserable business being on watch, but their precarious position guaranteed they stayed awake. That evening they each ate another Horlicks tablet washed down with a tin lid-full of water. Craving a pint of cold beer, they had seen nothing all day except the odd seagull.

The sea continued rough on the second day and they were kept busy baling water out of the flimsy dinghy which was always awash inside. The blustering wind kept up and Chandler thought if it did not ease it would kill them because at night there was no way they could get warm. For the rest of his life Chandler would hate any wind that rose above a breeze.

Towards evening the wind dropped and just before dusk they were excited by the sight of two Wellingtons no more than a mile away flying at 200ft. They tried to fire off the other distress signal but that didn't work either. The two bombers passed out of sight and their spirits dropped again. They each sucked on a Horlicks tablet and sipped their water ration. Chandler remembers:

'When it was too rough to lie round the edge of the dinghy, we all had to get inside under the Sidcot "tarpaulin" in an attempt to get warm, otherwise we would have frozen to death. Exhausted as we were, it was impossible to sleep for more than ten minutes at a time. Brian and Jock were both seasick, particularly poor Jock and even though he had nothing left to bring up but a little yellow bile, it still plagued him.'

Two of them managed to lie down facing each other, with the others crammed down either side, half on top of them, covered by the Sidcot. That night they heard the steady throbbing of what they believed were the diesel engines of a U-boat. They kept quiet, hoping it would not come any nearer and overturn them.

Next morning was calm and warm and they managed to dry out. No good for anything else, they used the flares as paddles, steering by the sun. It was backbreaking work for the wretched dinghy only wanted to go round in circles. The airmen believed they were making progress until that evening, when they bumped up against a piece of the Hampden's wing. It was a cruelly disheartening moment.

On the fourth morning, three Blenheims passed 200yds away at a height of 50ft. They waved, shouted and flashed mirrors and the bombers appeared to swerve slightly. They exchanged happy grins believing the aircraft had radioed in their positions and would return after completing their job. Only one came back and that was a long way off. As the day dragged on and no rescuers appeared, their dejection deepened. The Horlicks tablets and chocolate had all gone and Chandler suggested they try fishing to give them something to do.

They sliced a piece of cord off the sea anchor then spent the whole day unravelling it and tying the bits together to make a long line. Jock Wood had a pair of pliers with which he turned a safety pin into a hook. They hadn't any bait and weren't surprised when fish were not tempted to grab at the empty hook, but making the line had been useful therapy. Chandler, a keen fisherman, thought longingly of more carefree days near their quarters at North Carlton manor house, in Lincolnshire, where the only recreation was fishing for carp in a small lake. Carp were in short supply and they had tied worms on to pieces of cotton so that when caught, the fish could be replaced in the lake without being hurt.

Another way of passing time in the dinghy was by seeing who could keep their heads under water the longest. During a spell of this McKay suddenly shot up and gasped, 'There's a bloody great mine down there'. Chandler says:

'We thought he was joking and told him we had enough trouble without bloody silly cracks like that. Then we all looked down and there it was beneath us, a bloody great mine, four feet wide with horns sticking out all over it, almost certainly one of ours. We decided, in whispers, to paddle very gently away from it, but discovered we were drifting away anyway. Now we knew why we had seen no ships, we had paddled into a minefield.'

They kept a sharp watch out for more mines, but didn't see any. That day the water ration was halved. A little rain fell in the night and they tried to catch some of it in their handkerchiefs, but they were so thick with salt it was useless. Time crawled. The nights were raw, shot through with pessimism and despair. Each dawn brought a fresh glimmer of hope. Hope was all they had. Baling out was a continuous and laborious chore and when, somewhere, the dinghy sprang a leak, air had to be pumped into it as fears grew that it might collapse, throwing them into the cold water. They would then face a slow but inevitable death and no one would ever know what had happened to them.

On the fifth day they divided the paddling into half-hour shifts to save their flagging energy. It was demoralising knowing that most of their efforts were wasted because the dinghy refused to move in a continuously straight line.

At noon next day, 6 July, they saw three launches two miles away, heading straight for them. They became almost delirious with excitement, waving, flashing mirrors and kicking up as much row as they could, but to their bitter disappointment the boats turned north and were soon out of sight.

The appearance of several flies and wasps made the four drifting airmen believe they were getting near land. They had great expectations for the following morning. That night they heard another submarine and what they thought were several launches, but didn't see them. They did see darting searchlights and anti-aircraft fire from the English coast, which was farther away than they had imagined.

Chandler recalls: 'The dinghy needed pumping up all the time now. Before we had only done it once a day, taking it in turns. Now we could only manage about a dozen strokes of the tiny pump at a time. Despite being on half-rations we ran out of water.

The last drops came out of the hot water bottle white as milk, probably with bits of rubber in it, but it tasted oh so sweet.'

By the seventh day they were too weak to do much paddling. Their faces had been burned a deep brown by the sun and wind. They used sea water to wash out their mouths which were cracked and foul, covered by a white salty excrescence. For much of the time they were silent. They had reached a point when talking drained the little energy they had left. They began losing interest in survival, each imagining the dinghy drifting aimlessly in the North Sea until, one by one, they died. The following morning, parched beyond belief, they began drinking sea water, believing they might as well go mad as die of thirst. That evening a Hampden, escorted by two Hurricanes flew from the west at 2,000ft, turning north almost over the dinghy and the tiny frantically waving figures inside it. Again they were not seen. Chandler again:

'We decided that if the buggers were not going to pick us up we'd get to England under our own steam and that when we did we'd head for the nearest pub, line up eight pints of shandies each and drink them two at a time, one in each hand. But our strength was just about gone. That night as I lay on the side of the dinghy on watch, I thought if only I can just see people walking down a street once more – not to touch them or even to talk to them, just see some ordinary people – then I would die content.'

They were too exhausted to move at dawn on the ninth day and huddled lethargically together in the dinghy, covered by the Sidcot. At first they ignored the single Hampden which roared out of the sun at 8.00am a mile away. It was high in the sky on a mission that would not involve looking down for a speck of yellow and four dying men. So many aircraft and boats had not seen them, what was the point in getting excited about this one? Then their weary minds were flogged by the vague memory of RAF discipline to stir themselves as the bomber's engines drew nearer. They struggled to hold their skipper upright while he flashed 'SOS' with a mirror.

To their disbelief and delight the bomber circled while its wireless operator got a fix. It came in low and they saw a series of rapid splashes racing towards them which, for a horrifying moment, they believed was its gunners shooting at them. The 'bullets' were lead weights bouncing over the waves on the end of the 200ft trailing aerial which the wireless operator had forgotten to wind in. It nearly cut them in half, passing a few feet away.

The four airmen, almost resigned to death, were now close to tears as the Hampden circled above them and they exchanged upturned thumbs with the crew. 'We thought we wouldn't survive until the next day,' Chandler muses, 'we were at the end of our tether. It was that close. We were lucky too, because the Hampden hadn't been looking for us.'

The Hampden kept them company for more than an hour then flashed a message with an Aldis lamp: 'Boat coming.' The bomber turned for England and although they knew the Hampden was probably running short of fuel, they were again overwhelmed by loneliness. The next few hours seemed the longest they had spent in the dinghy, but at 2.30pm they heard engines and saw a welcome plume of spray on the horizon. It was an RAF high speed rescue launch.

The 60ft launch chugged alongside and they saw the bronzed, well fed crew staring down at them. A scrambling net was dropped into the dinghy but none of them had the strength to climb up it. A sailor came down the net and exclaimed: 'Jesus! How bloody long have you been here?' The launch and Hampden had been searching for the crew of a Wellington which had ditched the night before. The four airmen were half-carried up into the launch and helped below where they were given a mixture of Navy rum and water which almost exploded inside them. Chandler:

'After that first rum I was feeling a bit better and I thought I'd better get back top-side for some fresh air. The launch wasn't going all that fast, so I said to one of the crew: "I thought these things were supposed to do about 40 knots". The seaman grinned and said: "They do, but we only go at half speed through a minefield".

'The boats did not draw enough water, usually, to explode the ordinary mine that we saw, although an acoustic mine would presumably have been triggered by the launch's engines. But this was standard drill for the crash boys. They'd go anywhere to pick somebody up.'

Their dinghy was also brought ashore and examined by experts to see why it had remained inflated for so long. The rescued airmen had their first half-pint the following Saturday in a pub near the RAF sick bay at Great Yarmouth where they had been treated. The beer nearly knocked them out and they had to sit on the seafront for a couple of hours to recover.

Chandler, a bony seven stone after losing three-and-a-half stone in the dinghy, said: 'That night we were in the pub listening to the 9 o'clock news. There was a report about us being rescued, which ended by saying: "They are now sitting up in their hospital beds waiting for their next trip". But we weren't in hospital, we were pissed as newts in the pub next door.'

5

OVER THE HILLS AND FAR AWAY

Conditions were primitive on the Chaklala airbase near Rawalpindi which sprawled in the foothills of the Himalayas in India, when Wellington pilot Flying Officer John Sutton, aged twenty-two, arrived on 215 Squadron in January 1943. Air and ground crews were living uneasily in flimsy, flapping tents, splashed up to the eyeballs in mud during the monsoon season, remembering with nostalgia the dreary cats-and-dogs downpours of Britain which, by comparison, now seemed to have been no more inconvenient than gentle drizzle.

In India, rain was more spectacular. Here, RAF personnel claimed, with wry humour, that rain fell like an endless herd of stampeding and trumpeting elephants. Yet there was a considerable compensation for being trapped at Chaklala, now part of Pakistan's Punjab province. Just north of Rawalpindi, Murree brewery's wartime output of beer was substantially increased by the presence of thirsty Allied airmen, unaccustomed to the almost endless stifling and dusty heat. Beer was cheap, unlimited and vital to the war effort.

Sutton recalls more easily the cool nectar which flowed ceaselessly from the brewery to the air base than the swirling floods, sticky heat, mosquitoes and wretched unpleasantness of the monsoons, saying with a wistful sigh: 'We lived the life of Riley in Rawalpindi. We trained, dropped paratroopers from the 10th Gurkha Battalion, pinched signs and things from the regular Indian Army, who didn't take kindly to us, and had a lot of fun. We played liar dice, I read a lot and played Fats Waller and Mozart on my gramophone.'

Nothing valuable was taken from the Army, but RAF morale was undeniably boosted when official parking signs and potted plants from the Rawalpindi Club were gleefully rearranged in the officers' mess at Chaklala. The more adventurous aircrews clubbed together to buy a racehorse, Ripe Bananas, which they raced at Rawalpindi racecourse, even supplying the jockey, the diminutive Flight Sergeant Prendergast, an air gunner.

On 23 March 1943, before the racehorse syndicate could really get organised, the squadron was moved over 1,200 miles south-east to join 99 Squadron at the larger base set in flat, featureless land at Jessore, now in Bangladesh. It took them two days to get there. Sutton had been with 99 Squadron at Digri, Bengal, before being transferred to 215 at Chaklala.

At Jessore, where there was a small control tower and no formal station plan, conditions were marginally better than Rawalpindi, with accommodation in bamboo huts. They were later moved into fine requisitioned houses. None of them had windows, but no one really noticed in the extreme heat of India and after living in tents, these houses were like palaces.

In the midst of all this comparative comfort, there was a major drawback. The men learned they were each restricted to a miserable monthly ration of a single bottle of beer. After recovering from their stunned disbelief and shamelessly fawning on the teetotallers, officers and men turned to the local whisky and gin. This was cheap and raw enough to temporarily take your mind off the enemy who were entrenched across the border in Burma – the Japanese, whose shuddering reputation for ruthlessness and cruelty was unsurpassed among all the horrors penned about the Second World War.

Sutton carried a passenger in the Wellington X he flew down to Jessore. He was Abdul Bari, the pilot's faithful young Indian bearer, who crouched excitedly in the back of the twin-engine bomber with his bed roll. Each officer had a bearer, the Indian equivalent of a batman. Bari was supremely efficient. Sutton only had to open one eye in the morning for the ever watchful Bari to thrust a cup of tea at him through the mosquito net which was draped over his bed in the officers' mess. All the pilot's washing was done and laid out ready to put on, and the bearer did all Sutton's shopping in the nearby village. At mealtimes, Bari joined other bearers in the small kitchen to collect food prepared by Indian contract cooks and deliver it to their officer sahibs. The bearers needed to have their wits about them on the walk between kitchen and mess, otherwise birds the airmen called 'shitehawks' would dive down and snatch food off the plates. Bari worked for Sutton from early morning until the evening, all for 30 rupees a month, then worth about £2. This was the going rate for the best bearers until the arrival of the American GIs, who could afford to pay a good deal more.

John Sutton, from Shipley, Yorkshire, whose father had built a glider before the war, loved flying and had been a member of Oxford University Air Squadron before joining the RAF in 1941. He arrived in Jessore, with all the confidence of youth. His nickname, Jumbo, suited him. He stood 6ft 2in and, at over 13 stone, was broad and muscular. Like most young pilots during the war, he was afraid of nothing.

From July until October 1942, he was based on the operational training unit (OTU) at Moreton-in-Marsh, Gloucestershire. To supplement the bombers in the frontline squadrons many sprog (novice) crews were taken from OTUs, skippered by pilot instructors and thrown into battle before completing their training. Sutton lost the whole of his first crew who didn't return from a raid of 630 aircraft on Düsseldorf, while he was kicking his heels in Gloucestershire. The pain of that loss was deadened at first because there was always the hope that they had been shot down and taken prisoner. Later he heard they had all been killed.

Sutton left Lyneham, Wiltshire, on 20 November 1942 flying a new Wellington, with overload fuel tanks fitted in the bomb bay. He was to deliver the medium bomber to the Middle East via Gibraltar and join a squadron for a tour there before returning to England. When he arrived at the north Egyptian coastal town of Mersa Matruh, which had just been recaptured, he found elated airmen charging around on German motorbikes, some of them wearing Italian officers' uniforms, but no one knew why he had been sent there. No official papers had been received. Certainly, he was not needed on a squadron. Sutton and his crew, who expected to be welcomed with open arms, had been lost in an over-stretched system which was responsible for the movement of thousands of aircrews. After ferrying several aircraft about the Middle East, he was told to take a Wellington to India, where he eventually joined 99 Squadron in 221 Group.

Spearheading Bomber Command's night offensives against Germany until the heavy four-engine bombers came fully into service, the Wellington was designed by the brilliant engineer from Vickers, Barnes Wallis. He later achieved greater fame with his 'bouncing bombs' which were used on the Dambuster raids in May 1943, than for his years of work designing at first airships and then aircraft, which he continued almost until he died in 1979 at the age of 92. Wallis's ingenious geodetic design featured a lattice-work of steel which provided the Wellington with tremendous ruggedness and an ability to soak up heavy punishment, all of which helped to get its crew safely back to base. This skeleton of thin steel was covered by a fabric which caused some anxiety in the Far East because it absorbed moisture. The Wellington X, with its twin 1,675hp Bristol Hercules engines, had a portly appearance which led to it being affectionately nicknamed 'Wimpy' after the cartoon character Popeye's overweight friend J. Wellington Wimpy. The bomber carried twin belt-fed .303in Browning machine guns in the front turret, and four in the rear turret, although Sutton could not remember the front guns ever being fired in anger. The Wellingtons at Rawalpindi and Jessore had their front turrets faired-in with fabric to help increase the aircraft's speed.

On 23 October 1943 Sutton was one of twelve 215 Squadron Wellington X pilots briefed to bomb the railway station at Saigang, a suburb of Mandalay, occupied by Japanese forces. This was Sutton's nineteenth operation but he would eventually complete forty-five, including several daylight raids on Japanese positions, earning himself a DFC. He recalls: 'It was quite different in India compared to Britain where you generally kept a crew together for a whole tour of operations. I flew with many different people, particularly because I was flight commander for a lot of my time there.' Consequently, Sutton remembers little of his crew for this bombing trip.

Sergeant Yaw was navigator/bomb-aimer. Sutton comments: 'Around this time things were changing and we soon had straight navigators and a bomb-aimer instead of a front gunner.' Front gunner was Sergeant Jackson, and Sergeant Lappage rear gunner. Wireless operator Flight Sergeant Ted Singleton, a cheerful Australian, flew with Sutton again after they were both posted to Palestine. Sutton recalls:

'I enjoyed flying, but I didn't get to know how to really fly a Wellington until I finished my tour in India and was posted to Palestine as an instructor on an OTU, where I taught single-engine and flapless landings and became quite accustomed to doing so. I looked back to India and was amazed how lucky I was to get through that tour, knowing as little as I did at that time. I hadn't had that many hours' flying experience at the time of the trip to Saigang, and later realised how fortunate I was to get through that operation, the landing in particular.'

Sutton was pleased the monsoon season had petered out the previous month, believing bad weather was a more dangerous enemy than the Japanese. He had flown through torrential monsoon rain, a frightening experience when he could see little in front of him. 'I remember getting into tremendous cumulo-nimbus clouds, which built up massively, reaching well above our operational height, particularly when we were flying the early Wellingtons, the Ic's, which had two 1,000hp Bristol Pegasus XVIII engines. You couldn't fly over the weather, you had to go through it. We were thrown about in the most violent sort of way. This was an horrific experience.'

They took off from Jessore's single runway at about 3.45pm in Wellington LB141, F-Freddy. Each man carried a normal survival kit with maps and emergency rations, but they needed more survival aids than crews flying over Germany. The hazards facing men baling out were different in the Far East. Besides the Japanese, there were thick jungles and Burmese villagers who could not always be trusted. Sutton carried a kukri, a wicked looking Gurkha knife with a curved blade over a foot long. This was not only for hand-to-hand fighting if he was surprised by Japanese soldiers, but was also needed to hack a way through the jungle back to base, as some aircrews had done successfully.

Each man aboard carried a 'ghooli chit', printed in Burmese and English on white linen. It read: 'Dear Friend, I am an Allied fighter, I did not come here to do any harm to you who are my friends, I only want to do harm to the Japanese and chase them away from your country as quickly as possible. If you will lead me to the nearest Allied Military Post, my Government will give you a good reward.' John never needed to use his ghooli chit or the kukri. Neither helped one 215 Squadron pilot who did have the misfortune to bale out. A report reached Jessore that he had been caught and beheaded by the Japanese.

'I didn't see any Japanese eyeball to eyeball,' Sutton says, 'that's why I think the RAF was a relatively easy service to be in compared to the Army. Flying is such a clinical business. You took off and, unless you were hit or anything happened to you, you just came back to a relatively civilised world. You were obviously in some danger when you were flying, but you were not as emotionally involved in what goes on to the extent that you would be in a tank.'

Although the Allies regarded the Japanese with deep loathing, bombing operations against them were not as devastating to aircrews as those who flew to heavily defended targets in Germany. Anti-aircraft fire was less withering and localised over the main targets. Bombers did not face a gauntlet of flak when they crossed over territory occupied by the Japanese, whose searchlights were not as elaborate or as sophisticated as those of Germany. The Japanese had Mitsubishi 'Zero' night fighters but these, too, were mainly snapping and spitting over targets they were defending. Sutton again:

'It was normally an easy ride until we got to the target, which was reasonably defended. Generally speaking, we operated the Wellingtons at a much lower level than in Britain. There was no need to go particularly high in the Far East because there was less flak on the way to the target than in Europe. In any case, you couldn't get too high, especially in the early Wellingtons, which had a limited ceiling because of the lack of power and the fact that they didn't perform so well in the ambient temperatures that were current out there, and also because the fabric got very soggy, adding to the weight of the aircraft.

'We flew out at about 10,000ft over the Chin Hills to Mandalay. We didn't need dog-legs, we went straight to the target. It was, we thought, a routine, straightforward operation. The weather didn't present any problems, although there were cumulus clouds around.'

On the debit side were the navigational difficulties. There were few navigational aids in the Far East, no Gee or H2S; it was all DR (dead reckoning). Aircrews always hoped for clear visibility so they could see the aiming point. Yet even the return flight could be difficult because air bases did not have radio equipment to guide in their aircraft.

Yaw, who wore the observer's half-wing badge – its 'O' was known as 'the flying arsehole' – navigated them almost to the target, with front gunner Jackson acting as map reader when they drew nearer to the busy railway station. Yaw then briskly brought his maps forward into the nose below and in front of the pilot, where he used his bomb-sight looking through a glass panel. They met the first sporadic bursts of flak about twenty miles from Mandalay, which was an important railway centre and distribution point. They saw one fighter, but it ignored them. It was dark, heavy with cloud, but the leading Wellington carried only flares which had successfully illuminated the target area.

Sutton recalls: 'You were briefed where to go and where to drop your bombs and you went purely on an individual basis. It was entirely up to your navigator/bomb-aimer to find the target and bomb it. We rarely saw any other bombers and we didn't on this night, when we bombed from 9,000ft.'

Debriefed crews later reported bombs straddling the target, north and south of it and in the jetty area. Several fires were started, including a large one to the west of the target and another to the south. Yaw pressed the bomb-aimer's tit to release two 500lb and five 250lb bombs onto the railway station, and the aircraft jumped with the relief at getting rid of them. Seconds later, the starboard engine cut out and the aircraft automatically turned to the right.

Sutton checked all his instruments thinking there might be a fault that could be put right, but he couldn't find one. It was a mystery. They had not been hit by flak or a fighter cannon shell. All power in the engine had failed completely. Sutton feathered the starboard propeller to reduce the drag on that side, while increasing the power on the port engine.

Sutton explained over the intercom to his crew what had happened and that he had decided to press on. The Hercules engines were usually reliable and he thought they could reach Jessore on the port engine, which was running normally. He did not dwell much on the problems facing them. Stretching ahead were 285 miles of the Chin Hills, whose highest peak, Mount Victoria, touched 10,000ft; the Wellington's maximum ceiling on a single engine was 8,000ft. The only alternative to going through the hills was to bale out, with all the grim possibilities that might ensue. That was not a consideration at the moment, but it might be if the port engine became over-stressed. They were young, thousands of miles from home, and none of them could think of an appropriate black joke about baling out over such inhospitable terrain.

The navigator set a course for the disabled bomber through the mountains, avoiding the highest peaks. He aimed to be slightly north of track because he thought the highest peak, Mount Victoria, was on their left. They stabilised out on the one engine which managed to hold them steady at 8,000ft. One of the main problems was keeping the bomber on a straight course. They needed to use a lot more power on the one remaining engine and that tended to turn the aircraft to starboard. Sutton set the rudder bias to the extreme left to reduce the pressure required to keep the aircraft flying straight. Keeping on course also required him to put extreme pressure with his foot on the left side of the rudder bar. This was very tiring for Sutton's left foot as he recalls:

'I had a rudder bias, which I twisted on and off with my left hand. This helped keep the Wellington on course, but it wasn't sufficiently powerful to overcome the effect of a single engine on one side of the aircraft working at pretty near full power. The port engine still tended to swing the aircraft to the right unless constant heavy left rudder was applied. I was pushing down on the left side of the rudder bar with all my might.'

Jackson, the front gunner, helped ease the pressure on his skipper's leg by wrapping his parachute harness round the rudder bar and pulling on it. Sutton kept a close eye on the oil pressure and temperature gauges to make sure the engine was not being over-stressed.

'The one engine was probably more thirsty than two engines being used normally but, at first, fuel wasn't a problem. I never thought for one minute that we wouldn't get back. It was probably because of lack of experience, but in those days you thought you could overcome anything. We were in a difficult position, but I didn't consider the possibility of failure and I wasn't as apprehensive about it as I would be now with the benefit of hindsight.'

Cloud added to the pilot's difficulties. They tried to get their bearings when they occasionally saw through gaps in the cloud. At other times, which Sutton found most disturbing, they were enveloped in thick cloud. Flying in cloud for any length of time was an unnerving experience. The crew had great faith in their pilot and navigator, but it was unsettling to be flying blind through a range of mountains with only one engine, which all the time was trying to drag them to the right. If they were unable to hold their height or if that engine faltered, there was no question of Sutton attempting to crash-land among the Chin Hills, they would have to bale out. It was a depressing thought that Sutton pushed to the back of his mind.

Sutton again: 'The periods when we were in cloud were obviously more worrying than the times when we weren't. In cloud, there was a possibility that we might be off course. At least while we were flying in the clear, although it was dark, you could probably see something looming up ahead of you. In cloud, you had absolutely no idea. Both gunners were looking out, not only to see where we were going, but also to see if they could get any pinpoints to establish where we were and, of course, they were few and far between over that sort of country.'

It was a wild and barren landscape with one hill looking very much like another. Occasionally the ribbon of a river was seen and an attempt was made to find it on the maps pored over by the navigator and front gunner. Conversation was kept to essentials. In cloud they might have been flying through a tunnel, except the sides of a tunnel are reasonably predictable. Flying blind for any length of time over a landscape strewn with such massive obstacles, they really had no way of knowing if they had just missed a mountain top by inches or were seconds from smashing themselves into eternity.

They were over Allied territory when Sutton realised they would not have enough fuel to get to Jessore. He knew they were near the small fighter airfield at Chittagong, about 200 miles short of Jessore, and the pilot turned hopefully towards it. They were relieved to see the friendly lights of the airfield, six-and-a-half hours after leaving Jessore. They circled to reduce height to about 1,500ft.

'I flashed my downward identification light, but didn't have any conversation with the control tower,' adds Sutton. 'There wasn't the same sophisticated control situation that was normal in Britain. We more or less went straight in. The critical thing to avoid now was under-shooting, because once I got the flaps down I wouldn't have the power to lift it up and go round again. Also, if you touched down and overshot, that was not so bad as crashing on the approach. All the crew went to their crash positions. The short runway was lit up. We came in fairly fast, at about 120mph. When I was absolutely sure we were going to get in I put down the undercarriage and flaps and touched down. Unfortunately, as we slowed up, I couldn't centralise the rudder bias which had jammed after being in an extreme position for so long. I just couldn't get it back. It had been effective when I was on full power, but when you take off the power, it goes the other way. When the port engine was taken off, the rudder bias tried to swing the aircraft to the left.

'I was pleased with the touchdown, but we were going a bit on the fast side and my only worry was whether I would pull up in the length of the runway, but that didn't seem terribly important. If we ran off the other end we'd be going reasonably slowly and it didn't matter.'

Sutton need not have worried about having enough runway. The rudder bias swung the Wellington off the runway for a spectacular, screeching arrival. The 'clunk! clunk! clunk!' reverberated eerily around the airfield, sending a wave of panic surging through the scattered buildings. The bomber was brought to a sudden, crunching halt. Sutton froze in his seat. 'I couldn't see them, but thought they were aircraft. The Wellington just ploughed through them. There was nothing I could do about it. We stopped and there was complete silence. Then we got out in a hurry.'

The Wellington had halted on top of a wrecked fighter, preventing Sutton from getting out through the lower escape hatch. He left through the top of the cockpit, jumping 14ft to the ground, hurting his back, an injury which still bothers him.

'We just stood there and looked at the smashed fighters. They were Hurricanes, six or seven of them. They'd been parked in a neat line. Most had had their tailplanes removed. There was no fire, and the robust Wellington was still standing. Its under-carriage was badly damaged though, and it was later written off. Someone came and picked us up in a truck and took us off to the mess for a drink. I learned later that part of the fighter squadron had to be grounded because of the wrecked Hurricanes.'

Sutton and his crew were flown by Dakota back to Jessore, where his commanding officer, Wing Commander French, seemed very pleased by the way they had returned to base. F-Freddy was the only bomber lost on that night's raid.

Sutton was mentioned in despatches for getting his crew and himself back to Chittagong by showing 'remarkable skill and determination'. The Hurricanes, mangled beyond repair, were not mentioned.

Some time later, Sutton received in Jessore a letter signed by two pilots in Chittagong. They cheerfully congratulated him for being instrumental in them being re-equipped with Spitfires, and believed he should have been awarded the Japanese equivalent of the DFC.

6

ALIVE, AFTER
LANCASTER BLOWS UP

On the night of 18/19 March 1944, Bomber Command despatched 846 aircraft to hit the west German city of Frankfurt. Extensive damage was caused, 421 civilians were killed and 55,000 bombed out of their homes. Four nights later British bombers returned to Frankfurt to finish the job. This is the story of one of the 816 aircraft which took part in the second operation.

It was late afternoon on 22 March when Lancaster JB648, B–Beer, lifted into a clear sky from 106 Squadron's base at Metheringham in Lincolnshire. The Lancaster, backing up the Pathfinder Force, was to be among the first aircraft over the target, but it would play no part in the attack on the city. B–Beer did not carry bombs, only flares to mark the target area, and a mixed bag of incendiaries.

The aircraft was piloted by Pilot Officer Ted Rosser, twenty-two, a small thin Australian from Rutherglen, Victoria. Rosser was a quiet man, with delicate features, who appeared to those who did not know him well as someone wound up by nervous energy, taut and with a hint of volatility. Yet to his crew he was totally unflappable, calm and conscientious on the bombing runs, a dedicated flyer. Then something happened which changed the composure of his men. Returning from an op one night they overshot the runway and had to go round again.

After the next trip, Rosser's starboard wheel went off the edge of the runway and the Lancaster was ignominiously hauled off the grass by a tractor. There was a lot of fuss and, to their shame, the crew were put on circuits and bumps every afternoon. They were now more scared coming in to land than they were over the target, taking up crash positions on the approach to the airfield. Rosser, increasingly uncomfortable, had inexplicably lost his confidence about landing. Yet after bombing Berlin on only his second trip, 28 January 1944, he had displayed great expertise when faced with an emergency. With only three minutes of fuel left he landed perfectly at Middle Wallop, Hampshire – a fighter airfield then occupied by Americans – on a grass runway reinforced with wire mesh and much too short for a Lancaster.

Flight Sergeant Doug White from Sheffield was the navigator. A little on the plump side, he was a steadying influence, less boisterous than the rest of the crew, studious and keen on mathematics. He had been known to wag a cautious finger when some of them showed signs of drinking too much on nights when they were not flying.

There was no more than two years in age between the crew members, the only exception being flight engineer Sergeant Ernie Harris from Wellingborough, who was nineteen. His family had been twice struck by tragedy earlier in the war. His eldest brother, a Royal Navy seaman, died when his ship was sunk. Some months before, his younger brother had drowned in a swimming accident near his Northamptonshire home.

Sergeant Norman Goss, the bomb-aimer, had also trained as a navigator. Baby-faced Goss, sporting a public school accent, came from a farming family near Bicester, Oxfordshire. He had more money to spend than the others and enjoyed eating dinners at expensive hotels in which they would have felt uncomfortable. He was ambitious and, the others believed, looking for medals. It was Goss who wanted them to join the Pathfinders, which offered several perks worth considering, including more rapid promotion.

Wireless operator Sergeant Ted 'Hank' Sears came from West London, where his father had been bombed out and was now living in temporary lodgings. Sears, worried about his father, left the airfield more often than he should have done to make sure he was all right.

Sears also worried about the morality of bombing German cities flat and was often gloomy after returning from an operation. He once told a startled debriefing officer: 'Oh, yes, it was a good trip. We've probably done in a few children's homes and hospitals.' He talked of quitting flying, but would not have risked being accused of going LMF. Normally a very lively character, with twinkling dark brown eyes, Sears enjoyed mimicking the accents of the two gunners, both of whom came from Lancashire. All three were bosom pals.

Sergeant John Charnock, twenty-three, the mid-upper gunner, came from Darwin. A good swimmer, it was his unfulfilled ambition to swim across Morecambe Bay. An apprentice sheet-metal worker for Leyland Motors, this was his thirteenth operation, one more than the others. On the afternoon that he had arrived at Metheringham from OTU on 14 January 1944, he had been picked for one trip to join a crew short of a mid-upper gunner, and who were halfway through their tour. Charnock was petrified, not so much for being pushed so quickly on to a trip, but knowing that a veteran crew would not want to be saddled with a rookie gunner, although the skipper, Pilot Officer W. Lee, was kind and reassuring.

Returning from the raid on Brunswick in Lancaster JB562, they were hit by heavy flak. The aircraft was bouncing violently and in the mid-upper turret, Charnock could smell the smoke and cordite as shells exploded all around them. He opened fire on a Ju88 which veered off and Lee was pleased with him. Back at Metheringham, he told the gunner: 'Don't imagine for one minute that was a normal trip. I've never smelled cordite in the aircraft before in all our operations. It'll probably never happen to you again.' Lee and his crew later joined 617 Squadron.

This experience gave Charnock an edge on the rest of the crew skippered by Ted Rosser. He jokingly told them not to worry when the flak appeared heavy, only when they could smell and taste it, which he described as a bit like the after effects of Bonfire Night.

The rear gunner was Sergeant Dennis Steele from Southport. A handsome six-footer, he was a fine pianist who had once made a recording with Henry Hall. On a gunnery course at Bridlington, Steele also had a regular job as a pianist on the pier. Later, whenever the crew went into a pub which had a piano, Steele settled himself in front of it, guaranteeing them all free beer for the rest of the night.

This was their first operation since bombing Frankfurt four nights earlier and they did not expect an easy trip, but could not believe it could be worse than Berlin, which they had bombed three times already. The German capital was always fiercely defended, but tonight they would be among the first bombers over the target, one of five Lancasters from 106 Squadron supporting the Pathfinders. They were a little nervous about being a part of this small advance force, for there was safety in numbers. A force of over 800 bombers would overwhelm the German defences, which could not be expected to fire at each aircraft. A trickle of Lancasters would be easier meat for the gunners and fighters. Another thirteen Lancasters from 106 Squadron set off later for Frankfurt.

Before take-off they emptied their pockets in the crew room and put securely into lockers prized personal possessions and anything which might identify their station or squadron, even tickets for buses, cinemas and the laundry. Charnock left his new and expensive Irish Petersen pipe, given him by his father, and a fountain pen. He noticed Doug White admiring his new gold signet ring. Charnock commented: 'Surely you're not going to fly with that?'

'Why not?' said White in surprise.

'If anything happens to you, it'll be lost,' said Charnock, adding more gently, 'If you're taken prisoner, the Germans will have it off you.'

White grinned as he removed the ring and put it into his locker. 'I suppose you'd rather the padre got it than the Germans.'

They had been briefed to cross the Dutch coast north of the Zuider Zee, turning south to Frankfurt. To confuse the German defences several diversionary raids had been laid on to attack Berlin, Dortmund, Hannover and Oberhausen, while minelaying was carried out off Denmark and in Kiel Bay. The last flecks of light were fading as they crossed the Lincolnshire coast. That was a good start. Too often, they believed, Bomber Command cut it too fine for comfort, making them leave base in full daylight during winter, counting on it being dark as they got over the North Sea.

Lancaster B-Beer saw little flak and no night fighters. There was not even any flak or searchlights when they crossed over the outskirts of Frankfurt, and Charnock wondered if they were over the right target. White, the navigator, then reported that they had arrived nearly two minutes early and told the pilot to make a slight diversion so they would be over the exact spot at the precise second. There must have been other Pathfinders in the sky, but Charnock didn't see any. A few minutes ahead of the Main Force, they started the run at the end of which they would release the marker flares over the target. Beams from two searchlights began probing the sky and flak suddenly burst close around them. Bomb-aimer Norman Goss reported: 'Bomb doors open,' adding 'steady' as they droned over the centre of Frankfurt at 21,000ft. It was about 9.15pm.

Everyone was waiting for the words 'Bombs gone!' when the bomber leaped mightily into the air. Charnock was thrown violently from his seat and hit the top of the mid-upper turret. Before the gunner fell back, his canvas seat became disengaged from its socket and he dropped helplessly into the fuselage, wondering what the hell had happened. He had not heard an explosion and nothing had been reported over the intercom. As he stumbled to his feet a torrent of flames, like a gigantic blow torch, ripped with a fearsome roar through the fuselage from the front of the aircraft. The heat was intense and painful. In a single breath, Charnock consumed a mouthful of flames. His rubber oxygen tube caught fire. He tore off the oxygen mask, which dragged off his helmet, exposing his bare head to the full blast of the flames. His parachute had fallen from its straps on the side of the fuselage and was starting to burn. He clapped it to his chest and was clipping it to the harness, while crouching with his back to the mass of flames, when the photoflash went off, releasing a blinding white glare of one million candlepower. Charnock's last memory of the Lancaster is desperately fumbling with the parachute clips and stumbling backwards, away from the flames to get near the escape hatch.

At that moment the aircraft exploded into fragments, flinging Charnock out into the cold night sky. He recalls:

'That is as far as I remember inside the aircraft. I don't think I reached the hatch, I certainly don't recall going out of it. The next moment I was spinning like a top, in the foetal position, with my head in my knees, which is the correct position to go out, going round and round. I could smell my burned hair and flesh as I was coming down. My hands had also been burned. I still hadn't heard an explosion and didn't know what had happened to the aircraft. I was only conscious of the flames.'

It was much later at Fallingbostel, a prisoner-of-war camp in western Germany, that Charnock met a man who had been in the first wave of the Main Force and who saw the last seconds of Lancaster B-Beer. He told Charnock: 'We'd never seen anything like the incredible glare of light which suddenly appeared in the sky, with every colour under the sun coming from the blazing flares and incendiaries. Then the aircraft vanished. It just wasn't there any more. It was unbelievable.'

For Charnock, momentarily unconscious, probably through shock and lack of oxygen, his awakening came almost as if he had returned to his body after briefly leaving it:

'When I came-to I found myself falling. It really was like a strange discovery. I found my right hand struggling to fasten the second clip from the harness to the parachute. I knew exactly what I had to do, but I had no power at all. My mind was clear, but I was utterly useless. I had no strength and couldn't do anything. I suppose it was the G-force, but at the time I couldn't understand why I was unable to fasten that clip.

'How I wished I had listened properly when they had said at various lectures what happened if only one clip was fastened. I knew you could be all right, but didn't know whether there were any precautions you were supposed to take. I thought all this out and looked down, seeing the ground coming up and still no aircraft above. I don't know how long I dropped, thinking "I'm going to have to pull the ripcord soon".'

After he had pulled it at about 10,000ft, Charnock then worried that he had left it too late. The first sensation was of absolute silence and the cold air, which deadened the pain in his face and hands. The harness fed through his crotch so he couldn't fall out of it unless he twisted sharply. He could see no other falling parachute, nor blazing wreckage, and he hoped the rest of the crew had already landed safely. Charnock would not know for some time that he was the only survivor.

'Bits of my parachute, probably the knotted parts of the lines, were glowing red like cigars. They weren't supposed to burn. The canopy seemed all right.' He looked down and saw the river Main, twisting in a big horseshoe bend. Then came the fearful flashes of pounding anti-aircraft guns and searchlights sweeping the sky. He was no longer afraid of the searchlights, they were hunting juicier targets.

All aircrews had been warned of the dangers of being picked up by civilians, particularly in a city they had just bombed. Dropping into the centre of Frankfurt, he tried to swing the parachute towards the river. He believed the gun emplacements were near the Main and was confident he would be all right if picked up by the military. The gunner wouldn't mind even dropping into the river, that would probably be safer than hitting a house.

Charnock missed the river. He braced himself as he struck the ground and sank up to the tops of his thighs in soft earth. He had fallen into a freshly dug grave. Lying on its side beside him was a marble headstone, cracked in half by his shoulder as he landed, although he felt no pain. Terrible pain was erupting from his face and head. His hands were sore, too. He touched his raw swollen face with an exploratory finger and gasped at the agony it caused. His hair had gone and his eyes were rapidly closing. The gunner's head was swelling hugely, with pain so intense it almost seemed to be gathering itself before exploding. He scrambled out of the grave, discovered that he had lost one boot, and had to drag his eyes open with grubby fingers. He gazed about him. If he'd had a map of the city he might have had time to work out that he was standing in the

Niederrad, a section of Frankfurt cemetery. Little more than Schwanheimer Strasse lay between him and the river Main. Graves of an army of dead Germans stretched beyond him. Having fallen into the land of the dead, he could see no one from the land of the living and though that did not bother him much, it was an eerie place to be. Nothing moved. There was no sound and he shivered.

It was then the pain became temporarily anaesthetised by a thought that brought further horror to an already unbelievable situation. The bombing raid had not started. The night's target was the centre of Frankfurt and that was where he was, trapped in a graveyard. Over 800 bombers were due overhead at any second.

The grave was in the middle of the cemetery. He looked wildly round, fingers clawing at tortured eyes. He was afraid of going blind, but more frightened of being pulped by the bombs which began falling as he ran to the 3ft-high wall surrounding the cemetery. It offered scant protection, but he used his hands to frantically dig himself into the earth beside a corner of the wall. He thought he must be the only human being above ground in Frankfurt that night as the bombs poured down in a continuous and terrifying fusillade, a thunderstorm from hell. The ground shook and leaped around him. As the bombers passed high overhead, irregular lumps of red hot shrapnel screamed, whoosh-whoosh-whooshed through the air, thudding and clattering within feet of his crouched and trembling body. Jagged remnants of German shells joined those whirling and caterwauling from the British bombs. Charnock did not believe he could survive the raid, most likely ending up a victim of his own bombers. It was too much to expect two miracle escapes in one night. Yet he wished if he must die, that death would come quickly, without further pain. He thought of his family in Lancashire, probably comfortably listening to the wireless. Would they ever learn what had really happened to him? He thought, too, of the cruel absurdity of dying in a German graveyard.

Waves of scorching heat surged over the cemetery. The ground vibrated and shook as each bomb exploded. He risked occasional peeps into the nightmare world and saw walls leap intact into the air, falling as dust and rubble. Murderous splinters of brick and stone darted about him. A bomb fell nearby with an ear-splitting kerumph and he watched the wall of a big factory no more than 50ft away collapse with a curious sighing whoosh before flames and smoke poured out of it. He saw one building which carried a familiar sign, 'Messer'. He had used that company's welding equipment before the war. It was a scrap of bizarre nostalgia in that hostile city.

Just beyond the cemetery there was a house, brilliant white lights blazing from every window. Charnock thought a lunatic must live there, not putting up blackout in the middle of a raid. Suddenly, it was consumed by billowing flames. Other buildings caught fire as more incendiaries rained down. He tried to assemble his thoughts during the constant blast of noise, which continued for nearly thirty minutes. After the bombing stopped, gunfire rattled on until the defence commanders knew the bombers had gone. They had left a desolated city: 948 people dead, 346 seriously injured and 120,000 bombed out of their homes. Many timbered buildings, preserved since the Middle Ages, were in ruins. Hospitals and churches had been razed to the ground and industrial areas severely damaged. Charnock stared fearfully around, not expecting to find anyone prepared to offer assistance.

Between 9.45 and 10.00pm, Lancasters from Metheringham dropped 99.2 tons of bombs on the city, the highest total to date dropped on a single target by 106 Squadron.

German guns were still booming when Charnock rose from his pathetic sanctuary and turned hopefully towards their flashes. He needed medical treatment and thought he would be safer with the German Army. Then the guns stopped firing and he was lost. 'I had no sense of direction and no idea which way I should go. There was dead silence, then the all clear went, a siren just like ours. And so I started walking.'

Fires crackled fiercely around him as he left the cemetery. Flames tore through roofs and buildings collapsed in showers of sparks that cascaded high into the air. He saw no one as he started along a street in a daze then, after 30yds, two boys aged about twelve suddenly appeared, like startled rabbits bolting from a hole, skidding to a halt in front of him. They stared, mouths open, absolutely petrified. He was an alarmingly grotesque and dishevelled figure, with third degree burns to his head, puffed up and red raw, only a few bleak wisps of scorched dark brown hair left, and eyes which had disappeared into the abused flesh. He now needed both hands to open one blue eye. The gunner's American leather bomber jacket caused him further anguish. It had shrunk in the extreme heat until it had become a straitjacket, pinioning Charnock's elbows to his sides. He could only move his hands and forearms.

Charnock said hopefully: 'Police! Soldiers!' The boys, uncomprehending, continued to stare at him from round dark eyes, in fear and disbelief. Then, without exchanging a word, they turned and fled. Charnock stumbled on. Everything around him was burning or smouldering. He was in Bruchfeldstrasse, which led to the city race track when people, emerging noisily like trolls from underground shelters, spotted the injured British airman amidst the devastation of their homes, and rushed to crowd round him angrily shouting, screaming and spitting.

Among the crowd of about thirty distraught and vengeful Germans were two men in dark uniforms and helmets. Charnock believed them to be the equivalent of the British ARP (Air Raid Precautions) wardens. They stood next to Charnock, holding off the crowd, which was baying for blood, shrieking: 'Luftgangster! Terror bomber! Murderer! Schwein!' One of the wardens asked if he was English or American. Charnock did not know what to say for the best. 'I knew they had two points of view. One lot said the British were the real enemy and always had been, the other was that the British were involved and the Americans had stuck their noses into something that was none of their business. I said: "English".'

He was cursed for being an 'Englander schwein', the crowd began flinging stones and rubble at him. There were plenty of potential missiles lying around beside the ruins of bombed buildings. Others tried to punch and grab Charnock, while the wardens fought them off, trying to move him along the street. Then one warden spoke quickly to the other, and Charnock instinctively knew he was going to summon help. The remaining warden was himself hit by flying stones, but he never gave up, shouting at the crowd, displaying considerable bravery. Charnock saw one man on the fringe of the crowd, wielding a length of iron fencing, crying: 'Mein haus! Mein haus!' and knew he was the one to watch.

Charnock recalls: 'I should have been terrified, but I wasn't. It was nothing to do with courage. I was in so much pain, I didn't think anything worse could happen and probably didn't care if it did.'

A pretty girl of eighteen stood in the street beneath her family's fourth-floor flat where the roof was on fire. She was catching bedding thrown out by her father when she noticed the crowd hitting the British airman. She asked what was happening and was told he was an English terror bomber, getting what he deserved. She picked up a brick and joined the crowd.

Then a car screeched to a halt and several helmeted policemen jumped out. One of them asked: 'Englander or American?' Charnock replied: 'English.'
The policeman spat: 'Schwein!' He struck the airman a crushing blow in the face with his fist. Charnock sank, gasping to the ground. He saw the pretty girl appear, holding the brick. Totally expressionless, she loomed over him and dropped it. The brick smashed into his mouth, breaking two teeth and he almost passed out. A third air-raid warden, who had found a 4lb incendiary bomb which had not gone off, stepped forward and let it fall on to the body of the defenceless airman.

Suddenly, the man whose house had been flattened burst howling through the crowd, waving the piece of iron, which he brought down savagely on to the head of Charnock, who lost consciousness. When he came-to, the police had cleared the crowd in a wide circle around him. He was dragged roughly to their car and pitched inside. The car was driven a short distance to the police station in the same street. 'I was thrust into a room where they were all jabbering away. One could speak a little English. They didn't bother me, but the room was thick with cigar smoke. It was as if my raw face had been put into an acid bath. They were asking me questions. I just mumbled at them.'

The Germans lost patience and shoved him out of the room towards a staircase. He was struck brutally on the back of the head with a rifle butt and tumbled helplessly down the stairs into what seemed to be a cell. He has no idea how long he laid on the cell floor. It may have been just overnight, but at the time he thought he had been left there to rot.

Charnock was handed over to two armed soldiers who pushed and prodded him a short distance through the streets, where men toiled ceaselessly in the debris of the raid, to an Army flak unit at the city race track. He was passed to a grumbling doctor, who stitched up his wounds, while continually insulting him. The doctor clearly resented having to treat an enemy airman, and emphasised his feelings by pulling and tugging at the gunner's throbbing head as he inserted the stitches. The doctor completed Charnock's treatment by emptying a bottle of iodine over his head. The fiery liquid scorched through cuts and burns and trickled into his clothes. Charnock jumped, but did not murmur at the excruciating pain. The doctor laughed scornfully.

The next few days were hazy, as he passed in and out of consciousness, but he was eventually admitted to Frankfurt's City Hospital. A doctor cut away the shrunken flying jacket and gently cleaned up his face. He was stripped and put into a bath of gentian violet, his head being pushed under several times. He was then given several blood transfusions. His principal concern at this time was thirst. He created a few disturbances in his eternal quest for water until he located a water fountain near his ward. 'Nothing in my life has ever delighted me as much as this water fountain. I couldn't stop drinking.'

He left the hospital for Frankfurt railway station sitting on a flat cart drawn by a horse. The swelling had gone down and his vision had improved, although he was still worried about his sight. Charnock arrived at a Red Cross hospital in Ober Massfeld on 2 April, his twenty-fourth birthday. His face was saved by an Australian plastic surgeon, Major Sherman, who like himself was a prisoner-of-war. Sherman exclaimed: 'Oh, if only I'd got you earlier, but don't worry, we'll fix you up.' He was true to his word, operating every day, gently scraping away the dead flesh. He rebuilt Charnock's eyelids with flexible skin taken from under his armpits. Skin removed from his hips was grafted round the badly burned mouth and ears. He twice carried out the same operation on an American, but it didn't take. When he removed the bandages, the graft came away. Charnock observes:

'I was lucky. He said I had good healing flesh, it took well and I was the best patient he'd ever had. He used techniques which he learned in Germany as a POW, involving the use of blood plasma, rather than stitch grafts. The results astounded RAF doctors on my return to England. Major Sherman was a saint. He could have been repatriated but insisted on staying, working from 6.00am until midnight every day, carrying out all kinds of operations.'

The surgeon recommended Charnock for repatriation back to England for further treatment to his eyelids, which sprang open involuntarily when he was asleep. The Swiss Commission agreed, but the top German surgeon refused, saying the elasticity of the new eyelids would improve naturally. He was right.

After several months in hospital, he was sent to an RAF prisoner-of-war camp at Heidekrug in East Prussia, Stalag Luft III. When the Russians threatened East Prussia, he was moved to Thorn in Poland.

'We walked from Poland to west Germany, about 600 miles, sleeping beside roads, in fields, occasionally in farm buildings, or stationary trucks. Sometimes we were carried between country stations in cattle trucks, but mostly we walked. We were given three boiled potatoes each day. When we had cigarettes, soap, tea and coffee to barter we could buy bread, but when they ran out we stole vegetables from gardens and swedes and cattle beet from fields.'

Charnock was flown from Luneburg Heath – where German officers had signed the surrender document on 4 May 1945 – back to England with several soldiers in a Lancaster. 'A bright bloke came out of the rear turret, as perky as anything. He said: "Here you are, you can have your old seat back". I didn't want it, but he insisted. I stuck it in the turret for a couple of minutes. I couldn't get out quickly enough. I said I'd never fly again, and I never have. I thought I had used up all my luck.'

Charnock made an almost full recovery from his injuries, although he now receives a disability pension. Afraid of going bald, his hair eventually grew again and most of his scars faded.

Part of the wreckage of Lancaster B-Beer fell into Sommerhoffpark across the river Main. Three aircrew bodies were also found here. More wreckage was found by Schwanheimerstrasse. The remains of Ted Rosser, Norman Goss and Hank Sears were buried at Durnbach Military Cemetery, south of Munich. Ernie Harris, Doug White and Dennis Steele, who have no known graves, are commemorated on the Commonwealth Air Forces Memorial at Runnymede.

John Charnock visited all the families of the dead men, except the Australian pilot. Everyone drew comfort from his visits, except the mother of the flight engineer, Ernie Harris, who was her third son to die during the war. Especially pleased to see him were the parents of Doug White in Sheffield who had received his gold signet ring through the post.

7

BITTER AND TWISTED

If the skipper hadn't got his knackers in a twist, they wouldn't have lost the Halifax. Flight engineer Archie Fazackerley wouldn't have broken his leg, and none of the crew would have harboured such deep bitterness about the ineptitude of some RAF met officers after one of the more bizarre foul-ups of the war.

The pilot, Squadron Leader Misselbrooke, was 'resting' after completing a tour of thirty operations. He peered out of the cockpit into the blackness of the November night. Some rest, he thought, shepherding a bomber-load of sprogs on a cross-country training flight to the Shetland Islands. Beside him at the dual controls, in the first pilot's seat, was Flight Sergeant Charlie 'Chuck' Bateman, the pilot under instruction.

It was cold. Cold enough for snow. There had been a snow warning for much further north, well away from the bomber's flight path. With luck they'd have a decent run, putting the crew through their paces and be back in time for a pint, if the bar was still open. The heavy bomber was old, taken off an operational squadron, not considered safe enough to carry bombs hundreds of miles across Germany, but good enough for training. It was probably no wonder so many young men died before they had a chance to get at the enemy.

Misselbrooke shifted uneasily in his seat as the four-engine Halifax roared over north Lincolnshire. The seat harness was too tight under his crotch. He had noticed it soon after take-off. All the fidgeting since had made him more uncomfortable and now the harness was threatening to crush all the life and spirit out of his balls. That would be a disaster. A married man, he smiled grimly to himself.

Sitting beside him, Chuck Bateman, a Toronto lorry driver before the war, gazed ahead, his concentration broken only by the grunts and gyrations of the squadron leader who was not suffering in silence. It was Bateman's first trip in a Halifax. Behind the pilots stood the thin, wiry figure of Sergeant Fazackerley, twenty-two, earnestly studying the banks of dials and warning lights. Fazackerley had about three-and-a-half hours flying time behind him. Not a lot, but he had enjoyed every minute of it. He was part of a bomber aircrew, the proudest man alive. Although he didn't know it, the next half-hour would submit him to the severest test of character he would face during the whole of his five years in the RAF. Much later, after sixty to seventy hours on a Link

Trainer, he would occasionally take over the controls returning home over France and the North Sea while his pilot had forty winks on the rest bed. Now he was in some awe of Misselbrooke, who was like a teacher, putting him through his lessons.

Fazackerley had been born in Preston's Deepdale, surrounded by dour cotton mills, a cheer away from North End's First Division football ground. The family later moved to Morecambe, where the bracing sea air flattened even further young Fazackerley's crushed Lancastrian vowels, which were to confuse the officers at an aircrew selection board. Indeed, he believed his broad northern accent, combined with an abrupt manner and blunt speaking, probably led to his rejection and was nothing to do with his diminutive size.

In the first two years of war, he had been an apprentice cabinet maker in the Lancaster factory of Waring and Gillow, which had been diverted from its original function of producing quality furniture to making wings for the Airspeed Oxford, an aeroplane used for training, light transport and communications. Fazackerley had worked on the Oxford and, later, on the legendary Mosquito bomber. Both aircraft were constructed largely of wood. He had also turned his hand to building the giant Horsa gliders, first used in the airborne invasion of Sicily, and which later played a major role on D–Day, carrying men and equipment to Normandy. The aeroplanes had whetted his appetite for the RAF.

Although he was in a reserved occupation, he ached to be closer to the war. He desperately wanted to fly. He craved excitement and adventure. He joined the RAF on 11 January 1941, qualified as an aircraft fitter, and worked for a time on Whitleys with 57 Conversion Unit based at Whitchurch Heath (Tilstock), near Crewe, later volunteering for aircrew.

He was disappointed not to be accepted for aircrew. He passed the medical even though an eyebrow or two was raised among the doctors. Bollock–naked, Fazackerley resembled an animated hairpin. He was concerned about his height, but although he strained every fibre of his body to stretch another fraction of an inch, he was unable to yank himself much beyond 5ft 6½in. He discovered later, with some irritation, that the RAF employed pilots who were shorter than him and needed blocks fitted to their control pedals. Being thin did have its advantages. He could tuck into four good meals a day and know he wouldn't add any weight to his 8st 6lb frame.

Fresh from his flight engineer's course at St Athan in South Wales he was, at last, in the thick of things and the war looked like being around for some time. Happily, the young man from Lancashire, with his twinkling blue eyes, infectious grin and ironic sense of humour, was able to pursue his hobbies of girls and booze with continuing enthusiasm and success. He had not yet seen a burst of flak to justify the nickname he had been given, Flakackerley, nor had he seen a bomb fall. He had not even seen a bomb. He need not have worried. Once they started operations, RAF aircrews packed a lifetime of experience into a few weeks.

It was the night of 23 November 1943. The Halifax was some miles north of its base, 1667 Heavy Conversion Unit at Blyton, near Gainsborough, Lincolnshire. It had been a clear, crisp night when they had taken off. The mainly inexperienced crew were expected to carry out all the normal routines of an operational flight over enemy-held territory, without any of the inconveniences of flak or fighters. Nor was there a target to find. A doddle. Misselbrooke sighed, glanced at the intense young pilot sitting beside him and wondered if he and the other sprogs in his crew would survive thirty ops. The chances were against it.

Fazackerley was a bit disappointed not to be in a Lancaster. He had been on a five-week course at Avro's Woodford plant in Cheshire, and knew every nut and bolt of the big bomber. But Blyton did not have a spare Lancaster. Fazackerley had never seen a Halifax, but had been given the pilot's notes on the unfamiliar bomber to study during the week before his first flight. He just hoped he would remember enough to get him safely to the Shetlands and back. He could hear the mumble of Canadian navigator Sergeant Bill 'Spider' Buie, from Bradford, Ontario, talking to himself, working out their course in his small curtained-off office. Fazackerley recalls: 'Spider had the habit of saying "Woah!" before a change in course, as if we could put the brakes on and stop in midair.'

The engineer, together with the rest of the crew, heard the pilot muttering in a strained voice over the intercom: 'This bloody harness!' as he continued to squirm with increased anxiety to release his gasping testicles. At last Misselbrooke could stand it no longer and, with a grunt of pain and frustration, keeping one hand on the control column, he reached above him for the fixed handle to haul himself an inch or two out of the seat for a moment to make suitable adjustments. At that moment, an ambling routine training flight was turned into a grotesque nightmare. Instead of seizing the handle fixed to the roof, the pilot seized the lever for the escape hatch which was immediately jettisoned from the aircraft. 'Fuck me!' he gasped.

His sentiments were loudly echoed by the horrified Bateman and Fazackerley as icy air with dancing flakes of snow poured into the already cold cockpit. Then, as they roared into a thick cloud at 9,000ft, still climbing, the bomber was struck by a shuddering blizzard. The air turned blue with obscenities, swiftly becoming glistening white as snow blasted spitefully through the 2ft 6in square hatch, normally only used if the aircraft was ditched into the drink. Fazackerley heard further puzzled curses issuing from the navigator's office, where Spider Buie made frantic grabs at his equipment as it slid from the table on to the floor.

The snow got rapidly worse until it seemed as if a squad of vengeful janker wallahs must be above them shovelling it gleefully into the cockpit. Fazackerley remembers:

'The skipper had it in his mind to get out of the snow or turn back. He remained calm, although it was a desperate situation which he tried to keep from the rest of the

Right: Derrick Allen at the
fuselage door. (Allen)

Right: Before the war, Jack
Halstead, the flight engineer,
worked as a butcher, then in a
tank factory. (Halstead)

Left: Derrick Allen in the mid-upper turret, from which he stared into the hell of burning Düsseldorf in November 1944. He was photographed from the astrodome during a training flight over England. (Allen)
Below: The rear half of the crashed B-Bastard. (Allen)
Right: Düsseldorf burns during a heavy raid by British bombers. Hundreds of bombs and incendiaries were poured into the city and devastation was widespread. (Imperial War Museum)
Below right: Düsseldorf after the raid of 2/3 November, 1944. In the devastated northern suburbs, the large workshops of the Rheinmetall-Borsig engineering and armament works (left) are empty shells or heaps of rubble. (RAF Museum Hendon)

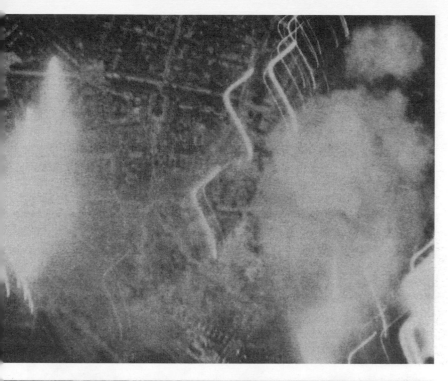

DICING WITH DEATH OVER PEENEMÜNDE

Left: Rear gunner, Patrick Barry, is flanked by his delighted father, James, and brother, Eugene, after receiving the DFM from King George VI at Buckingham Palace in June 1944. (Barry)

Bottom left: The injured Patrick Barry and admirers at hospital in East Grinstead. (Barry)

Right: Pilot 'Pluto' Wilson (right) and Charlie Cawthorne, flight engineer, look down from the Lancaster cockpit. The kangaroos on the side record the number of operations flown. (Cawthorne)

Right: After Peenemünde. From left: Harry Crumplin, navigator, Dave Booth, wireless operator, 'Pluto' Wilson, pilot, 'Swill' Campbell, bomb-aimer, Charlie Cawthorne, flight engineer and mid-upper gunner George Oliver. (Cawthorne)

Below: This makeshift tent, with pin-ups pasted inside, was shelter at dispersal for the groundcrew, including Curly and Snowy, seen here, who worked on 'Pluto' Wilson's aircraft. (Barry)

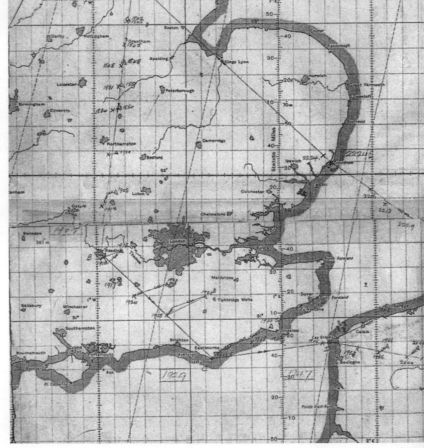

BATTLE ORDERS

Far left: At Scampton, on completion of their tour. From left: Flying Officer Ted Durman, Sergeant Vic Morandi, Flight Lieutenant 'Whizz' Wheeler, Sergeant 'Scotty' Scott, newly commissioned Pilot Officer Freddy Fish and Flight Sergeant Bill Turner. (Fish)

Bottom left: Navigator's chart for Cologne, 31 November 1944. (Fish)

Near left: Emergency landing fields on the Continent. (Fish)

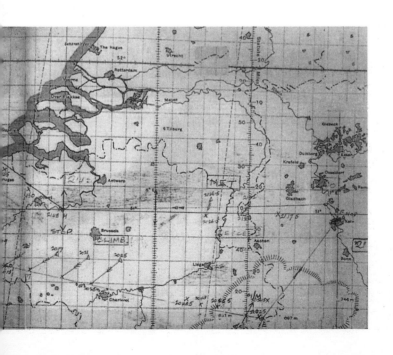

SQUADRON _153_ A/C NUMBER AND LETTER _A_ CAPTAIN _F/L WHEELER_ NAVIGATOR _F/S FISH_ DATE _24/3/45_

FORECAST W/Vs AND AIR TEMPS

STAGE FROM TO	2,000 FT From (T) Speed TEMP °C	5,000 FT From (T) Speed TEMP °C	10,000 FT From (T) Speed TEMP °C	15,000 FT From (T) Speed TEMP °C	20,000 FT From (T) Speed TEMP °C
BASE-52½	160 36	150 40	140 40	130 +5	120 52
22-B	166 35	160 35	160 35	150 40	150 40
B-1.30E	176 30	170 30	170 32	170 35	170 40
1.30-6E	180 26	170 28	170 30	150 35	190 37
6E-A-56	180 22	180 22	190 26	190 30	190 32
Δ	170 22	170 25	170 25	170 30	180 22
56-2E	160 70	160 30	160 30	160 35	160 40
22-A	170 50	160 32	170 25	160 35	160 40

POSITION	SUN RISES / SETS	MOON RISES / SETS	TWILIGHT A.M. / P.M.	FORM

WATCH _155_ slow AT _1025_ GMT. ON _24/3/45_ GD. RATE ___ sec./hr. gaining losing

ORDERS _A LANGENDEER (Mr. Browns) H.W. 16 30 H.4 RED_
TI" N.80 RED/GREENS & GREENS. LONGSTOP-YELLOW.
Bomb. W/V H-12 18500. Y on 0500E M.B. BOXRITE MF THUNDER
LONGSTOP LYSOL VHF "C" n.6 "B" T.o.T. 1630.   7/0 13.

TIME	REQD TRACK (T)	W/V USED AND COMPUTED DRIFT	Course (T)	VARN (T)	Course (M)	Compass Corrn for Devn.	Course (C)	ROUTE FROM:— TO:—		R.A.S.	HEIGHT & AIR TEMP.	T.A.S.	D.R. G/S	DIST. TO RUN	D.R. TIME	E.T.A.
	188	150/37	172	10	192			BASE	A—B READING	178	7600 190		161	120	48.4	
	121	170/30	128	10	138			B—EC		173	✓ 190		170	80	28.2	
	121	✓	128	9	137			EC—C 5020 0200		173	✓ 190		170	71	25.0	
	079	✓	087	8	095			C—0400		172	✓ 190		160	90	28.5	
	015	150/35	088	7	095			0400—D 5100 0645		165	16000 195		200	109	26.7	
	036	190/30	038	6	044			D—A 5130 0710		164	14000 205		234	42	10.8	
	035	150/30	039	6	045			A—E 6132 0721		168	✓ 227	250	5	.7	
	133	✓	138	6	144			E—F 5927 0729		168	✓ 227	260	6	1.7	
	199	✓	147	6	203			F—G 6112 0720		190	18000 252	205	19	5.1	
	243	✓	237	6	243			G—D 5180 0645		191	17600 244	232	29	7.5	
	281	190/37	278	7	285			D—H 5930 0330		190	16000 231	220	146	38.0	
	320	160/30	317	9	326			H—I 5300 0130		220	7000 244	220	136	30.2	
	272	✓	271	10	281			I—J 5306 0014		220	7000 244	256	54	12.6	
	292	✓	285	10	295			J—A		220	5000 237	265	36	8.5	
											-7			964		
								DEADLINE 13.40								

BST				W				NAVIGATIONAL OBSERVATIONS (Pin Points, Fixes, Position Lines, Actual T.M.G. Actual Drift, G/S and W/V Manoeuvres, etc.)	GENERAL (Met.Conditions, Bombing, Intell., Enemy Action)						
1025								Watches Synchronized W/T Go.							
1302								Airborne- climbing			170 7600 190				
1331	158	160/37	182	10	192			A & B			170 7600 190	158	130	49.2	14.20
1331								X	(Reset API)						
1337								X							
								G/S 165				165	113	40.6	14.1
1343								X							
								G/S 162				162	96	35.5	14.1
									162/40						
1349								X							
								G/S 157				157	82	31.2	14.2
									166/40						
1355								X							
								G/S 160				160	66	24.7	14.19
									172/30						
1401								X							
								G/S 162½				162	50	18.4	14.19
									176/34						
1407								X							
								G/S 161				161	32	11.9	14.18
									172/30						
1419	121	172/30	128	10	138			DB 8 & EC			165 7600 186	166	80	29.0	14.44
1414								X	183/37						
1425								G/S 165				165	59	21.4	14.44
									182/32						
1431								X							
								G/S 168				168	42	15.0	14.4
									Reduce EAS 165			158	42	16.0	14.4
									176/29						
1437								X							
								G/S 162		177 30			162	26	9.6	14.44

Signed _F. F. Fish_   Navigator.

	W/V USED AND COMPUTED DRIFT	Course (T)	VARN	Course (M)	Compass Corrn. for Devn.	Course (C)	NAVIGATIONAL OBSERVATIONS (Pin Points, Fixes, Position Lines, Actual T.M.G. Actual Drift, G/S and W/V Manoeuvres, etc.)	GENERAL (Met.Conditions, Bombing, Intell., Enemy Action)	R.A.S.	HEIGHT & AIR TEMP.	T.A.S.	D.R. G/S	DIST. TO RUN	D.R. TIME	E.T.A.
7	121	177/30	129	9	136		Oc EE %C C	Bombs fused	160	7600	150	161	71	26.5	15.13.6
							X	168/29							
3							X G/S 160					160	56	21.0	15.14
								Increase	165			165	56	20.4	15.13.4
								158/34							
9							X G/S 165					165	40	14.6	15.13.6
5							X G/S 175	206/16				175	22	7.6	15.12.6
5	679	206/16	282	8	090		DR C %C 4E		165	7600	186	196	90	27.8	15.70.8
							X	178/19							
10							X	168/24½							
					070		G/S 190 %C snod					190	66	20.4	15.40.4
26				110			G/S 190 %C TR ETA 1531	170/27½				190	48	16.2	16.41.2
37				557			%C					196	37	11.4	15.42.6
31							X	160/31				185	18	6.8	15.42.8
32	678	180/32	087	7	291		DR 4E %C D Climbing	163/47¼	160	15000	201	205	23	7.6	16.18
48							X G/S 205	176/43½				205	104	30.4	16.18.4
66							X G/S 190	172/73				190	85	27.0	16.22
61							X G/S 204					204	63	18.6	16.19.6
76							020 4E GE 13.								
79							X G/S 210	178/34½				210	340	9.7	16.18.7
								8 cast 170/35	156	14000	209	223	42	10.8	16.29.8
19	026	180/35	040	G	046		DR D %C D Switches switched. VPL 220 Δ 15 bombs gone, PPI	1625 5.470 %C down	170	14500				2	
2720				040											
3027				045											
31	133	180/35	139		139		DR E %C F		168		227	268	61.7		16.32.7
33	199			146			DR F %C G Hit R over GiS inner								
56							DR G %C D DR D P/C EINDHOVEN Emergency Drome								
49							EINDHOVEN. Permission to Land	Calling 'DARKY'							
22															
33							Landed.								
35							ORC OFF								

Nice work. It was a good thing you had noted the Emergency Landing Drome. J. O. Turner F/Lt

Signed E. Silbert — Navigator.

	SQUARE				SEARCH						HEIGHT.		T.A.S.		VIS.			MEMORANDA
	TRACK T.	W/V USED	Corrn. (T)	VARN	Course (M)	Corrn. for Devn.	Course (C)	D.R. G/S	DIST.	D.R. TIME	T.T.T.	DIST.	D.R. TIME	T.T.T.				

eft and above: Navigator's log for Harpenerweg, 24 March 1945. (Fish)

Headquarters,
No 5 Group, R.A.F.,
Grantham, Lincs.

04/17/0 of A.

5th. July 1941.

ar Mrs. Chandler,

As the Officer detailed to supervise
e collection of your son's belongings, may I be
rmitted to offer you my deepest sympathy during this
me of anxiety.

In accordance with Air Ministry
ders your son's kit has been carefully checked and
cked and sent to :-

The Central Depository,
R.A.F., COLNBROOK,
Slough· Bucks.

to whom any communications regarding it should
addressed. You are informed however, that no
fects can be released until certain statutory
rmalities have been complied with.

Your obedient Servant,

Officer i/c Committee of Adjustment,
Headquarters, No 5 Group, R.A.F.

s. Chandler,
in Cottage,
d Bosham,
r. Chichester,
ssex.

RIFT ON THE NORTH SEA
osite page, top left: 'Chan'
ndler faced the most miserable
al of his 96 operational flights
e summer of 1941. (Chandler)
osite page, top right: Air
ner 'Chan' can afford to smile
his proud mother Mrs Hilda
ndler, after receiving his DFC
bar from the King. (Chandler)
osite page, bottom: The war
ver. Flight Lieutenant 'Chan'
ndler, fed up and exhausted,
s impatiently on Tromsø dock,
way, for transport home.
andler)

CONFIDENTIAL NOTICE

The names of all who lose their lives or are wounded or reported missing while serving with the Royal Air Force will appear in the official casualty lists published from time to time in the Press.

Any publication of the date, place or circumstances of a casualty, and particularly any reference to the unit concerned, might give valuable information to the enemy, and for this reason, only the name, rank and Service number are included in the official lists.

Relatives are particularly requested, in the national interest, to ensure that any notices published privately do not disclose the date, place or circumstances of the casualty, or the unit.

The Press have been asked to co-operate in ensuring that no information of value to the enemy is published.

OVER THE HILLS AND FAR AWAY

Opposite page, far left: John Sutton learned to fly in Oklahoma in this Fairchild PT19. (Sutton)
Near left: Sutton at Jessore beside his new Wellington after the trip to Saigang. (Sutton)
Below left: Sutton converted from single-engine aircraft to twin-engine Oxfords at Spitalgate, near Grantham. Left to right: Pilot Officers Lord, Scrase, Smith-Carrington, Sutton and Wallis. (Sutton)
Right: All aircrews carried these 'ghooli chits' during Far East operations. (Sutton)

Dear friend,

I am an Allied fighter, I did not come here to do any harm to you who are my friends, I only want to do harm to the Japanese and chase them away from your country as quickly as possible. If you will lead me to the nearest Allied Military Post, my Government will give you a good reward.

AFTER LANCASTER BLOWS UP

Right: John Charnock was thrown out of an exploding bomber into the middle of an air-raid on Frankfurt. (Charnock)

Above: Bruchfeldstrasse, which has not changed much essentially since the war, looking west in the direction Charnock walked from the cemetery. He was attacked near this corner. (Gus Lerch)
Above right: No 4 Bruchfeldstrasse – the police station was on the ground floor. (Gus Lerch)

BITTER AND TWISTED
Right: Flight engineer Archie Fazackerley, the proudest man alive when he joined a bomber aircrew. (Fazackerley)
Below: This battered photograph travelled everywhere with Fazackerley. Back row: Brewer, Fazackerley, Byrne and Buie. Front row: Crooks and Bateman. Cut off in his prime is special duties operator Sergeant Docherty who, on bombing operations, fed false information to the enemy in fluent German. (Fazackerley)

THE ULTIMATE SACRIFICE

Above: The original five, from left: Jim Twinn, Buster Lister, Hugh Harvey, Dave Wallace and Pete Moore. (Twinn)

Above Right: The trip to Essen forced Jim Twinn to miss his honeymoon in North Wales, due to start the next day. (Twinn)

Below: Krupp's giant armament works in Essen after a raid by British bombers in 1943. (Fazackerley)

TARGET: E-BOAT PENS AT BOULOGNE
Left: Happy days. Roland Duck (left) and Mac Hamilton, trainee pilots at Eagle Field, California. (Duck)

Left: Boulogne harbour pictured after the raid on the E-boat pens on 15 June 1944. (Duck)

Left: Years after the war, Mac Hamilton receives thanks from Prince Bernhard of the Netherlands. Roland Duck (left) waits his turn. (Hamilton)

crew as long as he could. It didn't take them more than a minute or two to figure out what was happening. He released himself from the safety harness and left himself in his parachute. He said: "Right-oh engineer, we'd better get out of this lot." I thought we might climb out of it then go over the North Sea and try to come back under the cloud, if we could maintain height.

'He tried to keep climbing, but the snow had already got the better of us. Whatever you do in that situation, you mustn't lose height, but the snow was settling on the wings and freezing. We were losing our centre of gravity and being forced down. The engines were running rough.

'The skipper eased off the throttle to slow down the engines, diving 50 or 60ft then giving them a burst of throttle to climb, like a fairground switchback. It didn't work. I thought to myself we've got to get it down somewhere. I was shit scared. We should never have taken off. The bloody met officer had given us duff information.'

The snow was now swirling in, freezing on the floor and worse, covering the pilot's blind flying panel. Fazackerley slithered across the cockpit to scrape busily at the frosted dials on the panel with his gloved hands. Like the other crewmen, he was wearing three pairs of gloves. Silk gloves next to the skin, covered by chamois leather for warmth, with an outer pair of brown leather. He recalls:

'Spider had given the skipper a course back to Blyton, but the instruments were going haywire because the carburettors were icing up. Frozen snow began breaking off the wings and fuselage in lumps as hard as rocks; some smashed into the tail. There was a danger the tail might be ripped off. The wireless operator, Warrant Officer Eric Crooks, from Cheshire, had been in touch with base, giving them our position and explaining the problems.'

Crooks was one of only two other crewmen who had completed a tour. The other five were yet to finish training before going on their first operation. Misselbrooke tried to find a way out of the blinding blizzard, setting a zig-zag course, but it seemed hopeless and all the time the Halifax was losing altitude.

The pilot reported the situation in measured tones over the intercom. 'We are in a difficult position. I think the best thing is for us to prepare to abandon the aircraft. Get yourselves ready and when I say abandon aircraft, everybody go.' The crew immediately came surging forward. The rear gunner, Sergeant Brewer, had forgotten his own parachute and picked up Fazackerley's. The little engineer told the gunner sharply to sod off back to the turret for his own 'chute. Brewer was the quiet man of the crew who didn't mix easily, was a little homesick and seemed to prefer his own company in the sergeants' mess, reading a newspaper or a book beside the big coke fire when the others were playing crap or snooker. The gunner meekly did as he was told.

The younger men saw the panic in each other's eyes. They didn't talk about their fear of dying. To talk about it would be tempting fate. Nor did they want to be pointed out as pathological worriers, or worse, cowards. Thoughts were more difficult to control. Thoughts crowded in to scream at youngsters who didn't want to die at all, let alone die unheroically, ignominiously, many miles away from the nearest German gun or fighter aircraft before they had even seen the enemy.

An exception was the veteran mid-upper gunner, Warrant Officer Paddy Byrne from Southern Ireland, who had completed a tour in the Middle East. In his mid-thirties, the daddy of the crew, he carried himself with military composure, helped calm down the others and waited coolly for his orders. The trainees stared impatiently at their skipper who might yet perform a miracle for them.

Misselbrooke grated: 'Okay, just settle down.' He was still trying to get above the blizzard, but the aeroplane couldn't even maintain level flight and the pilot kept drifting it down to prevent the four powerful Hercules engines from stalling. Fazackerley remembers:

'All the engines were surging, even when I directed hot air into the carburettors. Then the starboard inboard (inner) engine began failing, rattling like a lorry full of scrap iron. The fuel warning lights flickered because all the pumps were icing up. We had very little time. Everything was icing up: props and controls. We hadn't been trained for this. It was freezing by now inside the bomber. There was no heating, except from the engines, and that couldn't get through.

'I glanced at the altimeter. It was showing 6,000ft. If we didn't get out soon it would be too late. The engines were about knackered. In a few minutes they'd pack up and the Halifax would dive into the ground. There was a smell of oil and aviation fuel which was leaking from somewhere.'

The big bomber was shuddering all over, like a great dog which had come into the house to shake itself dry after rolling in a snowdrift. No one hung around when the pilot gave the terse order to bale out. The first man out was bomb-aimer Sergeant Carl Brookes from Calgary, Alberta, waiting in the nose. He unfastened the escape hatch and was gone.

Fazackerley was like an orderly sergeant, lining the men up and sending them through into the nose one at a time, reporting briskly to the skipper as each man baled out through the escape hatch in the front of the nose. He watched Misselbrooke point the doomed Halifax east to the North Sea and flip the switch which activated the automatic pilot, before turning to negotiate the one step down into the nose. It was no wonder the youngsters were scared. Fazackerley explains:

'We hadn't jumped before. We hadn't got far enough on the course to have been taught how to parachute out of an aircraft. They'd just given us a parachute each at Blyton and let us get on with it. I was clueless. I tried to use my loaf but didn't even know whether I should go out feet first or head first. No one had told us which way to go. I looked through the hatch and met a great rush of wind. Feet first suddenly seemed a better idea. The other way might have led rather quickly to decapitation. In this situation there was no chance of a practice jump. We had to get it right first time. That was our problem.

'I had my right hand on the release handle of the parachute. I sat for a moment with my legs dangling out of the hatch and felt the cold wind dragging at them. At that moment I wished I'd never started in this bloody racket. I should have stayed safely on the ground as a fitter.'

The black mood passed and he slowly eased himself out. He was terrified of any part of him striking the fuselage or a wing and being seriously injured or killed. There wasn't a lot of him, but every bit was precious and worth preserving.

He hung grimly on to the far side of the hatch and lowered himself until his frail body was blown clear, almost parallel with the booming Halifax. Then he let go and counted to ten, rather hastily, before releasing the parachute. Fazackerley had a brief glimpse of Misselbrooke's slim body following him through the hatch before the blizzard wrapped itself hungrily around him. The screaming wind tore off his fur-lined flying boots as he heard the spluttering engines of the empty Halifax disappearing eerily into the frozen night.

'I wasn't sure if I would drop on to land, into the sea or the Humber estuary. I thought of the Humber and all that bloody mud, then I thought of the sea. I could swim like a pair of braces. I wouldn't have lasted long before drowning in that freezing water. It was only minutes since the skipper had let the snow into the plane, but it seemed hours. It was like a night without end.'

The engineer tried to see whether it was ground, estuary or sea rushing up to meet him, but his eyes were unable to penetrate the whirling turbulence of snow. The suddenness of landing in a field came as a great shock, although it was a relief not to be struggling in mud or water. Then winded, but exhilarated, he tried to get up and groaned as excruciating pain darted through him. He had landed awkwardly, in four or five inches of snow, no more than 50ft from the dark glacial waters of the river Humber, not far from the north Lincolnshire town of Goole. It was almost midnight and he had broken his right leg.

At first he thought he was miles from anywhere. Then, looking around, he saw the tiniest chink of light, winking at him through the blizzard. He rolled up his parachute and tucked it under his arm like a blanket. He had signed for the 'chute at Blyton and was afraid of losing it, believing he would have to pay for a replacement.

Fazackerley dragged himself eagerly on all-fours towards the beckoning light which was leaking through a hole in a blackout curtain hanging at the window of a farm labourer's stone cottage. The engineer thanked his lucky stars it had not been spotted by a vigilant air-raid warden.

He crawled up the short path, hauled himself onto his left leg and hammered on the door. The engineer heard a shuffle of slippers in the hall and the door was opened by a plump, middle-aged woman whose homely smile faded as she saw the little man, his face blackened by oil and muck squirted from the tortured engines of the Halifax.

She recoiled in horror and slammed the door, before he had time to speak. 'She must have thought I was a German invader.' The engineer, standing a whisker above 5ft 6in in his frozen stockinged feet, the skinny shivering frame almost buried inside bulky flying suit and helmet and a rolled-up RAF-issue parachute under his arm, was difficult to mistake for one of Hitler's battle-hardened stormtroopers. He had never been so cold. His feet were numb and his spirits at rock bottom. Yet the persistent image of his frozen corpse being discovered by the farmer next morning drove him on in his search for someone who did not believe he was part of the ruthless German war machine.

Fazackerley struggled along a lane and saw the dark bulk of another cottage nearly 50yds away. He knocked at the door, clung to the stone wall and prepared a little speech. The warmth from the cottage surged out as the door opened. A man stood there in his overalls. The words tumbled out. 'I'm English, RAF, I've just baled out.'

The man eyed him up and down, opened the door wider and grinned. 'Come in and sit down, son.' Fazackerley staggered into the warm sitting room. 'Tea's no good to you,' said his host, with admirable perception. He rooted around in a cupboard and brought out a half-full bottle of Scotch. He filled a tumbler and handed it to his shivering visitor. The engineer sipped it and felt the whisky scorching a delicious path down inside him.

The man sent a son to fetch the local policeman and asked the engineer what had happened to his shoes; he didn't realise aircrew wore slip-on flying boots. He invited Fazackerley to remove his sodden socks, squeeze them out and put them in front of the glowing fire, which he blazed up with another couple of logs.

Five minutes later the policeman arrived on his bike. Fazackerley told him that another seven men had baled out of the Halifax. There was a chance that some might be in difficulties in the Humber. The policeman left, promising to phone Blyton, while the engineer settled down to yarn with his host beside a warm fire.

He was picked up later by a three-ton Bedford military truck and rode in the back beneath the canvas roof, with another three men from the Halifax crew. Still in shock, marvelling at their survival, they didn't talk much. Fazackerley's bare feet were still icy cold and his leg hurt. The rest of him was snug in flying suit, service trousers and long-johns.

On the way back to Blyton he reached into his flying suit, drew out his lucky white scarf and tied a knot in one of its tassels. His mother had bought the scarf for half-a-crown at Marks and Spencer before the war. Each time he returned from a trip he added another knot. More than fifty years later he still has that scarf, grubby and disfigured with a profusion of knots at his bungalow home in Nottinghamshire. His wife, Joyce, whom he married in 1945, has never been allowed to wash it.

Fazackerley arrived back at Blyton where his broken leg was put in plaster and he knocked back a tot of rum before a bacon and egg breakfast. All the Halifax crew had landed safely and were reunited at the air base later that morning.

The Halifax, never seen again, was presumed to have crashed into the North Sea and then quietly to have sunk beneath the waves.

Fazackerley was later to be shot through the neck by a German Junkers Ju88 fighter, survive three belly landings and thirty-six bombing operations. He and the rest of that original sprog crew volunteered to make six extra trips so Brewer, the shy rear gunner, did not have to join a new crew to complete his tour. He had been in hospital with a chest infection when the others completed their thirty operations. Fazackerley, officially described as a 'non-combatant', was the only member of his crew not to be decorated.

None of the thirty-six trips would ever leave their mark so vividly in Fazackerley's mind as that terrible night in 1943 when his skipper got his knackers in a twist. More than fifty years later, Fazackerley says:

'They were the best years of my life. You lived from day to day and couldn't give a shit about anybody. I went off on one operation wearing a bowler hat for devilment. Someone had given it me at a pub in Market Rasen. An SP (service policeman) saw me on the airfield at Ludford Magna and screamed: "Take that bloody ridiculous hat off!" I yelled back: "Bollocks!" and kept on walking. He didn't say anything else. Perhaps he'd thought that I was off to bomb the shit out of the Germans, while all he was doing was making sure the airmen had creases in their trousers. That bowler hat became another lucky mascot. I took it with me on every operation.

'I wish I could do it all again for the excitement. I still dream about bombers. Now, when I go to an air show, I still think the sun shines out of my arse because I was in Bomber Command. Yet I was one of the lucky buggers who got away with it. A lot didn't.'

8

THE ULTIMATE SACRIFICE

On the morning of 27 May 1943, Sergeant James Twinn was awake early. He lay in bed, eyes closed, savouring the moment. Tomorrow he would start a week's leave, the extension of his honeymoon. He and Enid had been married four months already, managing only a long weekend together before he had to return to Warboys, the Huntingdonshire RAF airfield where he was stationed with the Pathfinders' 156 Squadron.

Later, as he washed in the accommodation hut, he planned for the following week. Bomber aircrews could rarely afford the reckless luxury of making plans. Although each of them secretly hoped he was invulnerable, they had known too many friends fail to come back not to believe it was possible for them to get the chop, too.

Enid, his wife, an electrician's daughter, had booked their week's honeymoon in a hotel at The Mumbles, South Wales. He would collect Enid the next day at her parents' home in Ealing, west London. Twinn spent a little time happily speculating about the hotel and the seaside resort before going to breakfast.

It was a warm, sunny day, hinting at a fine summer to come. Twinn, full of high spirits, looked into the blue sky, noting the fluffy white clouds and hoped there would not be an operation that night. He was to be disappointed. Soon the airfield resounded to the roar of Lancaster Merlin engines as the bombers were taken up for air tests.

Twinn, a bomb–aimer, was aged twenty-one, a month or two younger than his pilot, Sergeant David Wallace, who was an Australian. Five of them had been together as a crew for three months. They had trained on Wellingtons before converting to four-engine bombers, when they were joined by the flight engineer and mid–upper gunner. They had arrived at the airfield feeling awkward and inadequate at being drafted into such a senior squadron, mixing with highly decorated crews who may not have been much older than themselves but were obviously imbued with the experience and self-confidence the younger men lacked.

Twinn recalls: 'We were all so young. They were running short of Pathfinders with enough experience. We were told the idea was to train some of the more proficient and promising crews and post them directly into Pathfinder Force. That was the idea, although we never actually operated as a Pathfinder.'

70

Even now, after five operations – all to the Ruhr – they did not feel completely at ease among the veterans. Twinn described themselves as 'quiet and inoffensive', hardly the stuff from which heroes are made, yet they were earnest young men who cared deeply about each other, knowing there would always be willing hands to help them out of a crisis.

The Lancaster handled beautifully beneath the morning sun, but the test ended badly when they returned to Warboys. Wallace made a slight error of judgement and the Lancaster landed heavily on the runway, setting into motion a string of events that would culminate in tragedy.

Wallace climbed down the short metal ladder from the fuselage and made his way to the crippled rear wheel, which had received the whole weight of the aircraft as they touched down. He scratched his head ruefully. His ground crew who examined the wheel wouldn't pass it for flying and agreed there was not time for the damage to be repaired for that night's sortie. They were given the standby Lancaster, the squadron hack which normally stood alone, unwanted at her dispersal point, nose pointing sullenly in the air as if to say 'You must take me as you find me'. It was a bad omen.

Their own Lancaster, which had been brand new for their first operation, ran sweetly and they were used to it. It had, after all, brought them back safely from five operations. The old hack was battered and covered in metal patches, clear signs that she had many times fought her way gallantly across German skies. Yet it wasn't enough for them that she had survived more sorties than they. She wasn't theirs and that made all the difference. The change of aircraft deeply affected the pilot, Dave Wallace.

He came from Perth, Western Australia. An only child, his parents had emigrated from Scotland in the 1920s. They had been given a parcel of land in the bush from which they had hacked out a farm, where they grew corn. Their nearest neighbours were twenty miles away. The boy went to boarding school and at home never mixed with anyone socially. He was very shy and gentle. His diffidence showed on the squadron where he was always quiet and thoughtful although in the air, his authority was sound, never questioned. Over 6ft tall, he appeared slightly built, yet he had powerful arms with hard muscles formed from ploughing with eight horses in line since he was a boy.

After being briefed for that night's target, Essen – the principal city of the Ruhr and home of the giant Krupp armament complex – Wallace was not in his usual good humour. Twinn remembers: 'It was the only time before take-off that I had known Dave to be reticent and, for him, almost short-tempered. I don't think he very much liked the aircraft we had been given that night. There was, of course, a degree of superstition that it was not our own aircraft. No one liked using the old hack.'

They boarded W4943, Q-Queenie, as dusk was falling. She did not look much like a queen. She was more of a shabby old tart who had run out of clients. Their regular

Lancaster still smelled of new paint. This one was tainted with the sweat and fear of countless other crews who had flown with her. Many crews thought of their bombers as living creatures, coaxing, urging and pleading with them to get to the target and safely back home. Q-Queenie was not one of them even though she had survived many a skirmish over Germany. She did not have more than two or three ops left in her and they knew it.

They sensed she was a bitch as soon as they boarded her and Queenie herself might have felt their animosity. She handled differently from their own aircraft, with irritating little idiosyncrasies that Wallace had to get used to after a short test flight confirmed his suspicions of the aircraft. 'A real old cow,' he thought, frowning, as they took off from Warboys with two other Lancasters. The squadron's Pathfinders did not fly that night.

The night was very warm. Twinn was not flying with his snug Irvine jacket, he wore ordinary battledress without the heavy duty trousers. Only the rear gunner still had on his cumbersome, multi-layered gear, aware that without it, he would freeze at 20,000ft. At ground level he had tottered, gasping and perspiring to his turret. He was Sergeant Hilton Arthur Lister, a twenty-two year-old who, not surprisingly, preferred to be called Buster. Lister came from New Zealand where his family ran the only general store in a small village. He had once told them proudly: 'They sell everything from pins to telegraph poles.'

His fiancee lived in New Zealand and they planned to marry at the end of the war. Twinn says: 'He was very quiet, a man you could get on with very easily and pleasantly. That was true of the whole crew really, at least, the original five. It was harder for the other two to mix in with the rest of us who had established such a warm and close relationship.'

They carried a full bomb-load of high explosives, including a 4,000lb Cookie, but no incendiaries. All Lancasters had been briefed to bomb from above 20,000ft and leave the target area as quickly as possible, climbing to maximum height for the return journey, crossing the enemy coast at no less than 14,000ft.

Q-Queenie was among 518 aircraft: 274 Lancasters, 151 Halifaxes, 81 Wellingtons and twelve Mosquitoes, which set out that night to attack Essen. The Met men had forecast small amounts of stratocumulus cloud outward to the town of Den Helder in northern Holland, increasing to less than 5/10ths at Essen. The target was to be sky-marked by Oboe Mosquitoes. In reality, the cloud over the German city would be 6 – 8/10ths cloud, at times increasing to 10/10ths.

The Main Force consisted of ten waves, each of about fifty aircraft. They were to aim their bombs at release point flares dropped by Mosquitoes at five-minute intervals. All flares, red with green stars, plus one white for longer burning, were to be fused to ignite at 15,000ft.

It was when they crossed the Dutch coast, eyes peeled for flak and fighters, that all their fears about Q-Queenie were realised. The starboard outer engine suddenly packed up and the intercom failed. There seemed to be no reason for any of it except Queenie's sheer cussedness. Wallace tried in vain to restart the engine then caught the attention of his flight engineer to tell the wireless operator, Sergeant Pete Moore, to attempt a repair job on the intercom. Moore, aged twenty, nodded and set to work busily. From that moment the engineer, Sergeant 'Jacko' Jackson, became the pilot's only contact with the rest of his crew. When Wallace wanted a message delivered he bawled in Jackson's ear so he could be heard above the roar of the three engines. He told Jackson to tell the navigator, Sergeant Hugh Harvey, to get him a course back to base if it was necessary. At this point, they did not consider returning to Warboys, but it was as well to be prepared.

Twinn observes: 'You had to have two major things go wrong before aborting an operation, otherwise you risked being accused of lacking moral fibre.'

The Lancaster could continue to fly to the target on three good engines, but the loss of the intercom had robbed the pilot of the ears and eyes of both gunners, who would demand immediate action from him if they spotted a fighter heading their way. Twinn, the bomb-aimer, could no longer report landmarks to the navigator. The weight of responsibility rested even more heavily on Wallace's shoulders and he was annoyed with himself for damaging his regular aircraft.

Buster Lister might have seen the German fighter streaking towards them before yelling into the dead intercom for the pilot to dive. The shell sliced through the main rudder bar between the mid-upper gunner's position and Lister's rear turret. The Lancaster went into a straight dive from 18,000ft, its three engines screaming. Twinn, pressed by the G-force to the front of the nose, was convinced he was about to die. 'I said a prayer. There was no tension, panic or fear. You only get that when there's a chance of survival.'

The bomb-aimer lay calmly pressed against the nose by the G-force, waiting to be blown to pieces. Then, miraculously, the bomber levelled out. Twinn remembers: 'The pilot had used maximum trim to get the tail down and the aircraft's forward velocity had pulled it out of the dive.' The flight engineer stumbled, greyfaced, into the nose with a message from the pilot. He bellowed in Twinn's ear. 'Release the bomb-load! We're going home!'

Twinn operated the mechanism to open the bomb doors, but they remained tightly shut. He tried again and again and Jackson, seeing the desperate look in his eyes, climbed back to report to the pilot. He returned within seconds. His voice wavered with the tension of the moment. 'Dave said release the Cookie. The weight of it should crash open the doors.'

The bomb, weighing 1.79 tons, struck the bomb doors with a thud that sent a shudder rippling through the Lancaster. But the doors remained stubbornly closed. They stared in alarm at the unfettered Cookie as it moved uneasily over the jammed doors like a caged monster. Avro was rather proud of the strength it had built into its Lancasters, but the crew of Q-Queenie wished the company's chief designer, Roy Chadwick and his engineers, had paid less attention to the robustness of the bomb doors. Dave Wallace received the news with a sigh. His shouted instructions were brief and to the point. 'We'll head for home and bale out. I'll put her on George (automatic pilot) and turn her back over the North Sea.'

Jackson hurried to the navigator for a new course. Twinn and Moore received the news with relief. The op had somehow seemed doomed from the start. No one would mourn the passing of Q-Queenie. The new course was passed to Wallace and grins were exchanged as they turned towards England.

They were still over Holland when the bomber was hit a mortal blow. A cannon shell plunged into the starboard side which was raked by tracers, some of which smashed into the nose and passed terrifyingly close to Twinn's shoulder. The main fuel lines were cut and flames shot out twice the length of the aircraft. Both port engines had stopped. Only the starboard inner engine was working. Numerous holes had been torn through the fuselage. The aircraft had become a death trap over the flat green fields below. Q-Queenie creaked and groaned like a giant in torment as the single engine struggled to keep them crawling towards England and flames ate wickedly into the starboard wing to make sure they would not.

Jackson, Moore and Twinn rushed through the trembling bomber and found Buster Lister slumped over his machine-guns in the rear turret. There was no way of knowing in the dark if he was alive or dead; whether his oxygen lead had become disconnected, or whether he had received a fatal wound. The turret was at an angle, the guns pointing in the direction from which they had been hit. They all had the same thought. The gunner had seen the fighter, screamed into the useless intercom and fired his Brownings. The turret's sliding doors were facing into space. The hydraulics had gone with the rudder bar. Had Lister been conscious he could have turned his turret manually to move the doors into the fuselage.

Recalling how desperate things had become, Twinn remembers: 'We tried moving the turret, but couldn't get it back. There was no way of turning it. The sliding doors were over nowhere. We looked at Buster trapped inside and could do nothing for him. Buster was Dave's best friend on the squadron.'

Dave Wallace, grim-faced, told Jackson to pass the word to the crew to bale out. Wallace was, as usual, sitting on his parachute pack. Jackson wanted to release the pilot's canopy so he could get out, but Wallace waved him away and said: 'Buster is trapped in his turret. The only way we can get him out is by landing. I'm going to land this thing.'

Jackson told him he had no chance of landing: the extinguishers had been spent and the flames were out of control. Wallace retorted, grimly: 'I'll land it. You go with the others and bale out.'

Jackson left him, reluctantly, and joined Twinn in the nose. The escape hatch was jammed; Q-Queenie was being a bitch even in her death-throes. They could hear the roar of the flames and the eerie crackling as they ate into the bomber. The Cookie still rolled heavily from side to side in the bomb bay.

Twinn again: 'You pulled a toggle to open the escape hatch which you then pushed out of the aircraft. Unfortunately, it was difficult to pull up. When I got the hatch up I couldn't get rid of it through the hole so, in desperation, I jumped on it with both feet. The hatch disappeared and I went with it.'

Jackson, Moore and Hugh Harvey, the navigator, quickly followed Twinn, who immediately experienced more problems:

'The wind caught me under the closed parachute pack and broke the little cords which went across my chest and held it in position. It floated shut above my head, but I didn't know that. I reached for the parachute handle on my chest and it wasn't there. I assumed I had forgotten to put it on because I had left the aircraft in a bit of a hurry. I again experienced a great sense of peace and thought that was the end of it. Then I saw the parachute floating behind, still attached to me by the webbing. I pulled the parachute down with one hand and pulled the D-ring with the other. I had time to put my hands up and think I was just about to enter a cloud. But it wasn't a cloud, it was the ground. I was no more than 30 seconds on the 'chute.

'I hit the ground fairly hard, near the Dutch town of Ede. It was a shock to land so quickly, but I was utterly relaxed because I thought I was going through a cloud. Then I heard the roaring of our aircraft and saw the blazing starboard wing break off. The entire bomber was wreathed in flames. A moment later the sky was lit up by a gigantic explosion when it crashed about two miles away and the bomb load went off.'

It was 30 minutes after midnight. The pilot and both gunners died. Much later, Twinn learned from Hugh Harvey that after the first hit they had dived from 18,000 to around 10,000ft and had not regained height. He had baled out not much higher than 8,000ft and most of that time he had been in free-fall.

Twinn comments: 'Dave stayed at the controls trying to land that aircraft. I have never encountered bravery such as that. He was a fine man: modest, stoical, quiet and easily embarrassed. He deserved a posthumous award for his bravery, but got nothing.'

In their official report, Dutch policemen Wouter van Zwetselaar and Gerrit Jan Michels said the Lancaster had crashed near the village of Otterloo. They went to the scene where they found villagers and four German soldiers. The wreckage was a mass of flames and fragments of the aircraft had been scattered over a wide area. The Ortskommandant of Ede and the head of Ede's air-raid precautions service arrived, followed by a bus out of which piled numerous German soldiers who mounted guard on the Lancaster and blocked nearby roads. The two policemen reported that they could not find any of the crew, but the Germans later found partially carbonised bodies in the cold embers of the fire. The body of mid-upper gunner Dave Ross was also found. He had baled out after Twinn. His parachute had not opened.

Otterloo was shaken by another explosion at 1.30am when a Halifax from 51 Squadron crashed in flames a short distance south of the village.

Twinn landed in a field of maize three to four feet high. The light, sandy soil helped to cushion his landing. Lucky not to break any bones, his only injury was a black eye, caught by his knee as he hit the ground. 'I felt very lonely and hoped I would run across one of the crew. I was young and vulnerable. I heard all the other aircraft going through to bomb Essen. Eventually the aircraft were gone and I sat in that field feeling very sorry for myself thinking how, in a few hours, I should be going off on my honeymoon. Enid had complete faith that I would turn up, I can't think why, but she was right.'

Twinn hid the parachute in the field and made his way to the edge, startled by the amount of noise created as he passed through the maize. He slipped into the farmyard just beyond the field where he stood in the dark, near some outbuildings, listening to the snores of two people coming from the open windows of the house. It was a warm night. He wasn't searching for food. Fear drives away hunger. He looked for shelter where he might sleep for a couple of hours. He found a shed and inside it, a woman's bicycle.

He says: 'I thought, if I take this bicycle I shall be able to cycle somewhere. Then I thought of the poor woman coming down in the morning and not finding her bicycle. I sat on a box looking at the bicycle, thinking how useful it would be. Then I walked away, leaving it. Foolish perhaps, but you can't change the habits of a lifetime.'

He left the farm, then heard a gunshot. Imagining someone was firing at him, he sank to his knees, heart pounding, until he was sure no one was coming. Later he returned cautiously to the field of maize where he settled down for the rest of the night, alone, in a strange country occupied by Germans, and well after curfew.

At daylight he peered cautiously above the maize and watched the farmer hoeing potatoes. He sat there a long time, as curious and timid as a rabbit, trying to pluck up courage to talk to the man, wondering if he would be welcomed with kind words or a gun. The hours passed, the sun beamed down upon a scene so peaceful it did not seem possible this was a country terrorised by war. The man continued to hoe, watched all the time by Twinn who suddenly, to his astonishment, saw the farmer's wife walking towards him. She was middle-aged and smiling nervously. Twinn stood up. The farmer rested on his hoe, watching. The woman, nodding encouragingly, handed the airman a bottle of milk and a hunk of cheese so huge, he was unable to fit it into his pocket. She spoke gently and made signs for him to stay in the field. Twinn thanked the woman profusely and watched her return to the house. If the Germans knew the couple had helped him, they would be taken away, possibly shot. Twinn sank into the maize, nibbling cheese, and the farmer continued hoeing.

Later, Twinn bobbed his head above the maize and looked around. Seeing no one, he boldly left the field and walked more deeply into the countryside. Although he had torn off his RAF insignia, Twinn still wore his battledress. He soon found the wreck of an aircraft. He approached it tremulously, believing it to be the remains of Q-Queenie.

'I forgot that there would obviously be a guard on it. I went across to see if it was ours and an armed guard stood up and greeted me in German, "Guten morgen". I replied in best English, "Good morning", expecting him to do something, but he did nothing and I wandered away under a notice which said "Zutritt Verboten!" (Entry Forbidden!). I daren't look back and presumed he had sat down and finished his cigarette. I didn't have enough time to see if it was our Lancaster.'

This was the first of several curious little incidents which allowed Twinn to remain free for several days. He slept at night, mostly in sheds and barns, walking mainly during the day. The longer he was free, the greater his courage grew. One morning he was trying to orientate himself with his escape map, which was in the form of a handkerchief. Road signs had not been removed and he looked for the way to Arnhem, the only major town on his map, and he had ideas of catching a train south from there. As he lingered a small transport vehicle from the German Wehrmacht passed, carrying half-a-dozen men. They all ignored him, giving him a false sense of security.

A man driving a horse and cart stopped and Twinn said he wanted to go to Arnhem. The carter took him in the opposite direction, but Twinn decided not to protest and thanked the man two miles later. When he reached the outskirts of Arnhem it was Sunday morning, Twinn was scruffy, unwashed and unshaven. The Dutch were in their Sunday best, the Germans smart in uniform. No one took any notice of him. He slipped through a hedge and found two guards goose-stepping at a war cemetery. He retreated quickly and found a gap in another hedge which led to a field. Here, two teams of German soldiers played football, earnestly and noisily, encouraged by a crowd of onlookers. Twinn hastily withdrew. He found a park and looked for somewhere to lay down. He picked up a route map which he presumed had been blown out of a British bomber. It was unmarked. He thrust it down a rabbit hole and pretended to fall asleep in the warm sunshine beneath a tree, well away from people. He still carried the rather grubby remains of the cheese. Apart from the milk, long since finished, the cheese was all he had consumed since the last dinner at Warboys days ago.

Time passed slowly. Twinn was not sure what his next move should be. It was unlikely that his luck would hold long enough for him to walk through the entire German Army to the coast and hitch a lift to England. The decision was taken out of his hands when a middle-aged man approached him then walked briskly away calling out to the nearest German soldier.

Twinn remembers: 'He was a civilian, insistent that his name and address were taken. I believe rewards were offered for turning in Allied aircrew. I'd like to think that he was a German civilian, but one wondered. We'd been told that anyone who baled out would be picked up by the Resistance. That didn't happen to me.'

Twinn became the prisoner of a small reluctant medical orderly, who was out for the day with his girlfriend. 'He carried a revolver but was friendly and gave me cigarettes. I did consider my chances of overpowering him, but thought better of it. He took me to a biergarten and bought the drinks. Several Dutch people were there. They recognised my uniform and all stood, spontaneously, beaming, quietly raising their glasses to me. They embarrassed the little German.'

Twinn and the medical orderly travelled into the city centre on the platform of a tram. Here the German experienced some difficulty getting rid of his prisoner. They went to what Twinn believed to be the Wehrmacht headquarters. The orderly opened several doors but no one would help him. One German officer bellowed at the orderly to get out. Red-faced, the orderly peered down a corridor full of doors. Eventually, he left Twinn with a clerk, who compiled a list of everything in his pockets, including an Orlec Sports cigarette lighter Enid had given him. This was confiscated with his British and Dutch money. Twinn was astounded when, two years later, the lighter was returned to him at a prisoner-of-war camp in Poland.

Twinn was driven from Arnhem to Amsterdam that day in a Mercedes with a Gestapo skull and crossbones pennant on the bonnet. They travelled flat out on the crown of the road. Twinn sat nervously between two guards, one with a Luger pressed into his side, another holding a bayonet. He spent eight days in a civilian prison, passing the time playing patience with tiny squares of paper torn from a toilet roll.

After a year of incarceration at Stalag Luft VI in East Prussia, the prisoners were taken to Thorn just outside the Polish capital, where they were held during the Warsaw Uprising. In February 1945, they began walking through Germany. Twinn suffered from dysentery and pneumonia. Normally 11st, he now weighed seven-and-a-half. He recalls: 'There were 500 prisoners. We were skeletal. We were given only three small potatoes each a day. We had to walk 20km a day. Some died on the way. There was also a chance of being shot if you dropped out of the column. We were taken into Allied hands just outside Lüneburg Heath. Hugh and Jacko had been in the same POW camp, but we lost touch during about two months on the road.'

Twinn was recorded by the Germans as a casualty of the crash. They believed Twinn's remains had been buried with those of Dave Ross, the mid-upper gunner. Although the space left for his name was never filled in on the headstone, even today his name is included among Bomber Command fatalities by British writers who have obtained their sources from uncorrected German records.

After the war, Twinn became a secondary school headmaster in Mitcham, Surrey, retiring at 59 to take holy orders, becoming a Methodist minister in Cheshire.

9

TARGET:
E-BOAT PENS AT BOULOGNE

Swift German motor E-boats armed with torpedoes and guns, operating from Le Havre and Boulogne, had preyed remorselessly on Allied shipping since early in the war. After D-Day on 6 June 1944, they had become an even greater threat to the vast armada of ships supporting the invasion. The RAF were given the task of snuffing out the E-boat menace.

On 14 June, twenty-two Lancasters and three Mosquito marker aircraft of the crack 617 Squadron, armed with 12,000lb Tallboy bombs, made a daylight raid on the reinforced concrete-covered E-boat pens at Le Havre, thirty miles from the Normandy beaches, before the first and second waves of the Main Force arrived. The 617 Squadron bombers were followed in by another 199 Lancasters and ten Mosquitoes, supported by Spitfires. Few E-boats escaped damage. One Lancaster was lost.

The following night, 617 Squadron crews were briefed to attack the harbour at Boulogne, with similar tactics to those used at Le Havre. One of the Lancasters which left Woodhall Spa at dusk was DV403, G-George, piloted by Flying Officer Malcolm 'Mac' Hamilton. This was the thirty-first operation for Mac Hamilton and his crew:

'By the time you had done half-a-dozen trips, you were becoming a veteran. After twenty trips, you were an old man in a young man's body. By thirty trips, you were beginning to pace yourself and you knew more about the target than anybody else. My crew didn't want to stop at the end of thirty trips. They wanted to go on, as long as we stayed together as a crew. You got to the stage when you thought: "They're not going to get me". You felt you could handle almost anything.'

Singapore-born Mac Hamilton looked older than his twenty-six years. He had started going bald at nineteen, after suffering from mumps. A commercial artist before the war, his first assignment had been designing an advertisement for a condom, for the journal *Retail Chemist*.

On his first tour, he had learned a lot with 619 Squadron pilot, Squadron Leader Gerry Scorer, before the squadron was moved from Woodhall Spa to Coningsby, making way for 617 Squadron. Mac Hamilton recalls: 'My first operation was to Hannover with Gerry on what we called a "dicky trip". I went into briefing for the first time, wide-eyed and dead keen. There was no place for a second pilot to sit and I stood virtually at his shoulder.'

Mac Hamilton flew through his first flak with Scorer at the Dutch coast. A lot of it came up with tracer. Scorer moved to the left and the tracer moved to the left. Then he moved to the right and the tracer tried to follow him. Each time the Germans took about twenty-two seconds to realign their guns. Mac Hamilton again:

'He showed me a lot of tricks like that. He also showed me how you "corkscrewed" to avoid fighters. When you started corkscrewing you got ready for it and listened carefully to the gunners who would tell you which way to start. You predetermined that you were going to start diving to starboard or port, so the gunners could have the best advantage of getting whatever fighter it was that was attacking them.

'He also showed me how you didn't take any notice of searchlights unless they were coming on to you. With so many aircraft, the searchlights seemed to be weaving across the sky. Every now and then you would see some poor devil coned, and the flak began aiming at him. Sometimes you saw them get out of it without much trouble, but if they were coned, the fighters often jumped them very quickly.'

Mac Hamilton's navigator, Pilot Officer John 'Jacky' Jackson, quiet and serious, was almost a conscientious objector, having had a great battle with himself before deciding to go on. He became a fine navigator, and a good friend. When Hamilton was trying to get his wife Pat and their baby daughter Brenda out of London, Jackson arranged for them to stay with his parents in Solihull for several months.

Flight engineer Sergeant Len Rooke was a cheerful, round-faced man, always full of fun, with inexhaustible energy. Of Rooke, Mac Hamilton says: 'I never saw him tired. Bleary-eyed yes, but never tired. He liked to gamble. I had to tell him off once when he reported for duty after playing poker all night with Australian and Canadian crews. We didn't need to talk much during an operation. We just gave signals. We had got to know each other so well during training. He was a brilliant engineer.'

The father of Roland Duck, the bomb-aimer, expected his son to be an engineer. His mother wanted him to go into the Church. Duck, brought up in Swindon, France and Germany, only wanted to fly. He got his way, originally training to be a pilot. Now a flying officer, he was the crew's bomb-aimer, a position he filled with enthusiasm and considerable expertise.

Duck's philosophy was simple, and one shared by many of the young aircrews: bomb the shit out of the Germans then come back and have a good time. He remembers: 'As a young man one's only real thoughts were getting on with the job and doing it to the best of your ability. Some people suffered badly from conscience. I never did. As far as I was concerned, it was a question of doing as much as we could, as hard as we could and as fast as we could, getting it over and having a good time. Lots of beer and lots of popsies.'

Mac Hamilton again: 'Roly was very good at map reading and was able to pick out a target on the Ruhr. He'd watch as we crossed various rivers or canals, noting distinctive bits about them, and whatever else you could see at night. He knew immediately when the Pathfinders' marker flares had not quite lined up with the target we wanted.

'On Main Force, one of the big problems about bombing was that as we approached the target the bomb-aimers, particularly the inexperienced ones, would bomb on the nearest edge of the fire. You might have 150yds of flames from one bomb load. You'd have the Cookie in the middle surrounded by HEs (high explosive bombs) and then a whole mass of incendiaries, which set light to all the stuff you'd smashed up with your bombs. Then you got this very bright light, and the nearest edge was the one that they would aim at which, of course, was natural. And so the bombing would creep back, sometimes as far as a couple of miles from the actual target.

'Roly was able to work this out and he bombed quite accurately. Whilst training with the Mk XIV bomb-sight on 619 Squadron, we won the bombing trophy for 5 Group three months running. The Pathfinders wanted to have us on about our twenty-first or twenty-second trip, but the crew weren't keen. Soon afterwards, on 16 February 1944, the day after our tenth trip to Berlin, we joined 617 Squadron, where Wing Commander Leonard Cheshire was commanding officer.'

Wireless operator Flight Sergeant Tommy Thompson was very adept at picking up signals which less able men could not find. During training flights, or long, tedious legs of trips to Germany, he and Jackson played chess, passing a pocket set between them.

Mid-upper gunner Flight Sergeant Taffy Dadge, a cheerful former cook from the Rhondda Valley, had assumed unofficial control of the bomber's guns. Rear gunner Warrant Officer David Hamilton, an Irishman who was quiet and extremely shy, and who in peacetime was a teacher, wouldn't have said boo to a goose.

The bomber carried an extra man on the trip to Boulogne. He was front gunner Warrant Officer Tom 'Ace' McLean, later to be awarded both the DFM and DFC. The guns in the front turret were usually operated by the bomb-aimer. Mac Hamilton says: 'I was very glad to have him. He had flown with me on several occasions, teaching my gunners how to cope with fighters during fighter affiliation training.'

The crews went up in the morning for training sessions, testing guns and turrets, returning for lunch and briefings. Boulogne was not a long trip and less daunting than a flight deep into Germany. Mac Hamilton again:

'When you saw the target go up at briefing and you knew it was Berlin, your stomach very often turned over. God, not another Berlin! You remembered previous trips, the fighters that came up to get you, and the bombers you'd seen going down. Anyone who says they weren't scared were either lunatics or had no feeling at all. You didn't let your feelings show, although you jolly well knew each time there was a chance you were not going to come back. I was more scared of being injured or burned, or coming down in enemy territory. Fortunately, we didn't have the problem of fires, although we were hit many times by flak. The Lancaster was a beautiful aircraft, lovely to fly and very sturdy, with this great girder through the middle, the main spar, which was a damned nuisance to climb over with all your kit.'

Twenty-two Lancasters left Woodhall Spa for Boulogne at 9.15pm and climbed slowly to 20,000ft, each with a Barnes Wallis Tallboy filling its bomb bay. The bomb, 21ft long, 3ft 2in in diameter and packed with Torpex could, from 20,000ft, penetrate 100ft into the ground. If dropped accurately, the damage from the resulting underground blast was devastating.

They crossed high over the river Thames, where visibility was good, and over the Channel, to the French coast where thick cloud had built up. Heavy flak met them over Boulogne.

Duck comments: 'We used a device called SABS (Stabilised Automatic Bomb Sight). In order to use that properly, you needed a long run during which time you kept the aircraft straight and level and adjusted your ground speed and height. But you had to keep the target in visual, and we kept losing it.' Mac Hamilton:

'We circled the target, but couldn't see it through the cloud. Cheshire suddenly broke radio silence, which he seldom did. He said: "Okay, back to base." We hated this because it meant us returning with the Tallboys aboard. They were too expensive to jettison in the sea. It also meant getting rid of some fuel, anything to make the aircraft lighter.

'We were between the sea and the Thames Estuary when we had a call to say the target was clear at 8,000ft. That was the minimum height you could drop a Tallboy to get the terminal velocity to damage U-boat pens, where the E-boats were hiding. They had something like 18-20ft of concrete above them. Only the Tallboys could tackle those, it was a very accurate bomb. The tail unit was aerodynamic, beautifully designed. The bomb used to vibrate when it stuck into the concrete and worked its way in a little bit, then went off with a hell of a bang. Accuracy was important. We didn't want to damage the town. We just wanted to hit the pens.'

A reduced force returned to Boulogne. Cheshire, marking the target in his Mosquito, had said: 'Come down to 8,000ft and follow me in.' Mac Hamilton's aircraft was the fifth to go in, diving from nearly 20,000ft. By this time, the German gunners realised the bombers were coming in one after another and the flak was a hectic box barrage. About twelve miles from the dropping point, G-George began its bombing run, immediately plunging into a sky torn by murderous gunfire. A shell burst underneath the Lancaster, smashing the hydraulics and cutting off the mid-upper and rear gun turrets from the rest of the crew. The starboard flap was also damaged.

A second shell severely damaged one of the open bomb bay doors and tore off an engine nacelle. A third disturbed the lock of the starboard undercarriage and the wheel dropped down and hung there, spinning uselessly. Another shell blasted straight through the starboard inner fuel tank – luckily, without exploding – otherwise the wing would have been blown off and eight more names added to the casualties of war. Mac

Hamilton later discovered that a tennis ball could easily be dropped through the hole, giving the tank no chance to self-seal. Four hundred gallons of high octane fuel poured out, drenching the fuselage, while the aircrew waited tensely for a spark from the exhausts to start a fire. It didn't happen.

The tail unit, an elevator and starboard aileron were also damaged. Now on its bombing run, the Lancaster was difficult to keep straight and level. One of the aircraft's batteries had been put out of action, the r/t had gone and the pilot was unable to contact the rest of the crew. They switched to emergency, maintaining the link between pilot, navigator and bomb-aimer.

The gun fire eased and Duck cried: 'Bomb gone!' The Lancaster, suddenly over five tons lighter, leaped skittishly, like a prize bull turned into a field full of heifers. Cheshire darted about below, keenly observing the accuracy of the bombing. Mac Hamilton, eyeing the intense flak ahead, thought that was enough and was preparing to turn for home when the bomb-aimer roared: 'Hold it, Mac! I want a picture!'

They waited for the automatic camera to record the impact of the plunging Tall-boy. Mac Hamilton observes: 'And so we went on. It felt like a fortnight we were sitting there. And then from Roly, quite excited: "We've hit it!" He always got a bit excited when we went in.'

At that moment, a shell burst in the front of the aircraft. The entire perspex nose of the Lancaster exploded into thousands of fragments, some of which accompanied Roland Duck in a blizzard of wicked shards as he was blown half-way up the three steps from his bomb-aiming position. He sprawled gasping in front of the flight engineer. The bulbous nose of the bomber had gone, tearing away part of the structure, leaving it open to the sky. A tremendous draught rushed through, making the handling of the aircraft even more of a problem. The navigator's maps and equipment became airborne, while packets of 'Window' – metal strips thrown out to confuse enemy radar – blew all over the fuselage. The emergency intercom line was severed. From now on, the crew in the cockpit could only communicate by shouting or passing notes.

Mac Hamilton: 'There was devastation below my seat. I can't understand how I wasn't hit, yet I could look down between my feet into open air. The front part of the aircraft had all gone, it felt very 'dirty' – not aerodynamically clean. Ace McLean came back to help. I don't know how he and Roly were not thrown out of the aircraft.'

Dozens of pieces of shrapnel had smashed into Duck's legs and he was bleeding badly. The flight engineer grabbed Duck by his parachute harness, hauled him on to the floor of the cockpit and cut away the injured man's trousers. Duck growled: 'What the hell is wrong?', to which Rooke replied: 'Well, you've got a hole in the front of your leg and a bigger bugger in the back.' Later, the engineer observed wryly to his skipper: 'I don't know what he's making such a fuss about. I could only find one hole. My finger only goes in that far.' He pointed three inches from the end of his forefinger.

Duck recalls: 'There was no pain at first. It was like being hit on the back of the legs with a football on a cold day. My legs were numb. The pain came when some bloody fool tried to inject me with morphine. I was bloody cross with the Germans.'

Rooke tried in vain to inject an ampoule of morphine into Duck's leg, causing him more pain than the injury. Duck cried out and his flailing legs demolished the flight engineer's tip-up chair. Mac Hamilton says: 'Roly thrashed around as Len tried to give him morphine. On my right-hand side was a pillar on which were the exactors, throttles and mixture controls. One of Roly's legs shot up and cut out my starboard engines and we went into a violent right-hand dive. I knocked his foot off and there was a scream from Roly. I pulled the selectors up, reset the engines, got out of the dive, then told the engineer to keep the bugger away from my controls.'

The Tallboy had been held by two huge steel shackles, which now dangled into space. One bomb door was damaged, the other door wouldn't close. It was the wireless operator's job to use two cables to pull the shackles in, out of the way of the closing bomb doors. It was impossible and Mac Hamilton told Thompson to leave them, although the open door and drifting chains caused considerable drag.

Over the Channel the Lancaster lost height. Mac Hamilton daren't put on too much power because they were running out of fuel. Thompson was sending off a series of radio messages on w/t, explaining their position. Speed was about 185kts. Mac Hamilton asked the navigator for a course back to Woodhall Spa. Jackson handed his skipper a sheet of paper and said: 'Here's the course to steer, but I should keep the boys in crash position, because I doubt if we'll make the Thames Estuary.' Mac Hamilton prepared to ditch if the engines cut out.

During the tense journey across the Channel they were overtaken in the dark by several German fighters which they could not identify. Hamilton believed the first to be a fighter which had been hit and was on fire, although it did not lose height. They all ignored the stricken Lancaster and appeared to be heading towards London.

G-George was directed to West Malling. A terse message came in quickly from the Kent airfield: 'Land 100yds north of the east-west runway. Do not use lighted runway. Repeat, do not use lighted runway. We'll put out flares.'

As they crossed the Kent coast, the warning lights did not indicate if the undercarriage had locked down. Rooke got the Aldis lamp going with the second battery and shone it on to the wheels. Both were turning nicely. Mac Hamilton told him: 'Look, I'm going to risk it, keep everyone in crash positions.' They were all relieved to see the line of West Malling flares. Mac Hamilton says:

'We came into land at 11.30pm. There's an emergency air bottle which you can use to blow down your undercarriage and flaps. We couldn't get more than fifteen degrees of flap down, instead of the whole thirty, so I came in on the grass. As we were coming down, I noticed the fire engine with all the men in their white kit and helmets, led by a

Jeep. A meat waggon (ambulance) followed behind. These ran along beside us as we came down and landed. It seemed to me one of the smoothest landings we had ever done in a Lancaster, because it just greased in. I was so dead scared of the undercarriage collapsing, but we settled down quite nicely. The ground crew came running round the front and when they saw the damage to the aircraft, they said: "How the bloody hell did you get this thing down?"'

An officer apologised to Mac Hamilton for not letting them down on the main runway. Squadrons of fighters from Kent bases, he explained, had been scrambled that night to meet the threat of strange new German aircraft which had been streaming in over the coast on undeviating courses. They discovered later that these new German weapons were not night fighters. They were the first V1 flying bombs to be launched against London. The flames they had seen spurting from the rear of the 26ft long 400mph V1s came from their propulsion unit. Each flying bomb carried an explosive charge of 1,870lb.

The injured bomb-aimer was carried on a stretcher through the aircraft, over the main spar and out of the back door. Rear gunner Dave Hamilton was covered in fuel which had erupted from the hole in the wing tank. One spark from an engine could have turned him into a human fireball.

Mac Hamilton switched off all the electrics before leaving the aircraft. Fuel was still dripping from the starboard wing. Outside Roland Duck lay on the stretcher which was gradually filling up with blood. The doctor, who had managed to give him some morphine, looked at the bomb-aimer who was tenderly holding his crotch, and said: 'Christ! I've never seen so much blood. Are you sure you haven't been hit in the balls, old man?'

Horror infiltrated the pain etched on the face of Duck, a young man only two weeks away from his twenty-first birthday and who loved the company of pretty women. The crew of G-George who had helped get Duck out of the Lancaster heard him gasp 'No!' as he disappeared into the ambulance.

Duck watched the puttering flying bombs from his hospital bed in East Grinstead as they passed over the town at 800 to 1,000ft. He remembers his operation with a shudder. 'There was no anaesthetist and so they dragged this woman out of retirement. She made a mistake with the anaesthetic and I woke as they were cutting me up.'

Next morning, the crew went to see him in hospital where surgeons had operated during the night. A NAAFI pint mug stood on his locker. It was half full with twenty-seven pieces of shrapnel which had been dug out of his legs.

The raid on Boulogne had been the town's worst of the war. The port and the E-boats it sheltered had been severely damaged and about 200 people killed. Only one Halifax was lost from the force of 297 attacking aircraft.

When gangrene began eating into both Roly Duck's legs doctors wanted to remove the left one and were concerned about the other. Then it was decided to get him to

Rauceby Hospital, a few miles from Woodhall Spa, where top orthopaedic surgeon George Braithwaite might be able to save both legs.

Nearly a month after the raid on Boulogne, on 14 July, Mac Hamilton volunteered to return to West Malling in a Lancaster to pick up his friend and former bomb-aimer. Including the crew, medical officer Flight Lieutenant Richard Matthews and a WAAF nursing orderly, thirteen were aboard, a mixture of off-duty aircrew and ground crew, enjoying a gash (free) ride on a fine, sunny day. Duck's replacement, Flying Officer Freddy Atkins, settled in the nose. (The Canadian bomb-aimer would stay with Mac Hamilton until the end of the war.)

Lancaster ME560, H-Harry, crossed the Thames Estuary east of London and landed mid-morning at the fighter base. The crew got a cheerful Duck nicely settled on a stretcher just inside the back door, aft of the mid-upper turret. The little WAAF orderly sat on a parachute next to him, making sure he was comfortable. He told them he was feeling much better and proudly displayed his damaged legs, one of which was covered by plaster up to his hip. Nurses and all his visitors had signed the plaster, and there were the usual rude remarks about how far up the girls had managed to get their pens and pencils.

They took off into a strongish wind. Dr Matthews sat in the flight engineer's seat beside Mac Hamilton, and they chatted about the war. The pilot had been briefed to fly straight across London through a corridor which would be created for them by barrage balloons being lowered. As they thundered down the runway, Mac Hamilton asked the control tower if he should climb above the balloons he could see ahead. The tower instructed him to stay at 1,000ft.

The forest of balloons which lay before them were being lowered in plenty of time. They resembled obscenely fat duchesses offering the bomber massive curtseys. The gunners reported the balloons bobbing up again behind them. Mac Hamilton remembers:

'It was a beautiful clear day. We crossed Mitcham Common, near my mother-in-law's home, and saw a lot of London, including the Thames, the Houses of Parliament and Westminster Abbey. A wind was blowing almost straight down the runway at Woodhall Spa, about ten degrees off, nothing to worry about. We came in to land and I said to Doc Matthews, who was standing next to me: "OK, I'm going to do a wheel landing and make it as soft as possible, in case I upset Roly."

'When we got to the runway there was a violent, juddering noise. I looked at the engineer and he looked at me and pointed at our port wheel racing across the grass on its own. I thought: "What the bloody hell do I do now, because there isn't very much time?"

'I put a little bit of power with the two motors on the port side, just to give it a bit of a lift. I got the aircraft at a slight angle, and it went down slowly on to the main runway. The stub of the undercarriage was still hanging down. There were sparks, and as the wing went down, crumpling the propellers, we left a trail of fuel which had leaked from somewhere. We did the most beautiful skating turn to port, ending up facing the direction from which we'd come.'

Dr Matthews, who had been amazed to see the horizon spinning as they careered down the runway, scrambled through the fuselage to supervise the evacuation of his patient. Mac Hamilton and Rooke immediately turned off all the switches, activated the fire extinguishers in the engines and, in their excitement, pressed the propeller feathering buttons. The pilot cried: 'Everybody out!' as flames began licking ominously between the port engines.

Mac Hamilton looked out of the window and saw Roland Duck sitting up on his stretcher, borne by six men, beating them eagerly with his hat as they ran briskly from the aircraft. Behind came the little nursing orderly, hung about with gas masks and bags, one hand holding up her tight skirt so she could run at top speed. Mac Hamilton made sure everyone was out then, as he squeezed through the window on the engineer's side, he thought the fuel tank would explode and blow him across the airfield. He hung by his hands before letting himself drop on to the grass, landing like a Walt Disney cartoon character, his legs pumping, putting a safe distance between him and the burning wing.

Dambuster survivor, New Zealander Squadron Leader Les Munro, the flight commander, climbed into the aircraft and went into the cockpit, checking that everything was all right, by which time the fire crews were spiking the fuel tanks with their axes and covering the bomber with foam. They found one of the fuel tanks had been ruptured by the crumpled undercarriage.

A back injury was added to Duck's problems and engineer Len Rooke cut his thumb getting out of the cockpit. No one else was hurt. Mac Hamilton says: 'I told the Woodhall intelligence officers I was surprised so much trouble had been taken to lower the barrage balloons as we crossed London. They said it was good exercise for them. The aircraft was taken in and rejigged. The ground crew got another wing and undercarriage on to it and the Lanc was flying again in about six days.'

Roly Duck's legs were saved after receiving several bone grafts at Rauceby, but he would always walk with a limp and many years later was classified 100 per cent disabled. Squadron adjutant for a time after his discharge from hospital, he did fly again, including twenty-two operations in Vietnam.

Mac Hamilton completed 52 operations and holds a DFC and bar. None of his crew was decorated. He said: 'This was one of the things that always upset me. I had a brilliant crew, who worked very hard. We did a lot of operations and they never got a mention.'

10

COLLISION OVER WADDINGTON

German troops had already marched into Prague when Wing Commander The Hon Ralph Cochrane went to New Zealand, early in 1939, to help select suitable men for that country's air force. Some of the eager young men he recommended later served under him when he became air officer commanding the RAF's 5 Group, Bomber Command.

There was no shortage of volunteers, too many as it transpired. A war in Europe seemed inevitable and they all wanted to be part of it. One of them was Jim Verran, from Auckland, a well-built fellow of twenty-three, who already had some flying experience at Auckland airport. Verran had all the qualifications bar one, his name was too near the end of the alphabet. The New Zealand Air Force had filled its quota long before getting to the Vs.

Verran, bitterly disappointed, had an unquenchable adventurous spirit and desperately wanted to fly. And like so many other New Zealanders whose forbears came from the old country – his mother was Scottish, from Campbeltown, his father came from Cornish stock, tin and copper miners – he wanted to help protect Britain from the Nazis. He and eleven like-minded friends decided impulsively that if their own air force didn't want them, they would try to join the RAF. They sailed to England on the RMS (Royal Mail Ship) *Rimutaka*, which was carrying a cargo of butter and frozen meat products. They arrived at London docks at the end of July 1939, went to the Air Ministry for interviews and were all recruited on the spot. Later, one of them did not complete the pilots' course and another, who became ill, was sent home.

By the spring of 1943, Verran was a veteran pilot of twenty-seven, a flight lieutenant with 9 Squadron, based at Waddington. He had already served with distinction on forty-five operations, having been awarded the DFC on 5 June 1941 after his first tour on Whitleys.

The following January, after instructing for two years on Wellingtons, Verran and other officers were recommended for Air Force Crosses (AFC). Only a limited number could be awarded, so the decision about who should receive them was made by the toss of a coin. Verran lost. Instead of receiving an AFC, he had to be satisfied with being mentioned in despatches.

On the night of 1 March 1943, Verran's Lancaster, ED490, was among 302 aircraft whose crews had been briefed to bomb Berlin. Verran had been to Berlin several times before but, however experienced, aircrews did not relish the long trips to Hitler's capital, which was more fiercely defended and surrounded by a greater concentration of gun power than any other enemy city. He was routed over Lincolnshire to Mablethorpe, across the North Sea to Schleswig and Berlin, before returning on Gee lattice lines via The Wash to Waddington. Gee was a radio-based short range navigational aid.

Marking was difficult for the Pathfinders because individual areas of the city could not be clearly identified on the H2S ground scanning radar screens. Even so, more damage was caused by this raid than any previous operations against Berlin. Twenty factories were hit, twenty-two acres of railway repair workshops burned out and 875 buildings, most of them houses, reduced to rubble, while 191 people died.

It was between 2 and 3.00am next morning when Verran's Lancaster nosed out of thick cloud at 800ft over Waddington and a sleeping countryside. Verran and his crew were satisfied after a job well done. Physically drained, although still mentally alert, they peered eagerly down at the welcoming flare path, looking forward to a bacon and eggs breakfast, followed by several wonderful uninterrupted hours of sleep.

Verran recalls: 'We were in the normal left-hand circuit. I could see the flare path. I was talking to the control tower. I was down wind about 800ft, reducing speed, with the undercarriage down. All I had to do was go across wind and then turn in on to the final approach, just before landing.'

All the hell of Berlin then paled into insignificance as another Lancaster, at the same height, burst out of cloud and hurtled towards them. There was less than a second to decide that it would be futile to put the nose down and risk plunging into the ground. Instead, Verran heaved on the control column, hoping they would climb over the other aircraft. It was too late.

The two bombers, at a closing speed of about 300mph, collided in a nightmare of tearing metal and exploding ammunition. The sky was filled with bits of burning and exploding wreckage and the fragile bodies of men, plummeting to earth. Miraculously, four of the fourteen men aboard the two Lancasters survived, all from Verran's aircraft. None had had their parachutes clipped on. Even if they had, at 800ft the 'chutes would have been virtually useless at such a low height.

At the moment of impact Verran said to himself: 'That's your lot mate, you won't get out of this.' Then the control column was snapped back and cracked the pilot on the chin, breaking his lower jaw and knocking him out.   Surprised to be still alive, he woke up in a ploughed field near Waddington after being catapulted through the cockpit canopy. He landed clear of the main fuselage, and crawled several yards to get further away from the leaping flames and exploding ammunition. The tail section of his aircraft was ripped off aft of the mid-upper turret. The front half of the bomber had shattered into several pieces. The four great Rolls-Royce Merlin engines were scattered over a wide area, none of them within a quarter-mile of another. The aircraft burned fiercely and the sound of exploding ammunition resounded through the shattered night, wrenching from their beds people who staggered to windows to peer anxiously into the sky.

Verran was badly hurt. His left femur was broken. His right arm was paralysed and there were gaping wounds in his head and face, the result of being punched violently through the cockpit canopy. Rear gunner Sergeant K. E. W. Matthews, bomb-aimer Pilot Officer Jimmy Geach, and flight engineer Sergeant A. D. Smithson, were all dead. Smithson, who had been sitting to the right of Verran, in the position of the second pilot had there been one, had been projected helplessly straight into the nose. He probably fell out of the bomber a moment after Geach, who seconds before the collision had been preparing to climb into the cockpit ready for the landing. Matthews was trapped inside his rear turret which broke off the shattered fuselage and went careering across the countryside. It was badly mangled.

Navigator Pilot Officer Frank Johnson, who was sitting sideways to the line of flight, was alive, but his head sustained such a fearful pounding that his brain came partly away from its anchorage points within the skull. He recovered after treatment and was sent home to Perth, Australia. The Canadian wireless operator, Flying Officer John Moutray, walked away from the wreckage with a few scratches and minor burns. Mid-upper gunner Sergeant Kenneth Chalk blinked, shook himself and climbed uninjured out of his turret. Verran understates matters when he says: 'It was a miracle escape for the four of us.'

Chalk, then a flight sergeant rear gunner, was killed on 28 September 1944 over Germany when his 77 Squadron Halifax collided with a Luftwaffe night fighter, the wreckage crashing into houses. Only two bodies were recovered, neither was Chalk's. Verran comments: 'He was killed in a second mid-air collision. You can't get more tragic than that.'

The Lancaster which smashed into Verran's bomber was R5894, piloted by Flying Officer John Greenan, a Canadian from 57 Squadron, based at Scampton on the other side of Lincoln. The crippled aircraft struck power cables and crashed at Riseholme, near Scampton, incinerating the seven men inside.

Verran says: 'I don't think the other crew saw us. No one has ever given me a satisfactory explanation about what they were doing over Waddington that night. They were going the wrong way round our circuit. Nobody saw the collision from the station, but they would have heard and seen the explosions. A station ambulance was there to pick us up in a very short space of time.'

Greenan, aged twenty-two, had also been returning from the raid on Berlin that night. A dapper man with reddish hair and a small moustache, from Calgary, Alberta, his remains and those of his crew were buried in the graveyard at Scampton parish church. Verran was in hospital for eight months, recovering from his injuries. A year and four days after the mid-air collision he was back in business with 83 (Pathfinder) Squadron at Wyton, Huntingdonshire.

The idea of a special force to find and accurately mark targets had been discussed at the Air Ministry since 1941. A high proportion of bombs dropped at night, some claimed up to 75 per cent, were not even striking the cities targeted. Bombing accuracy was imperative if the war was to be brought to a speedy conclusion. Most squadrons had crews who excelled at finding targets and hitting them with their bombs. It seemed obvious to gather together the best of these crews into elite squadrons. The name originally suggested for such squadrons was the Target Finding Force. Sir Arthur 'Bomber' Harris, Commander-in-Chief, Bomber Command, rejected the idea, believing new techniques, particularly in radar, would soon lead to an improvement in bombing accuracy. Harris was supported by group commanders who were anxious not to lose their best crews which, they warned, might lead to a loss of morale in the squadrons.

Meanwhile, German defences were improving and strengthening, and an increasing and unacceptable number of British bombers were being shot down. Eventually, it was Sir Charles Portal, Chief of Air Staff, who ordered Harris to set up the new force and the name chosen for it by Harris was the Pathfinder Force. The four squadrons which formed the new force – 7, 35, 83 and 156 – were based in Cambridgeshire and Huntingdonshire. The Pathfinders' commander was Group Captain Don Bennett.

Their task was to locate and pinpoint the targets with different coloured pyrotechnic markers. The last raid by 83 Squadron as a Main Force squadron was on 11 August 1942 to the German city of Mainz. Four days later the squadron moved from Scampton to Wyton, the first all-Lancaster squadron of the Pathfinder Force. After serving with distinction at Wyton, 83 Squadron transferred to Coningsby on 18 April 1944.

Later that year, on the night of 26 August, Verran piloted one of ten bombers from the squadron which joined another 164 Lancasters heading for Königsberg, the capital of East Prussia. The city is now known as Kaliningrad and is in Lithuania. The target was a large supply port and railway centre, a base for German armies attempting to halt the advancing Russian troops, who were now within 100 miles of the city. This was the first of two raids on Königsberg planned by 5 Group at this critical time. Another successful attack on the city was mounted three nights later.

Königsberg was an exhausting 950 miles from 5 Group's bases. Verran only needed to return from this trip to complete his third tour. He remembers: 'It was one of the longest flights we'd ever flown, our fuel tanks were full. Our instructions were to land at Waterbeach, about three miles north-east of Cambridge, on the way back.'

With full fuel tanks, the 174 bombers were restricted to a total bomb load of less than 500 tons. Verran's Lancaster, PB292:S, with forty-six flying hours behind it, carried a 4,000lb Blockbuster bomb together with a load of markers. Verran, one of the squadron's specialist blind marker crews, left in the first wave. He recalls little of the grinding flight to Königsberg but he says: 'It was pretty much a routine trip, although the total distance involved was a very long way, 1,900 miles. The run to the target was straightforward, with no fighter activity. We had two functions, we were marking and bombing as well. We carried high explosives and incendiaries. After the bombing run had been completed, we turned for home. It had been a satisfactory trip.'

Most of the bomb damage was concentrated on the east of the city centre. Four Lancasters would not return to their bases.

Many routine bombing sorties could so swiftly turn to disaster. And there were many disasters. About 125,000 aircrew served in Bomber Command during the war. Of this number, a horrifying 55,500 were killed. The routine trip of Verran and his crew ended abruptly soon after they crossed the Baltic coast and were flying over Jutland with unserviceable radar equipment. A Messerschmitt Bf110 night fighter suddenly screamed up from below and behind and unleashed a rapid burst of cannon fire which ripped wickedly through the belly of the Lancaster. Rear gunner Pilot Officer Keith Tennant squirted off a quick shot into the fighter. The fighter, like the Lancaster, was mortally wounded. Tennant's elation at his accurate shooting was short-lived. Seconds later he would be dead from his injuries.

The night fighter was equipped with a gun mounting which the Germans called 'Schräge Musik', meaning slanting music. Its twin Oerlikon 20mm cannon were cockpit-mounted with their muzzles pointing upwards at a fixed angle, enabling the fighters to attack from beneath the bombers' vulnerable bellies. Both the Bf110 and Junkers Ju88 were fitted with this arrangement. These fighters usually aimed first for the bomber's wings, which contained the fuel tanks and not, as many aggrieved rear gunners believed, at them. The fighter pilots were guided to their prey by their radar operator or the bombers' flaming exhausts. Sometimes the fighters became caught out by their own tactics when they hit the fuel tanks and were obliterated together with the bomber by the devastating explosion. Verran comments:

'I am not sure if the gunner got the fighter as he was coming in or streaking away. What I do know is that he shot the Bf110 down. The 20mm German cannon had incendiaries, and the hydraulic header tank above my wireless operator was hit. Hydraulic oil was spilling from the tank on to the cockpit floor. This caused the hydraulic systems to fail. The undercarriage and the flaps came down, the bomb doors opened and the turrets were useless. There were holes in the cockpit floor, used by the ground crew when they wound the bombs up into the bomb bay with cables. Burning oil poured through these holes and streamed back into the bomb bay.'

Verran told the bomb-aimer, Warrant Officer Raymond Page, to bale out before the bomb doors opened. Page landed safely, was captured and held as a prisoner-of-war at

Stalag IIIA, Luckenwalde, to the south of Berlin. In England, after his release, Page says:

'Over Sweden, I asked the flight engineer, Flight Sergeant Bert Smith, to change places so I could have a look at the lights of Sweden. I took my parachute with me and was kneeling on it watching the tracer. One of the gunners reported seeing another aircraft and thought it was another Lancaster. The next second our Lancaster was sprayed underneath from head to tail by cannon fire. The front turret where I was kneeling burst into flames from ruptured hydraulics. Jim, our pilot, twice called: "Open the hatches!" I clipped on my 'chute, opened the hatch and fell out. I didn't think anyone else had survived.'

Verran again: 'By the time I had inspected the damage and checked how many crew I had left, most of the oil had been pumped out of the hydraulic system and, of course, the fire was spreading rapidly. The engines were still going and I was able to trim the aircraft to fly straight and level. I went down to the front hatch which Page had used. I slipped through the hatch but was immediately swept up into the bomb bay and held fast by the tremendous air pressure. The burning oil was torching back on to me. I wasn't in good shape and knew I was in a spot of trouble, but there was nothing I could do.'

Verran was held in the bomb bay as inextricably as a moth stuck to flypaper, watching the flames roaring towards him.

'The aircraft was pitching a little bit. Then, as it came up to what we called an incipient stall, the air pressure reduced and I fell out. Your mind races around all sorts of things, but when I finally dropped out the next important thing was to pull open the parachute, but I couldn't find the D-ring. It should have been in the little pouch in front of me, but it wasn't there. Of course, it was dark, the middle of the night. I would have had trouble seeing in normal circumstances, but my eyelids were burned and swollen and I had to use my fingers to open them. Then I saw the D-ring spinning around in front of me. I was able to grab the ring and pull it and the canopy opened.'

Verran heard the Lancaster, with five dead aircrew aboard, flying around above him. He did not hear or see the bomber crash. He heard other Lancasters overhead, heading for home, and hoped his expiring bomber would not create any problems for them.

The men who died in the Lancaster that night were navigator Squadron Leader Albert Perkins, DFC, from Wallasey, Cheshire. He was the daddy of the crew at thirty-two, and the squadron's navigation leader. Flight Lieutenant Bill Frew, DFC, the mid-upper gunner, aged nineteen, left a widow Kathlyn at their home in Newbury, Berkshire. He had been 83 Squadron's gunnery leader. Pilot Officer Keith Tennant, twenty-two, the rear gunner, came from Rockhampton, Queensland. Flight Sergeant Alwyn Howarth, twenty-seven, the wireless operator, had lived in Blackpool. Norton, near Stockton-on-Tees, County Durham, was the home of the nineteen-year-old flight engineer, Flight Sergeant Bert Smith. Their broken bodies were left lying strewn along

93

the ground for up to a week by the Germans as an example to the Danish people of what happened to anyone who incurred the wrath of the Third Reich.

The Germans later buried them in a single grave near where their Lancaster had crashed and burned out. The grave was marked by a small wooden cross, bearing the words 'Hier ruhen 5 unbekanate englische Flieger gefallen am 27.8.44'. In the autumn of 1945 the grave was found by a Danish hunting party. The bodies were later identified by the RAF and the grave was soon marked by a piece of granite bearing the men's names. The bodies were exhumed and reburied just after the second anniversary of the crash, on 31 August 1947, at a churchyard in the centre of Randbøl, a village 2km south of the main road from Vejle westwards to Grinsted. Over 100 people attended the ceremony, which is repeated here every May. The inscription on the men's grave reads: 'They died for their native country and it was for our liberation. We thank them for what they gave, we will take care of their tomb.'

It was between 3 and 4 in the morning when Verran landed in the desolate Danish countryside, near the village of Hogsholt. It was not until 1948 when he returned to Denmark that Verran discovered he had dropped within 100yds of the edge of a fjord, narrowly avoiding a sheer drop into the sea. In pain from burns, he picked himself up, disposed of his parachute and walked to the door of a white single-storey farmhouse. He knocked on the door, but no one came so he waited.

Presently, Farmer Jensen appeared. He and his wife and son Erhart had been awakened by Verran's circling Lancaster in its explosive death throes. They had run terrified from the farmhouse into the fields, believing their world was about to come to an end. Verran remembers:

'I was in a pretty sorry state. I had third degree burns to the lower part of my right forearm and my right hand. My face was burned, especially around the outer edges of my ears. I was also burned round my eyes and the tops of my eyelids. Parts of my uniform were also burned. It was summer and I was only wearing my battledress and shoes. If I'd had flying boots on my legs would not have been as badly burned. Luckily, I was still wearing my helmet. The farmer and his wife took me inside and made me coffee. They were pretty shaken and knew I was what the Germans called a 'terror bomber', but did all they could for me. They sent for an ambulance but of course, all the time they were fearful of the Germans arriving.'

The ambulance was driven by former merchant seaman Hans Stienbrenner. His burly assistant was Ejvind Damsgaard. They both lived in the nearby town of Vejle. The two men gently helped Verran into the ambulance and set off for the town's cottage hospital, where the Germans had already established a name for ruthlessness by shooting dead the senior doctor. On the way Verran heard gunfire. The driver told him later the Wehrmacht had opened fire on them, even though it was clear they were in an ambulance. Stienbrenner put his foot down and they arrived safely at the hospital.

Here the injured pilot met the charming and sensitive Dr Carl Svenstrup, who spoke good English and wore a white coat made of parachute silk. The good doctor told Verran that they had the right connections to smuggle him to neutral Sweden, where he could be treated and sent back to England. Svenstrup, however, feared his injuries were so severe Verran might not survive the journey, which could have involved an uncomfortable and dangerous trip across the Kattegat in an open boat, covered by a tarpaulin. The Danish doctor decided, reluctantly, to hand the pilot over to the Germans, who would be better equipped to treat Verran.

Verran recalls: 'The Germans treated me well. They were not at all rough with me. They started off by putting a guard on the door of the cottage hospital, later moving me to the German Army hospital which was based in a convent a few miles away on the coast at Fredericia. German soldiers who had been injured on the Russian Front were treated here. The German doctors looked after me no differently than their own men.'

Major Hoefele, the pilot of the Bf110 which had been shot down by the Lancaster rear gunner Keith Tennant, was also a patient in the hospital. His gunner, Oberleutnant Walter Scheel, of Nachtjagdgeschwader (NJG) 3, claimed to have shot down Verran's Lancaster in quadrant NT at 3.15am. Hoefele arrogantly refused to see the RAF pilot. Verran believed the reason was because the German thought his victory was the greater for his aircraft, which had only two engines, had shot down a bomber with four. This was an unusual attitude at the time, opposing aircrews normally showed chivalry towards each other.

Verran believes he owes his recovery to a German general practitioner from Kiel, who carried out skin grafts on the pilot. The grafting was excruciatingly painful because the hospital was short of anaesthetic and had only paper bandages. Verran says: 'The doctor used an instrument like a crochet hook which he dug into my thigh, swiftly twisted off a circle of skin and put it on my arm or legs.' Today there are dozens of circular marks on his thighs, arms and legs where the surgeon worked deftly to put new skin on areas which had third degree burns. The remaining skin which was burned is now like tissue paper. Verran again:

'After landing I was not aware that I was badly burned apart from around my eyes and hands. I experienced extreme pain after I was taken to the German hospital where burns on my arms and legs were cleaned up, and after the skin grafts had been carried out. The donor areas on my thighs were extremely painful as were the open areas on my face, arms and legs which had third degree burns. I could only sleep lying on my back and each breath caused skin tension and pain.'

The patients at the hospital had a daily cigarette ration. Verran, a non-smoker, gave his cigarettes to a German nurse, whose husband had been killed on the Russian Front. She sold the cigarettes to other patients and used the money to buy Verran delicious Danish cream cakes.

When Verran was fit to travel, two armed Luftwaffe NCOs took him by train to Frankfurt-am-Main via Hamburg. 'Whilst I was on a stretcher at Hamburg railway station, a badly injured German naval officer came over, spat in my face, snarled: "Schweinhund!" and walked away.' He also met at the station an Englishwoman, married to a German, anxious about their soldier son, a prisoner in England. Verran reassured her that he wouldn't be badly treated. The woman was so delighted she hurried away, returning to give him a cup of Lipton's tea.

Verran remembers: 'During an air-raid I was taken down into a shelter at the station. There was a group of little German schoolgirls who had blonde plaited hair down their backs, playing ring-a-ring-a-roses. That was bloody hard to take, realising these were the kind of people we were bombing.'

The pilot, who still had open wounds which needed dressing, was taken to the Dulag Luft at Frankfurt-am-Main and left in a cell. Eventually he was interrogated by an English speaking German officer. Verran refused to tell him anything, apart from his name, rank and number. The German smiled thinly and said the Luftwaffe had a recording of Verran's voice made while he was taking part in bombing trials over Wainfleet Sands, Lincolnshire. The German provided details of times and dates. The interrogator, whose idiomatic English was far from perfect, added, smugly: 'Maybe you think I know bugger nothing, but when you have been here just a while, you will discover that I know bugger all.'

Verran was a prisoner-of-war at Stalag IXC, at Moosburg, near Munich, until he was released by an American tank destroyer unit in April 1945. The unit's commanding officer, Colonel Harry Charter, gave Verran a splendid Mercedes drophead coupe which they had liberated from a wealthy German family. Verran and former Spitfire pilot Flight Lieutenant Bill Creed drove it to Brussels, calling in at German hospitals on the way to get his wounds dressed, and at Army units for food, fuel and rest. Verran stored the car in a farmer's barn and hitched a lift back to RAF Manston in a Mosquito with a New Zealand friend, Flight Lieutenant Bill Kemp. Months later Verran returned to Brussels and collected his Mercedes.

Verran was awarded a bar to his DFC on September 18 1945. His citation reads: '... he has set an example to all crews. His fine record of achievement and unfailing devotion to duty merit high commendation.'

11

STRETCHING LUCK
TO THE LIMIT

On the morning of 12 March 1941, thirty-five young men, fresh from training, reported to the adjutant of 102 Squadron at Topcliffe in North Yorkshire. A little over seven months later only one was still alive, Sergeant Philip Brett, a wireless operator/air gunner. It is impossible to say why Brett alone survived, but luck played a significant part for those who lived and those who died in Bomber Command. Brett had his full measure of luck and more besides. He also had for most of his twenty-eight operations a pilot, 'Big' Bill Wilson who, claimed Brett, handled an Armstrong Whitworth Whitley twin-engine bomber with amazing natural instinct, almost matching that of a predatory bird.

When most twin-engine bombers had been phased out of the war, Brett believed no one else in the RAF could match his record of three SOS trips and five times returning from a bombing operation on only one engine. Years afterwards, just thinking about such luck made him perspire freely.

The thirty-five rookie aircrew who squeezed into the adjutant's office had been trained at 10 Operational Training Unit (OTU) at Abingdon, Berkshire. There were pilots, navigators, wireless operators and gunners, enough to form seven crews. They arrived at Topcliffe with the enthusiasm of bright-eyed young men who had been thoroughly prepared for war without actually being part of it. Veterans at Abingdon had spoken casually to them about bombing, flak, German night fighters, probing searchlights, and the many friends who had not come back, yet somehow it had all seemed so unreal. The reality of war struck them forcibly as they listened to the adjutant give his usual pep talk for new arrivals, spelling out how much was expected and how their King and country would be proud of them.

It was not, however, his words of wisdom which dragged them into the war, but the noticeboard behind the officer's desk. It contained rows of names, neatly written in alphabetical order, names of the men of 102 Squadron. Against many of the names, which seemed to swell in number as they stared horrified at them, had been inserted a single strip of white card bearing one word, 'Missing'. Staring mutely at that noticeboard, they knew their days of playing at flying were over.

Another notice, larger and more decorative, greeted them at the entrance to the crew room: 'Abandon Hope All Ye Who Enter Here'. This was a message not meant to be taken too seriously, although Brett remembers the words contained too much truth not to chill the marrow of the new arrivals. Inside, however, they found not abandoned hope but the unquenchable spirit of youth and comradeship.

Norwich-born Brett met 'Big' Bill Wilson on B Flight in the spring of 1941. The pilot was a 6ft 4in Australian beanpole, who spoke in a slow Queensland drawl which belied his swift reaction to mid-air crises. He had the soft responsive hands of a man born to be a pilot and many times dragged crippled bombers back to England. His calmness was extraordinary. As flak poured up to meet them he was often heard to murmur: 'Jeez man, they're shooting at us'. He and Brett were both twenty-three years old and, quite soon, they had acquired legendary reputations as men who could stretch their luck to the limit and beyond.

Brett had already been on two operations to Kiel Canal and Hamburg with other pilots. On 3 June he took off from Topcliffe at 3.15pm with Wilson in a Whitley Mk V bomber. It was a training flight during which Brett had to carry out two radio controlled landings to finally qualify him as a squadron wireless operator. The Whitley, powered by two 1,145hp Rolls-Royce Merlin X engines, headed for Linton-on-Ouse, an RAF station near York, which had excellent flying control facilities. They would make their approaches and landings directed solely by radio. Brett remembers:

'At that time we had no way of landing in bad visibility. We had no radio beacons or anything like that. That came later. We used to try and land by what they called a radio controlled landing, a ZZ landing. They tried to bring you in with a radio operator on the ground talking you down. I was extremely apprehensive of my ability to perform such a difficult exercise but once in the air, and with my radio behaving in a delightful manner, I soon forgot all my fears and revelled in the satisfaction that everything was going smoothly.'

The Whitley made its first approach to Linton with absolute precision and Brett was calmly informing ground control that they were coming in for the second time, when a thunderous explosion erupted from the port engine, which then disappeared in a belching cloud of smoke and flames. 'It all happened in a flash. I couldn't seem to think properly but I managed, with very shaky Morse, to ask ground control to wait as our port engine was on fire. They were extremely helpful and suggested we turned back into the airfield to land immediately, but that was impossible because by now we were several miles away and only about 100ft from the ground. We were gradually losing height with only one engine.'

The fire was put out by the automatic extinguisher and Brett left his seat to see if he could help the pilot. He was staggered to see the tops of trees passing a few feet below them. Wilson shouted that they were about to crash. Brett returned to the radio and told ground control they were going in. He switched off the sets, then returned to the pilot. The Whitley, its single engine roaring, getting lower by the second, scraped over woods and houses. Brett stayed with the pilot long enough to strap him tightly into his seat before lying flat on the floor, feet braced against the side of the fuselage. Brett recalls:

'We seemed to fly for an eternity after that, although it was probably only a few seconds. Then came a horrible grinding and tearing of metal as we nosed our way into – thank God – a ploughed field. The flooring just in front of me was completely torn away and I was blinded and choked by the clouds of dust and earth that came pouring into the fuselage. We charged across one field, through a hedge and across another small field, scattering a long trail of wreckage behind us, narrowly missing a telegraph pole and a clump of trees. There was a final ghastly bump, the grinding and tearing ceased, and we were still, but not for long.'

Hearing the sound of petrol gushing from ripped fuel tanks, they scuttled from the escape hatches. Brett scrambled through the torn and battered fuselage to a door, trapping his foot in the wreckage and freeing it with a desperate jerk. Then he was outside gasping in fresh air, amazed that apart from the pilot, who had cracked his head against the front panel in the cockpit, none of them were hurt.

With Brett and Wilson were the navigator, Sergeant Bobby Adamson, a blond Canadian, who also doubled as bomb-aimer, and the Geordie rear gunner, Sergeant Bill Nichols. Brett looked at his watch. It was 4.20pm. Surveying the twisted wreckage they realised the bomber had buried its nose into a high bank and was lying across a main road near Green Hammerton, four miles south-west of Linton. Wartime civilian traffic was sporadic, but a couple of cars had stopped a safe distance away, the drivers thanking their lucky stars.

A blood wagon, fire tender and crash crew arrived quickly, with one man detailed to remove what was then secret radar equipment, the IFF (Identification, Friend or Foe), a device to differentiate between friendly and hostile aircraft. Brett was not required to go up for a second test. He was now a qualified squadron wireless operator and did not take part in any further operations as a rear gunner. He was not sorry about that.

He only flew operationally in the Whitley V, known as 'the Flying Coffin', which Brett describes as 'a basic tub', but regarded it with genuine affection:

'The Whitley V was an ugly old thing, designed to fly with its nose down, an awful attitude of flying. Its secret was its Merlin engines and the stressed steel skin construction which gave it incredible strength. You could blow holes in a Whitley and it would still fly, providing the flak missed all the vital parts. After one raid I counted over twenty holes just on one side from the fuselage door back to the tail assembly. You could put your fist through some. It was incredible the amount of damage it could sustain and still fly. One disadvantage was that the Whitley was so slow. Official speeds were always very exaggerated. The Whitley's cruising speed was usually no more than 125 to 130mph with a full bomb load. We got one up to 145mph, which we thought was fantastic. With a stiff breeze against us, the ground speed could be as little as 80mph.'

The Whitley carried four .303in Browning machine guns in a Fraser Nash rear turret and a single Lewis machine gun in the front, operated by the second pilot. Its maximum bomb load was 7,000lb, its ceiling 20,000ft and it was the first heavy bomber to go into large scale production for the RAF.

Topcliffe aircrews were billeted at Skellfield House, a large, serene, ivy-covered mansion three miles from the airfield. The contrast between war and peace was bizarre. At Skellfield there were woods, attractive gardens, summer houses, a swimming pool and a river passing 20ft behind the back of the mansion, where some of them fished. It was a sylvan paradise where aircrews could forget the war and relax before going off to kill Germans, or themselves be killed.

In the summer of 1941, Wilson was given his own Whitley. He and the crew christened it 'E-Eagle of Ceylon' – 102 Squadron was known as the Ceylon squadron. They designed a crest which was painted on the nose of the aircraft. It was a fierce looking eagle, grasping a bomb in its claws, surmounted by the name, with space left for small bombs which would be painted on after every trip.

Brett no longer surveyed morbidly the empty beds of comrades lost on operations. He was used to the strange behaviour and remarks of more experienced chaps. He knew they were not being callous when casually dismissing someone who had 'gone for a burton' the night before; unkind when roaring with laughter at an unfortunate pilot's terrible landing or take-off; or flippant when taking bets on who would be first back from an operation. Ribaldry and black humour were necessary safety valves for young men who tried to pretend that the word 'Missing' would never appear against their names behind the adjutant's desk.

Few of Brett's bombing trips lacked drama. Many were packed with moments of absolute terror. On 5 August the target was Frankfurt and the Eagle of Ceylon endured a nasty ten minutes from flak over France before flying well south of the Ruhr Valley. Here they picked up landmarks before being harassed by more anti-aircraft fire until finding the target and dropping their bombs. Then, inexplicably, they went badly off course, accidentally flying alone over Cologne and along the Ruhr instead of heading on a more southerly course. Not surprisingly, for there was nothing else to shoot at, every gun and searchlight for miles around was pointed at them. Remembering the incident, Brett says:

'We ran a gauntlet of flame, fire and hell which even now makes me shudder when I think of it. For thirty-five long drawn out minutes we were the sole target for such flak and searchlight opposition that I think very few people have experienced. I just shut my eyes and clenched my teeth in an effort to stop shaking with real and horrible fear. Having to just sit and operate our radio equipment made it even worse. An age seemed to pass, a never ending age in which the sky around us was filled with the sickening crumps and whoofs of exploding shells. It seemed impossible that any aircraft could survive such a barrage. Our evasive action brought us down to 5,000ft and it wasn't long before we had been driven to 2,000ft. As far as we could see in the distance, searchlights were coming into operation against us. At this height, clearly visible in the glare of the searchlights, light flak was coming up in a constant stream, and then machine-gun fire was turned against us from the ground.

'In desperation, we opened fire at their ground defences with every gun we had, while I scrambled along the corrugated metal floor of the fuselage to the flare chute to throw out some screaming incendiary bombs to try and shake them up a bit on the ground. This went on for a further five or six minutes, then every gun and searchlight seemed to be swept into oblivion. We found ourselves flying along in a world of unusual quietness, broken only by the pulsating throb of our engines.'

Completely lost, they eventually pinpointed Emden on the starboard bow and set a rough course for the French coast and home. The Eagle of Ceylon landed at Topcliffe after a trip which had lasted ten hours. Twelve days later the Eagle was grounded for repairs after being badly mauled by a Bf110 on a trip to Hannover.

They borrowed an inferior Whitley from A Flight, J-Johnny, for the trip to Bremen on 17 August, Brett's thirteenth operation. By now only twenty of the original thirty-five were alive. Second pilot was a Canadian, Sergeant Johnny 'Ropey' Roe, so called because of a disconcerting habit of bouncing the aircraft on landing. He was a cheerful, tubby individual who occasionally went drinking with Brett at the Golden Fleece in Thirsk. During these early days of the war crews were shuffled around to fill gaps left by men who had been killed. For this trip their rear gunner was another Canadian, Sergeant Sumpton.

Take-off was at 11.45pm. They had been briefed, together with aircrews of thirty-nine Hampdens and nineteen other Whitleys of Bomber Command, to bomb the Focke-Wulf aircraft factory and the railway goods station. J-Johnny negotiated the heavy flak and searchlights straddling the Dutch coast and droned on towards Germany. Its engines had a distinctive vroom–vroom! vroom-vroom-vroom-vroom! Excepting the rear gunner, the crew sat between them and when landing, exhausted, after eight or nine hours, and peeling off their helmets, their heads continued to throb long after the engines had been switched off.

They were still over Holland at 12,000ft when the starboard engine began to show signs of packing up. The oil temperature was going off the clock and pressure was dropping. There was suddenly a tremendous flash outside the cabin and Brett saw flames streaming from the starboard engine. Wilson told Brett over the intercom to contact base to say they were preparing to abandon the aircraft.

Brett made sure his parachute was handy, ready for a quick exit, then sent out the code 'WFZ, WFZ' (preparing to abandon aircraft) together with the letter 'J' to identify themselves, before turning to help put out the engine fire, which had only been partly quenched by the automatic extinguisher. Everyone except the pilot used hand extinguishers through the side window in an attempt to put out the fire, now licking round the wing and fuselage. The aircraft lost height quickly, blazing a trail of flame and smoke through the sky. The bombs were jettisoned and they turned for home. As the aircraft crawled through the flak and searchlights of the coastal defences, the rear gunner reported: 'Fighter coming up to attack'. Brett recalls:

'That was the last straw. However, during briefing, our signals intelligence, known as "Y" Branch, had told us the Jerry recognition signal for that night. The armourers only had time to make up two sets of cartridges for the Very pistol, and we had one of them. Bobby grabbed the pistol and fired a cartridge while we all kept our fingers crossed. The miracle happened, it worked. Almost immediately the flak and searchlights stopped and the fighter pulled away, thinking we were one of his own aircraft. The fire was out and right ahead was the comparative safety of the North Sea.'

J-Johnny was only a few hundred feet above the sea and sinking fast as they began to jettison all spare equipment. They needed to lose weight to give the port engine a chance to get them home. Out went the flares, ammunition, flame floats and loose incendiaries, but the altimeter showed that the single engine was losing the battle. The aircraft was still falling.

It was 12.45am when Brett sent out an SOS call, at the same time getting a radio fix to give their exact position. The skipper told him to clamp down the radio key so their position could be taken by radio stations at home if the Whitley suddenly dived into the sea. The others unhooked the dinghy from beside the door on the port side and began getting it ready for ditching.

Only twenty miles from the Dutch coast, with 125 miles of sea to cross to Norfolk, the altimeter registered zero feet. Bill Wilson and Ropey Roe, the second pilot, fought to keep the dying bomber above the water as the others sat by the open fuselage door, flashing their torches at the waves rolling underneath no more than 15ft away.

Brett reflects: 'I had always been particularly fond of the sea, but my feelings turned to a real deep hatred at the sight of the cold uninviting waves of the North Sea below. There was a bitterly cold wind blowing in through the fuselage door, chilling us to the bone and whipping a fine spray from the waves, just waiting to draw us into their cold embrace.'

They were waiting tensely for the nose of the Whitley to plunge into the sea when Big Bill Wilson remembered the fuel which had not been used for the long haul to Bremen. They stared at the two auxiliary tanks, on either side of the fuselage, each containing 100gals. Brett seized the axe to hack at one of them, but each tank was self-sealing as a protection against enemy bullets and flak. The quicker he chopped holes, the quicker they resealed themselves. Johnny Roe spotted the fuel leads on the floor, took the axe and chopped them open. A stream of aviation fuel cascaded towards the back of the aircraft, escaping through many cracks and holes in the floor. Roe, delighted by his good work, turned his attention to the clamps holding the heavy oxygen bottles, muttering 'Let's get rid of these, too'.

His first eager swing missed completely and the axe, biting into metal, sent a shower of sparks a few inches away from the high octane aviation fuel. Brett remembers how his 'blood ran cold when I realised how near we had been to going up in flames and diving into the sea.' The flow from the auxiliary tanks ceased. The fuselage stank of petrol but the loss of 200gals did not seem to have made any difference to their plight. They could still see the waves heaving beneath them and Brett was convinced it was only a matter of time before the aircraft ditched.

Half-an-hour passed and they were still skimming the water when Wilson called Brett into the cabin. He said the port engine was holding out well and he intended to put down in Norfolk. Brett sent out another SOS, getting a further radio fix and reporting their intentions. Navigator Bobby Adamson plotted Brett's bearings from a network of three long range D/F (direction finding) fixing stations. Bircham Newton, a radio station in north Norfolk sent back a very comforting message: 'Keep your chins up, only 75 miles to go'.

The note of the engine changed slightly as the pilot gently eased more power into it. He remembered the operation on 15 June, returning after bombing Schwerte marshalling yards in the Ruhr. The starboard engine had cut out after being hit by flak. The port engine had got them home but the ground crew found that two of its cylinders had blown and parts of it were fused together from the tremendous heat and strain. That had been another lucky escape and Wilson had learned from the experience. Another time, returning from a raid on one engine, the second cut out 30ft above the runway at Coningsby. Now, frighteningly close to ditching in the North Sea, Wilson listened carefully for any harsh, rasping protest from the Merlin engine, but although strained without its partner, it sounded healthy enough.

Their climb was sluggish at first, but Wilson was a man of infinite patience and calm, and after being so close to dropping into the drink, he knew it would be foolish to throw away their good fortune. He smiled happily as the altimeter needle flickered weakly above zero. The pilot cajoled, nursed and sweet-talked the Whitley up and up, away from the sea, so nearly their grave, every foot of height gained and every mile negotiated a testimony to his supreme flying skills. Flying a Whitley on one engine was difficult, impossible even for some pilots.

Brett was now getting regular radio positions, plotting their course, making sure they took the shortest possible route and telling Bircham Newton they had clawed their way up to 500ft. 'Bill's achievement was superb, surely the greatest test of any pilot. I certainly owed my life to his coolness and exceptional flying skill on many occasions, but his efforts went unrewarded. He was never decorated. Bill was cheated, he deserved some recognition.'

Within twenty miles of the Norfolk coast and still climbing, the altimeter showed a healthy 900ft. Bearings were being received in a constant stream from D/F stations. Brett was close to tears when he saw the Norfolk coast. It was then the crew gave three cheers of joy and thanks to 'Big Bill and his Bushwhackers'. Brett, too, received a slap on the back for the part he had played in keeping the crippled Whitley on its correct course.

Approaching Docking, just north of Bircham Newton, at 1,000ft, they landed safely 4hr 20min after taking off from Topcliffe. Exhausted and scruffy, they had never before made a landing in such a state of happiness and exhilaration after battling against what had seemed to be overwhelming odds.

Next day the whole squadron was called together. J-Johnny's dilapidated dinghy, held up in front of them, contained forty-three holes. Brett recalls: 'Some chaps thought it was a huge joke. Others didn't think it was funny at all. Our crew were shocked and horrified. If we'd ditched, we'd have had it. After that we always examined our dinghy before each op.'

The tightly packed dinghy, hanging up on the side of the fuselage, had been struck by shards of flak during an unknown number of operations. One piece of flak tearing through it might have created a dozen or more holes. Aircrews were instructed to examine their dinghies more regularly.

On 20 October 1941, after returning from Wilhemshaven, his twenty-third operation, Brett was the only survivor of the original thirty-five rookie aircrew. He was also the senior man on the squadron. It was at this time he developed 'the twitch'. This condition was a state of mind which affected many aircrew who had lived through horrors too numerous to enumerate, and whose nerves had been shot to pieces. It built up emotional layers of worry, pessimism and fear, and many of those who suffered could not stop their heads and sometimes their limbs from twitching.

Brett says: 'I didn't notice it when I was flying. But on the ground I couldn't eat soup or hold a cup and saucer. My hands shook so much the tea slopped everywhere. I went to see the MO (medical officer) and he advised me to drink a pint of Mackeson just before I went to bed and that would do the trick. It jolly well did, too.'

His tour ended after twenty-eight operations. 'Although at one time we were officially supposed to do thirty, we went on longer trips in Whitleys than say, the Wellingtons or Blenheims. We were told to do 300 operational hours or thirty trips, whichever came first. I clocked up 300 hours on my twenty-eighth trip, to Hamburg on 30 November 1941.'

A little over eleven months after arriving at Topcliffe, Brett checked the squadron records and found that 350 aircrew had been lost in that time.

A few days before Christmas 1941, Brett learned to his surprise and delight that he had been awarded a DFM. The citation read: 'He has been instrumental in the safe return of his bomber on at least five difficult occasions'.

Brett saw the rest of the war out with his feet fixed firmly on the ground. After passing a course for technical signals officers at Cranwell, he was posted to Scampton as assistant station signals officer, where he helped 617 Squadron in their training for the dams raid.

12

TOO CLOSE FOR COMFORT

It was 6.50pm on 2 October 1942, when Lancaster W4238, C-Charlie, of 106 Squadron, lifted off the tarmac runway at Syerston and ploughed a tumultuous furrow through the cold, fine night. All four engines were running sweetly as the seven-man crew looked down at the darkened Nottinghamshire countryside. No one in the stone cottages and farms which squatted among the spidery lanes below would have envied them their task that night: to bomb Krefeld in the Ruhr Valley. The heavily defended industrial heartland of Germany demanded the highest concentration from bomber aircrews at all times.

They faced a tough flight over the North Sea into northern Holland and Germany, turning on a dog leg and swooping south to Krefeld, with another 187 bombers. It was a trip which went wrong in more ways than one.

This was the twenty-second operation for flight engineer Sergeant John Humphreys. Brought up in Eastbourne, Sussex, he volunteered for the RAF shortly after the war started on 3 September 1939, and was put on deferred service until he was called up in April 1940. He was now aged twenty-one, three years younger than his Rhodesian skipper Flight Lieutenant Bill Whamond.

Humphreys, a lean and bony six-footer of 10 stones, carefully surveyed the instruments, then stared intently into the night, knowing that when the bomber crossed the Dutch coast they would be greeted by flak and possibly fighters, hungry for RAF scalps. Humphreys had exceptional night vision. A man who could pick up a darting speck in a murky sky and quickly identify it as a German fighter was an asset to any bomber crew. Later in the war he would remuster to bomb-aimer when his sight became invaluable to the Pathfinder Force. Most of the crew had been together some time when they were joined by Humphreys, a spare bod, who had served five different pilots in 106 Squadron.

Fair-haired, blue-eyed Whamond was from Bulawayo and, like his squadron commander, Wing Commander Guy Gibson, maintained a strict officer/NCO relationship between himself and his crew, all sergeants. Humphreys says: 'He was a bit dour and distant with us, but he was a good pilot, very capable and calm in stressful situations, which gave us a lot of confidence, and that was important.' Whamond was also a close friend of Gibson, who appreciated his rib-rattling sense of humour. Whamond was later awarded a DSO and DFC.

Navigator 'Mac' McLelland, from Saskatchewan in Canada, was easy going, helpful and likeable. He became even more popular among the aircrew when his regular parcels arrived from home and he shared out goodies, including packets of 200 Sweet Caporal cigarettes.

The bomber's wireless operator was 'Happy' Hanson, always cheerful, always laughing, and full of jokes. Hanson flew a lot with Gibson, who always called him Happy. He was one of the few NCOs with whom the taciturn wing commander had an easy and friendly relationship. Hanson and Brian Sutton, who both qualified as wireless operators/air gunners, regularly swapped positions before an operation. Happy Hanson was killed with 83 Squadron when his aircraft was shot down later in the war on a Pathfinder sortie.

Birmingham-born Sutton occupied the rear gunner's turret on this his sixteenth operation. Sutton had been a clerk in a coal and coke merchant's office before the war, and had joined the RAF on his nineteenth birthday in 1940.

The mid-upper gunner, Nobby Clarke, was a bright and breezy Londoner from Eltham.

John Cunningham, the bomb-aimer, was tall and good looking, with wavy fair hair. He was an off-duty lady killer, a regular visitor at the Palais de Danse in Nottingham. The city's Flying Horse pub was another popular rendezvous for many aircrews stationed at Syerston and at Newton, an airfield about five miles to the south-west.

Humphreys had been to the Ruhr before and knew what to expect. He remembers:

'We normally met a fair bit of flak when we crossed into Holland. You always knew from that point onwards that you were open to anything and everything. You were liable to be attacked by fighters or run into a sudden barrage of flak. Mainly you were concerned about fighters.

'Then, as you approached the target, following other aircraft which had already bombed, you saw the searchlights and, all of a sudden, puffs of black smoke. That's when you knew you were the subject of German interest.

'As you proceeded further into the target area, the flak would be much more intense, the real heavy stuff. The worst part was on the bombing run when you had to hold the aircraft straight and level and there was no chance of doing any weaving. You hoped you wouldn't get coned by searchlights. If you were coned, after the master searchlights clamped on to you, your chances of survival were going down and down. The German gunners just fired continuously up the cone at you. This was where a lot of our bombers were lost.'

The roar of a Lancaster's engines masked the noise of bursting shells, except those which exploded nearby when the unnerving 'whoomph!' got through to them and the crew held their breath. Tracers seemed to come up very slowly, almost laboriously, before accelerating past.

All aircrew feared a box barrage. No matter which way the bomber turned, it was boxed in by the criss-crossing lines of fire which slowly closed in until a shell struck. Humphreys says: 'You felt apprehensive on each trip, and the apprehension grew as you drew nearer to the target. Everybody was concerned about getting there, dropping the bombs and getting the hell out of it. The gunners were all the time watching out for fighters. The navigator was still checking all his headings, the wireless operator was on the r/t, while the bomb-aimer was busy trying to steer the aircraft to the aiming point.'

On this night they didn't see any flak. Nor did they get near the target. They had barely penetrated German air space when Hanson received a message from 5 Group headquarters in Grantham recalling 106 Squadron to base. They had been airborne 2hr 35min. Sutton remembers: 'There was a haze over Krefeld. No one complained about a recall when we were flying to the Ruhr'.

They droned back over the North Sea, jettisoned the bombs, thinking positively about returning from the Ruhr without a scratch, then debriefing, a leisurely meal, and some shut-eye. They had time for a drink before reaching the Midlands. They took hot coffee on each trip, and sometimes a bar of chocolate. It could be difficult choosing the right time to gulp down a mouthful of coffee. Bending to pick up a flask might be the moment a fighter chose to attack. Humphreys usually preferred a quick swig of orangeade.

The Lancaster joined the circuit over Syerston and patiently awaited permission to land. They were relaxed now. Germany was part of another world, someone else's world, not theirs; not until tomorrow or the day after.

Syerston was very close to Newton and the outer circle lights encompassed both air-fields. On the ground there was a very considerable difference in the Nottinghamshire bases. Syerston had a 1,900yd tarmac runway; Newton's was only 700yds, on grass.

Rear gunner Sutton recalls: 'We joined the circuit over Syerston and were told to go round again. We saw the runway lights below and the navigator called out "there it is".' Whamond lined up with the runway lights and came in. Cunningham had left the nose and was standing behind the flight engineer. Humphreys remembers: 'We flared out (pulled out from the approach angle and got level with the ground). Immediately we touched down at 120kts I knew something was wrong because the aircraft was bumping all over the place. Then, all of a sudden, I saw this dammed great gun emplacement.'

Sutton again: 'We realised it was the wrong 'drome and wrong runway and the skipper couldn't stop in time. He got to the end of the runway and turned the plane right over to the left.' They had landed at Newton, then a base for Polish fighters. It was 11.25pm. The careering Lancaster smashed into the brick and concrete emplacement with a great roar of tearing metal. The tail was smashed wide open as the aircraft split into three pieces and burst into flames. Sutton was flung out of the rear turret, which crunched sickeningly into the emplacement. Whamond pulled the lever above his head to release the escape hatch. He stood on his seat and shot out, jumping down on to the port wing and disappeared into the night.

Humphreys, desperately trying to yank his intercom lead out of the plug socket, reached the escape hatch, but the soles of his flying boots were soaked with hydraulic fluid which had flooded into the cockpit. He slipped on the perspex canopy and fell backwards, the intercom lead plug catching in the hatch. He hung upside down by the lead as the fire spat and crackled around him. Humphreys repeatedly tugged at the lead until it broke loose and he dropped back into the cockpit. Driven by the fear of being incinerated, he clambered on to the pilot's seat, climbed through the escape hatch, slid down beside the fuselage on to the starboard wing and fell to the ground.

He landed heavily on his back. Winded and gasping he looked up at the starboard inner engine and saw the magnesium alloy of the engine casing melting in the searing heat and running down towards him. All engines and wings were blazing, with fire spreading rapidly to the fuselage. There was a stench of burning oil and melting metal. The rest of the crew had escaped. Humphreys was on his own.

He tried to leap to his feet, then discovered he was hooked up on coils of barbed wire which were protecting the gun emplacement. The more he struggled, the more tightly he became entangled. He couldn't move. He stared for a second in horrified fascination at the stream of molten magnesium alloy pouring down the side of the engine cowling. 'I thought I'd had it. I thought I was going to be burned alive.' It was one thing getting the chop over Germany, but the craziest of bad luck being killed after touching down on the wrong airfield.

The ammunition was now going off, increasing the risk of an explosion and the bomber becoming Humphreys' funeral pyre. He flung everything into a frenzy of movement, tore himself free then noticed that where two thick coils of barbed wire met there was a small gap. Fire wagons were on their way now, but there was no time to wait. He had only seconds to spare before the Lancaster was consumed, taking him with it.

He crawled, agonisingly slowly, through the gap, feeling his battledress and fleece-lined flying jacket tear and the wire bite into his flesh. Luckily Humphreys was skinny, a bulkier man would have struggled to drag himself between the two long cylinders of barbed wire. Then he was free and running. He saw the fire tenders and behind them, the outline of some buildings. As he ran towards them the Lancaster erupted in a huge fireball.

Amazingly, all the crew escaped with nothing more serious than scratches. Seven aircraft were lost on the Krefeld raid, including C-Charlie.

The same crew faced an entirely different kind of ordeal when they left Syerston for Turin on the night of 9 December 1942. There were compelling reasons for and against being part of an operation on Turin. The flak was less fierce over Italy than in Germany, while the Italian fighters lacked the fanaticism of the Luftwaffe. Aircrews who had been told that the night's target was Italy normally left briefings in a lighter frame of mind.

On the minus side were the gruelling eight or nine hours in the air. Even worse, the heavily-laden British bombers had to hoist themselves over snow-capped mountains towering almost 16,000ft in the Alps. Some aircrews regarded Italy as a piece of cake. Experienced aircrews knew they could not afford to relax. Aircrews who became complacent were very often the young men who ended up in cemeteries far from home. A shell fired from an Italian gun in Turin had death written on it just as assuredly as one fired from the thousands of weapons which defended the Ruhr.

Humphreys says: 'The Italians did not put up such a strong defence as the Germans. They would fire at you, but when our aircraft were actually bombing, their gunners eased off. Then, when you'd finished bombing, they started up again, a bit half-heartedly. With a German target, you knew you'd be in for a really rough ride, and losses could be high. The Italian targets were easier. You still got people shot down and people missing, but it was nothing like a German operation.'

Lancaster R5697 took off from Syerston at 5.55pm to link up with another 226 bombers for the long flight to Turin. The crew faced a longer and wearier night than they could have imagined. The weather was cold and moonlit. They had a comfortable trip across France, with no trouble from flak or fighters. The snow-capped, inhospitable peaks of the Alps were an awesome sight and no one relished the idea of having to bale out in the mountains, or making an emergency landing.

The Alps seemed to drop away quickly as they approached Turin, the Lancaster descending to 12,000ft for its bombing run. The measured calm of the crew's routine was abruptly shattered as the Italian gunners opened up and got their range. Smoke and flames poured from the starboard outer engine. They had to act quickly before the fire got out of control. The pilot briskly throttled back, Humphreys feathered the damaged engine and pressed the fire extinguisher button. Foam squirted into the engine, blanketing the fuel pipes and carburettor. The fire went out and, luckily, the Italians did not press home the attack on the wounded Lancaster. They flew on, completed the bombing run and dropped their bombs on a target partially obscured by smoke from a raid on the city the previous night, which had damaged industrial and residential areas.

Turning west, the Lancaster headed for England. There was an immediate problem. The aircraft, reduced to three engines, was unable to gain sufficient height to climb back over the mountains. They would have to fly through them, a daunting, almost suicidal prospect. The alternative, baling out, was briefly considered, but they decided to fly on. At the time, they were not sure which course of action was the most frightening.

Ordinarily, a Lancaster could return to England on three engines after bombing Germany, while maintaining a comfortable cruising height. Here, not only did they have to stay as high as 12,000ft, they would occasionally have to climb out of trouble.

There was no long debate on whether they could make it. They simply threw out any equipment that would not be needed for the return journey, including 500lb flares, normally used for illuminating targets.

Skipper Bill Whamond asked the navigator, Mac McLelland, for a course away from the highest peaks, which the Lancaster could not have attempted to climb. The Alps suddenly looked a good deal more formidable than on the outward journey and the powerful Lancaster seemed even more vulnerable than when it was flying through Germany, chased by flak and fighters.

Tension grew aboard the bomber as they plunged into the Alps, searching for ravines and gullies which might adequately accommodate a crippled heavy bomber. They flew through gaps with mountains towering above them on both sides, some of which seemed close enough to reach out and touch. It was like being part of a monstrous slalom, with the glittering prize at the end of it being a clear course for home.

Pilot, engineer, gunners and bomb-aimer maintained a long vigil as they weaved and slipped through the blackness of deep gorges, with the need for sudden jerks on the control column to miss menacing outcrops of rock, which had unexpectedly become part of the enemy's more subtle armoury. There were times when the aircraft seemed to be flying through the vaulted walls of a monolithic cathedral, as Humphreys recalls:

'It was a case of nose up, nose down, tack left, tack right, slip and weave. We couldn't fly straight. We were going through ravines, dog-legging, flying round outcrops of rocks at a speed of around 150 to 160kts. We couldn't do very sharp manoeuvres and the rocks looked pretty sinister. In the moonlight they were awe-inspiring. We knew one slip would spell disaster. We came close to hitting the rocks several times. If a wing tip had grazed one we would have had it. There was a bad moment when we hit some turbulence and the aircraft reared all over the place. I thought "this is it, we have no control and no room to manoeuvre".'

The skipper regained control and the tension eased, but only for a moment. 'I stood looking out of the starboard side, making sure we were not heading too close to the mountains. The gunners and bomb-aimer were doing the same and relaying information to the pilot, calling out "left!" or "right!" if the Lancaster strayed too close to the rocks. The pilot was kept informed all the time.'

There was an unspoken fear that they might find themselves trapped in a narrowing ravine with a gigantic insurmountable wall at the end of it. 'Fortunately, we could always see far enough ahead to realise that you had to lift up or drop down. You flew down one ravine and had to find a gap in another to keep going. We tried to maintain the navigator's course, but had to zig-zag to keep us going in the right direction. We could pull the aircraft up, but obviously not to negotiate a tremendous angle.'

Even with its three Rolls-Royce Merlin engines surging, the bomber had to be lifted over the top of a lesser mountain and they were forced to fly off at another angle, while the frustrated navigator swiftly worked out a new course. There were anxious shouts from some of the crew when they thought the pilot was getting too close to the rearing mountains. Whamond could not afford to have a panicking crew around him and snapped: 'Shut up! Stop shouting! Calm down!' Humphreys comments: 'He didn't mind the crew telling him about the situation as they saw it, but he wouldn't have anyone panicking. It was difficult enough flying the aircraft in that situation.'

Once more a strangled cry rang out and Humphreys gasped 'Blimey!' as they appeared to be charging towards a cliff face. The pilot banked to port lifting the starboard wing, the end of which passed no more than 20ft above the massive craggy outcrop of rock. Humphreys remembers the tension of the moment:

'That was very frightening. I didn't know if we were going to miss it or not, but I knew it was going to be pretty dammed close. As we slid past I took a backward glance and realised it had been too close for comfort. It was certainly the worst moment. It probably took not much more than twenty minutes to get through the higher mountains, although it felt much longer. Apart from that one hairy moment, it went fairly well under the circumstances. It was pretty straightforward after we reached the lower reaches of the Alps and then it was a question of nursing the aircraft home. We came down to 10,000ft so we didn't need oxygen and reached France where we could keep to a straight and level course. The last thing we wanted was anything else going wrong. We did see some flak in the middle of France. It was a single burst, some distance away.'

They were still over France when the starboard inner engine suddenly caught fire. Humphreys immediately feathered the engine and activated the extinguisher and the flames were put out, but it was a bad moment. Whamond re-trimmed the aircraft, which plodded on. Humphreys recalls: 'People had got back from an op many times on only two engines, but we now had no margin for error. We couldn't gain altitude. It's possible the engine had been damaged over Turin. Luckily it survived long enough to get us through the Alps.'

They crossed the North Sea, listening intently for the slightest change in the note of the two port engines. Humphreys' vigilance on fuel economy was constant, but their petrol was running low. Dodging through the mountains had been thirsty work for the Lancaster. After a call to Syerston, they were given permission to put down at the nearest airfield, Tangmere, the fighter airfield just north of Chichester.

Humphreys again: 'Fire engines came out to meet us but the landing, at 3.30am, was a good one. Even then we hadn't finished with the excitement of that op. We'd just left the runway and were taxiing round the perimeter when the two engines cut out and we came to a halt. The aircraft had run out of fuel.' They had been airborne 9hr 35min. Just one more wrenching haul over an obstruction in the Alps might have forced them to ditch in the sea. One bomber was lost on the Turin raid, and Lancaster R5697 had cut it a bit fine.

After a meal they were given blankets and bedding, and directed to a building where they slept soundly on the floor of a large room. Next afternoon they were debriefed at Syerston by the squadron commander, Wing Commander Guy Gibson, of which Humphreys says:

'He wanted to know what had happened. Why had we landed at Tangmere? Why hadn't we come straight back to Syerston? He didn't like it because he wouldn't have the aircraft for ops that night. The engines had to be changed and other work needed doing. He wasn't very happy because it would reduce his effort for that night. Gibson was arrogant, a martinet, not very approachable. I always felt uncomfortable talking to him. You were always made to feel that if you said something not quite right, he would pull you up. He believed in firm discipline and ruled us with a rod of iron.'

Guy Gibson VC, DSO and Bar, DFC and Bar, was killed on the night of 19/20 September 1944, when 227 Lancasters and ten Mosquitoes raided Monchengladbach and Rheydt, near the Dutch border. By then, Humphreys had been commissioned and was a flying officer bomb-aimer with 97 Squadron PFF at Coningsby. Gibson, then base operations officer at the Lincolnshire airfield, had pleaded to be given one more trip. Gibson was master bomber for the operation, flying a Mosquito from 627 Squadron. His navigator was Ulsterman Squadron Leader James Warwick DFC. Humphreys remembers speaking to Gibson that night:

'He asked me if I was flying that night and wished me a good trip. I was in Lancaster L-Love in flare force. I saw two Mosquitoes over the target. Gibson was to drop the red spot on the aiming point. He could see the aiming point, but couldn't release his red spot. The other Mosquito could release his flare, but couldn't find the aiming point. Gibson said over the r/t: "Follow me in. When I reach the aiming point, I'll flash my navigation lights." In other words, that would be the point for the other Mosquito to drop his red spot. That's what he did. I saw him whipping across the aiming point, flashing his navigation lights. I saw his aircraft veering off. I guessed that he'd been hit. I didn't know if he'd been hit by flak, because he was quite low at the time, or by a fighter. We were dropping flares and were ourselves hit by flak.

'When we got back to Coningsby, the news went round like wildfire. Gibson's missing! We couldn't believe it. We thought he was immortal. I thought if he had copped it what chance did the rest of us have?'

Gibson and Warwick lie buried in the cemetery at Steenbergen, Holland, not far from the field where their Mosquito crashed.

John Humphreys received a DFC for his work during the Turin trip. He survived over 60 operations and became a chartered engineer in Civvy Street, working on aeroplanes. After the war, Bill Whamond qualified as a doctor and eventually moved to Keighley in Yorkshire.

13

RUNNING A DEADLY
GAUNTLET OVER WARSAW

Poland's spirit was never broken, not through grim centuries of occupation by Austria, Germany and Russia, nor even during the barbaric ravages of the Second World War. Many Polish Jews had already been exterminated in concentration camps, and their ghettos destroyed in 1943. Then, with the Germans in retreat from Russia, the Polish Government in exile saw the chance of an uprising in Warsaw on 1 August 1944.

The Poles believed the Russians, who had halted their advance 10km from the centre of Warsaw, would give them supplies to fight the Germans. They were wrong. German forces began ruthlessly crushing the Polish resistance in Warsaw. The Poles appealed to London for help with air supply drops.

Stalin refused all co-operation and landing rights for UK-based flights or to provide supplies from Russia. Winston Churchill's decision to rush aid to Warsaw was opposed by the Air Staff, who considered this would lead to great loss of aircraft and aircrews and seriously weaken the bomber offensive in support of the Italian campaign and supply drops in Yugoslavia. They claimed the small amount of supplies dropped would not affect the outcome of the fighting in Warsaw.

Churchill over-ruled them. He said the UK had declared war on 3 September 1939 to support Poland. Britain had an unavoidable obligation to support the Polish people, despite inevitable casualties. Other resistance uprisings essential to the Allied cause would not be effective unless it was seen that all possible support would be given by the Allies. Churchill turned to the Balkan Air Force based in southern Italy at Brindisi and the Foggia airfields with 205 Group Wellingtons, Liberators and Halifaxes. The only aircraft with enough range for the gruelling round trip of 1,750 miles were the Halifaxes of special operations units in 148 Squadron RAF and the Polish No 1586 Flight; and the B-24 Liberators of regular bomber squadrons – namely 178 Squadron RAF and 31 and 34 Squadrons of the South African Air Force (SAAF).

On 4/5 and 7/8 August, aircraft from 1586 Flight and 148 Squadron, who had earlier made supply drops into southern Poland, flew to Warsaw, but with severe losses. Of the seven aircraft sent by 148, four were lost and two crashed on landing. They were further reduced to one effective aircrew. Flight Lieutenant Gordon Prior, the only officer pilot left, took over A and B Flights, as both flight commanders had been lost and the Warsaw supply drops could not be sustained.

Air Vice-Marshal Sir John Slessor, Air Officer Commanding Balkan Air Force, then proposed that 178, 31 and 34 Squadrons should be used. Brigadier J. T. Durrant, who had taken over command of 205 Group on 3 August, considered this a potential disaster. He protested to Slessor and in a personal interview with Churchill said the squadrons had taken severe losses on the raids to the Ploesti oil refineries in Romania. Many replacement crews had little operational experience. As bomber crews, they had no experience or training in low-level supply drops even by day, let alone by night over defended targets. Durrant was over-ruled.

The main operations took place on the nights of 12 to 17 August 1944 by 178, 31 and 34 Squadrons, together with what could be mustered from 1586 Flight and 148 Squadron. Fewer raids called for greater skill and commitment from aircrews than these epic air supply drops into the embattled city of Warsaw, yet they remain among the least known and most scantily recorded operations of the war.

This account by one crew is probably typical of the conditions they met, but others had a worse time. Many were killed, wounded or taken prisoner after crashes. The survivors of one Polish crew were executed after crashing behind German lines.

Conditions were spartan for men stationed at the Foggia airfields. One aircrew was skippered by Flying Officer Jack Fletcher. They and everyone else lived in tents. This was fine in summer but in bad weather the airfield became a sea of mud. Packing cases were scrounged for flooring and making beds and tables. Drip stoves created from petrol cans sometimes caught fire or blew up. Farmhouses were used for squadron headquarters, administration, intelligence, briefing, communications and emergency first aid. Outbuildings served as stores, mess rooms and repair shops.

The air strips were made from perforated interlocking steel sheets which became hazardous during severe rain, and useless in ice and snow. If the sheets became unlocked they ripped the tyres of landing aircraft.

With the exception of the second pilot, Fletcher and his crew had joined 178 Squadron in 205 Group as a replacement crew on 1 August. This was a general purpose squadron equipped with twenty B-24 Liberator Mk VIs and twenty-seven complete aircrews, with ground staff and transport. The aircrews were mostly English, with some Canadians, South Africans, and a few Australians.

They had been given a mixed bag of jobs, which included night bombing of airfields, oil refineries and marshalling yards in northern Italy, Romania, Yugoslavia, southern Germany, Bulgaria and Hungary. They also carried out supply drops to partisans and mined the Danube as far down as the Iron Gate, a narrow gorge cut through the Carpathian mountains on the borders of Romania and Yugoslavia, causing considerable disruption to river traffic.

The bombers had dropped mines into the Aleusis channel to hold up the German evacuation from Greece. They bombed them on the mountain roads and passes when they tried to leave, and when they reached Yugoslavia, on directions from partisans, destroyed the small town of Podgorica, where the Germans had halted. Those not killed in the bombing were attacked by a strong, vengeful force of partisans.

American aircrews were also stationed at Foggia with Flying Fortresses and Liberators. They carried out daytime bombing raids, mainly on southern Germany and Romania.

N-Nuts' pilot, dark-haired Fletcher, a dairy farmer from Kerang, Victoria, was strong, wiry and quietly spoken. His parents had emigrated from Brighton to Australia when he was eight years old. Later, after joining up he had been an instructor on multi-engined aircraft in Southern Rhodesia with RAF Flying Training Command before being posted to Italy. Nearly all the friends with whom he trained had been killed in action. At twenty-six he was the oldest man aboard.

The aircraft only carried a second pilot on long trips. Flight Sergeant George Graves had been a trainee teacher before the war. This was one of three rehabilitation flights for him with Fletcher, after a crash in which he was the only survivor. The other crewmen were destined to stay together through forty operations.

Warrant Officer Bob Adams, twenty-two, navigator and bomb-aimer, had also been brought up in Brighton, although he could not remember meeting Fletcher as a boy. An architecture student at the town's college of art, he had enjoyed cycling around the Sussex countryside and drawing local buildings. Some of his time off in Italy was spent studying for an RIBA intermediate architectural examination. This was his twenty-eighth operation. Both his previous pilots had been killed in non-operational accidents. He would survive to complete another thirty-seven. The rest of the crew had only flown together for a short while.

The official bomb-aimer was Pilot Officer Eric Seddon, from Leeds, another teacher. He spent that night manning one of the waist guns. Adams had previous experience as a bomb-aimer which he combined with navigating them to Warsaw. The skipper decided to leave Seddon where he was, rather than have a gun unmanned if he came forward into the bomb-aiming position to relieve Adams.

The other crewmen were all flight sergeants. Flight engineer Bob Jackson had been a motor mechanic before the war. Adams says of him: 'He was extremely efficient. He managed to keep the engines going when it would have been very difficult for anyone else to do so.' Jackson had a mechanic's feel for the engines, instinctively nursing them, adjusting their revs and speed to keep down the consumption of fuel so they would have enough for the long return flight to base.

Wireless operator Len Eades was a long way from his civilian trade as a butcher, but he had become extremely competent at picking up wireless bearings. In Italy at that time navigation relied on the early radio navigation aid known as Gee, which only extended to northern Italy and part of Yugoslavia. After that it was necessary to use dead reckoning and astro-navigation with wireless bearings.

Eades was a quiet man and slightly nervous, a condition possibly influenced by his understandable hatred of a shuddering task which occasionally he had to fulfil after a bombing run. On some ops not all of the bombs were released. It was then up to Eades to lean out over the open bomb bays, holding on by one hand and either releasing the hung-up bombs with the other hand or kicking them into space. After the bombs had been fused, it was too dangerous to land an aircraft with them aboard. A stumble or the sudden need for the skipper to avoid an enemy fighter might have seen the bomber very quickly losing its wireless operator. Eades always had a parachute clipped on, but at low level he stood no chance of survival if he fell.

Mid-upper gunner Jack Butters was a taciturn Scot, with a harsh accent which made him very difficult to understand over the intercom. The regular beam gunner, Flight Sergeant Duggie Houghton, did not go on the Warsaw raids.

The rear turret contained the most intriguing member of the crew. This was the diminutive 'Snakebite' Butler, an ebullient Cockney, who often kept the others cheerful when there seemed nothing to laugh about. He had flown in Egypt and earned his nickname in the desert, after being bitten by a snake. A jockey before the war, he was no more than 5ft tall, thin and wiry. He was very good at his job, although he tried to pretend he was not. No one knew why he enjoyed pretending to be a sloppy gunner.

If wartime bombers contained none of the comforts of home, the rear gunners had the worst deal of all. On a long flight, the gun turrets became inhospitable freezers, despite heated flying suits for their occupants. An aperture in his perspex bubble allowed Snakebite clear vision of night fighters, with the obvious disadvantage of a continual blast of icy air. Once, after a long trip, he was unable to move and had to be hauled out of his turret, close to being frostbitten. His nickname was not, however, changed to Frostbite.

The American-built B-24 Liberator KG942, N-Nuts, piloted by Australian Jack Fletcher, took off from Amendola airbase in Foggia on 14 August at 7.45pm. It was only Fletcher's fourth operation. The bomber carried 2,100 gals of fuel and twelve 500lb cylindrical containers of arms, ammunition and medical supplies.

N-Nuts was a modified Liberator, with guns removed from the front turret, and without its ball turret, which weighed nearly a ton. The aircraft was powered by four Pratt and Whitney air-cooled radial engines, with superchargers, each developing 1,200hp at 2,700rpm for take-off. It had six 0.5in Browning machine guns – two each in dorsal and tail turrets, and one in each waist position.

Eight Liberators from 178 Squadron set off at two to three minute intervals for Warsaw. While climbing to altitude it was found some electrical circuits had failed aboard N-Nuts: the rear gun turret could only be partially operated by hand, while circuits to the electrically heated flying suits of the navigator and rear gunner had failed; and to make matters worse the reserve fuel tank cocks could only be operated manually.

Fletcher and Graves, conferring briefly across the flight deck, agreed the rear gunner could call for evasive action if a night fighter showed any interest in them, and decided to press on. They also decided that Graves should fly the Liberator to the river Vistula, so his skipper would be fresh for the supply drop into Warsaw. Later on, it would be flight engineer Bob Jackson's job to change the fuel cocks by hand.

Information from Warsaw was scanty and misleading. The crews were assured at briefing that the Polish uprising had been successful. Much of the capital and the air defences were said to be in Polish hands. There wouldn't be much flak. The most dangerous part of the operation would be the journey to Poland because they would be flying over enemy territory nearly all the way.

Nothing could have been farther from the truth: much of the resistance in Warsaw was already overrun, and the Germans had secured all key defensive points which had been armed with heavy, medium and light flak and searchlights around and within the city. They had also been given advance knowledge of the supply operations. All fighter and ground defences were on the alert, waiting for the Allied supply aircraft.

One of two Polish officers, who had assisted at the briefing, said they would encounter intense flak at Kracow. At least that was right. Casualties had been heavy on the two previous nights' supply trips by 148 and 1586. The crews were briefed to fly over Kracow, follow the river Vistula and turn at the third bridge into Warsaw over the citadel. Because of the great distance, the aircraft could not stay together as in normal raids. They arrived singly over Warsaw, a decision which assisted the German gunners who could concentrate their searchlights and fire on one bomber at a time.

Adams had more astro-navigation experience than other navigators on that night's operation. He believes inexperience may have been the cause of some casualties, when aeroplanes got lost and ran out of fuel.   N-Nuts climbed to about 15,000ft to clear the Carpathians. They did not want to risk going any higher because fuel needed to be conserved.

The long journey to Warsaw was largely uneventful. Some air-to-air firing was seen, but no night fighters came near them, even though they knew some had been diverted from the Russian front because of this operation. Over Kracow, where flak was heavy, they turned for the capital and began losing height. Fletcher recalls: 'At briefing, we were ordered to drop to a height of 300ft, wheels and flaps down at a speed of 135 to 140mph. This gave us no chance of avoiding the light flak.'

They saw the glow of fires in Warsaw at least thirty miles away. As they drew nearer at 800ft, the entire city, shelled and set on fire by the Germans, seemed to be burning. Flames and smoke soared hundreds of feet into the air. Ahead of them were night fighters and considerable light and medium flak, aided by searchlights. Flak came at them too, from the Russian-held bank of the Vistula. The Russian gunners probably believed the aircraft were German, attacking Russian forces nearby. The Russians had not officially been given details about these air drops.

Adams saw the citadel over which they had been briefed to turn and get into the dropping zone. He saw German gunners, crouched on the citadel roof, firing tracer at them. Shrapnel and bullets ripped through the Liberator, without causing serious damage. The Liberator was driven off by the intensity of the fire and turned back to where the flak seemed less withering. A searchlight picked them up on the port wing, but was shot out by their gunners, who continued to return the ground fire throughout the action.

They felt very exposed, illuminated by questing searchlights and huge roaring fires on all sides. Graves covered the controls in case Fletcher was wounded. The aircraft was difficult to control, with wheels and flaps down, flying at just above stalling speed. On the second run in, they saw another bomber disintegrate, 300ft above and 1,500ft ahead of them. The blast rocked their aircraft, but they were probably saved further damage by the huge mass of blazing wreckage falling on to the Germans below.

They dropped to 300ft and into this inferno, with flames darting up fiercely from the stricken city, scorching the belly of the aircraft, while acrid smoke poured into the fuselage. Second pilot George Graves thought it was like rushing through the open door of a furnace: 'Flames seemed to be reaching higher than the aircraft'.

Believing the bomber had been struck a mortal blow and was on fire, they flew on through the madness of that summer night. It was then they began to worry. Shouting broke out over the intercom from all parts of the bomber, as Adams recalls: 'It was a bit chaotic with some screaming for us to get out of it. Suddenly, we were no longer well organised and disciplined. All of us were scared.' Pilot Jack Fletcher shouted angrily once for everybody to 'Shut up!' His voice was enough to quieten them down, but their situation seemed hopeless.

Adams, kneeling over the bomb-sight, had little time to think. He saw two other low-flying bombers, caught in the glare of searchlights, which would have totally disorientated their pilots. Both aircraft crashed into the burning city. 'I was very frightened; we all were, but we could only carry on doing our jobs.' Adams believed he had no more than a minute or two to live as he watched intently for the cross of lights laid out by the Polish resistance, marking the dropping zone.

The crew knew from their briefing that the Polish resistance had been suffering and were now desperate. There was a chance the vital supplies they had aboard might help them continue the fight against the Germans. It was much later they learned of the barbaric battles on the ground. As they flew over the city, below them Hitler's ruthless troops and the resistance fought street by street, house by house, room by room, and then in stinking sewers beneath the city after the Germans had razed every building to the ground in the Old City.

The drop zone was difficult to identify through the numerous fires but at 1.06am, through the smoke, Adams saw a lighted cross in the centre of the old Warsaw ghetto in an area the size of a football field. Their speed was now below 140mph as Adams pressed the button which released the containers in groups on a heading of 210 degrees. He saw figures on the ground, starkly lit by the fires around them, running out from the rubble of buildings as the precious supplies fell towards them. Rear gunner Butler reported that all parachutes had landed on target. Graves raised the wheels, held the four throttles forward, and locked them by tightening the friction nut.

Once the bomb doors were closed Graves began raising the flaps in stages as they flew across the burning city. The Liberator was now being hit repeatedly by ground fire which cut the hydraulic lines to the tail turret. The wings, tail assembly and fuselage were ripped in several places but, amazingly, there was no serious damage to air frame, self-sealing fuel tanks, or engines. After landing, they found the aircraft had been hit forty-one times by shrapnel and bullets.

Adams comments: 'The worst time was when you stopped doing something. We had all been busy but now, with the containers gone, there was nothing more to do except get out. I became terrified.' Graves points out the danger of their situation: 'This was probably the time of greatest danger. The crew tended to relax, having dropped the containers successfully, their night vision impaired by searchlights and the fires. Furthermore, this was the time and place when the night fighters knew where we were.'

Fletcher dived to 100ft through billowing clouds of thick smoke and flames to gain speed and, perhaps, to confuse the ground fire. They had no idea of any obstacles which might lie ahead. There was always the chance a church spire or other tall buildings might loom into their path, but they could only ride their luck. It probably took no more than five fearful minutes to clear the blazing city. The gunners suddenly reported they were almost out of ammunition. They had kept up an almost continuous fire at the ground forces throughout the action over the city. Fletcher recalls:

'We were in no condition to engage in action. I commenced climbing towards our ceiling of 30,000ft in order to avoid, if possible, the numerous German gunners and night fighters. We did not encounter any at our level, although we observed some aircraft in flames below. When crossing the positions held by the Russian forces we were again fired at, and as we passed Lake Balaton in Hungary, ground forces had a few shots at us, but did no damage.'

Second pilot George Graves says: 'Time passed very slowly on the return trip. Each apparent hour that passed seemed to register only twenty minutes on the aircraft's clock. As we crossed the Yugoslav coastline it began to get light, but darkness descended again as we lost height over the Adriatic Sea.'

They landed safely at dawn in Amendola and taxied to the hard-standing. After shutting the engines down and making the aircraft secure, they opened the bomb doors and stood outside on the quiet airfield, gulping in fresh air. It was 5.45am. They had been airborne ten hours. Flight engineer Bob Jackson had done his job juggling the fuel. There was only enough left in the tanks for another half-an-hour's flying.

After waiting twenty minutes for another crew to land they joined them in the three-tonner which took them back to squadron headquarters for debriefing. They learned that three of 178 Squadron's eight aircraft which had set off for Warsaw were missing. Another two were badly damaged but had got home.

Among those who were lost that night were the two flight commanders of 178 Squadron, together with several of the more experienced crews from other squadrons. Replacement crews were brought to Amendola from Porticci and new aircraft ferried in from Maison Blanc in Algiers. The squadron resumed bombing operations on 21 August.

The crew of N-Nuts were among those briefed for Warsaw on the night of 10 September, with the same loads, but dropping from high level. N-Nuts took off without a second pilot, Eric Seddon handled the release of the supply containers, while Adams remained at his navigation table.

Bad weather was forecast en route. In fact soon after crossing the coast, the Liberator was over solid cloud and the outside temperature was plummeting. Luckily they did not encounter any German fighters but upon breaking through the cloud over Warsaw they could see that the city was still on fire, with flak and searchlights just as active.

An even greater concern was a blinding snowstorm. The Liberator rapidly began to ice up. The de-icing equipment was unable to cope and the aircraft became difficult to handle. Glazed ice built up on the wings and even with full boost and throttle, the bomber refused to climb. Ice on the propellers caused vibration and pieces flew off, striking the fuselage and tail assembly.

None of the guns would fire because their electric heaters failed and the firing pins contracted and failed to strike the rounds. Then, as they circled at 8,000ft, looking for a break in the cloud, Seddon saw the target through the swirling snow. Fletcher recalls: 'I attempted to lower the wheels and flaps. The wheels went down, but not the flaps, which must have been frozen. The bomb-aimer directed us to the target and released the containers and the tail gunner reported that the parachutes opened. Throughout this time we were fired at from the ground and hit a few times.' He believes the German gunners' aim was adversely effected by the heavy snow.

N-Nuts was one of three aircraft to drop on target that night. The wheels were raised and they attempted to climb away, but the aeroplane was sluggish and wallowing badly. The Liberator crept with difficulty up through the cloud and reached a colder, but drier level at 18,000ft. Five aircraft were lost from the eleven which took off, with two badly damaged.

They were briefed for a third trip to Warsaw, but it was called off because of severe weather and risk of icing. All four Polish aircraft sent the previous night had been lost. During these operations to Warsaw, 205 Group continued bombing northern Italy, dropping supplies to Yugoslavia and mining the Danube. The SAAF squadrons were so depleted they were temporarily removed from operations to reform.

Polish crews with 1586 Flight, based at Brindisi, continued making desperate and suicidal missions to Warsaw and to resistance groups outside the city. As their loss of aircraft mounted, they borrowed replacement machines from 148 and other squadrons, but they were eventually grounded to preserve their aircraft and crews which were needed for other operations.

Navigator Bob Adams' brother Walter worked on political intelligence at the Foreign Office during the war. He was closely involved with London and Washington, and with the resistance groups, trying to work out what the future pattern of the political situation would be in Europe after the war. Bob Adams remembers their discussions: 'Walter and I talked about the Warsaw uprising. It seems very likely that someone betrayed the whole of the uprising to the Russian authorities who, by devious means, got that information to the Germans, who were then able to quell the Polish resistance, particularly in Warsaw, very efficiently and with great cruelty, leading to the loss of thousands of Polish lives.'

The Russians misled captured Polish officers, whom they briefed with uprising details and dropped into occupied Poland – but into the hands of the Germans, who tortured out of them information about the resistance revolt. When the uprising began, the Germans went straight to the known resistance centres, thus preventing any effective opposition. All the sacrifices of the Polish people had been in vain. Of this tragedy Adams says:

'It is probable that Anthony Blunt, then the MI5 officer responsible for liaison and political co-ordination of Allied governments in exile and resistance movements in eastern occupied Europe, later exposed as a spy, had betrayed the details of the Warsaw uprising to the Russians. Stalin wanted all resistance forces to be eliminated so he could install puppet regimes in all countries as far to the West as possible. He delayed all help to the Poles in the Warsaw rising until their resistance forces had been destroyed by the Germans.

'After Blunt had been discovered as a spy, he traded his knowledge for immunity from prosecution and continued to work as an art historian for fifteen years, until publicly exposed. He said he had not betrayed British forces, but would not deny that other Allied forces had been betrayed. In retrospect, it is a bitter conclusion that the Warsaw uprising never had any hope of success.'

When Allied aircraft crashed in Poland, the resistance or local people rescued crews still alive and buried those killed. Many of the simple monuments erected by the Poles over aircrews' graves were made from parts taken from their downed aircraft. Some aircrews, especially the Poles, continued to fight with the resistance, although the non-Poles were advised to give themselves up to the Germans. Had they been caught with the resistance, they would have been shot.

On the 186 sorties flown with supplies to Warsaw, thirty-one aircraft were lost and many other aircrews killed or injured. Some flew three or more times. On only 92 of the sorties flown were supplies successfully dropped. The loss rate was 16.8 per cent, three times the casualty rate over Germany.

Polish aircrews were still trying to get supplies to the resistance on 22 September, almost at the end, as any hope of success dwindled. General Tadeusz Bor-Komorowski, commander of the Polish resistance, surrendered to German forces on 30 September 1944. Many of his men were executed or sent to concentration camps.

The Russian armies only resumed their advance when they knew all Polish resistance had been crushed. They entered Warsaw on 17 January 1945 in triumph as the liberating army, installing a government of their own supporters when the Germans had been driven out of Poland. Many of the resistance were hunted down by the Russians and executed or sent to forced labour camps and prisons in Russia.

Pilot Jack Fletcher and navigator Bob Adams were each awarded a DFC at the end of their tours in 1945. With their co-pilot, George Graves, they received the Polish Cross of Valour, the Warsaw Uprising Cross and the Polish Home Army Cross. Later in the war, Snakebite Butler was awarded a DFM.

14

PILOT ABANDONS CREW

The night before Jack Fletcher's Liberator stumbled bravely in and out of Warsaw, the flames in the burning city were less intense, although the German guns and night fighters were just as malevolent. The morning of 13 August 1944 was warm and dry on Celone airfield in Foggia, southern Italy, as bomb-aimer Sergeant Alan 'Basher' Bates ambled into a requisitioned farm outbuilding to inspect the aircrews' noticeboard. He was not displeased to find that no operation was planned for that day. Twenty-two year-old Bates, from the small Yorkshire town of Bolton upon Dearne, strolled across the airfield to the dispersal point where the Liberator VI, K–King, was waiting, its four 1,200hp Pratt and Whitney engines silent, fresh from a thorough inspection by the conscientious ground crew.

Bates, a former clerk with Liverpool Savings Bank, climbed leisurely into the bomber and walked through to the nose. A day off at the Italian base could not be compared to England, where local pubs and cinemas were available and the company of girls enjoyed. The war had passed through Foggia and most of the city was in ruins. There was no camp cinema and no kind of entertainment for off-duty aircrews. Bates was bent over the bomb-sight, which he checked with assiduousness, when he heard his name yelled from outside the aircraft. He looked out, saw an airman waving and caught the word 'Brindisi'.

Brindisi was the base of 148 Squadron and the Polish Special Duties Flight, 1586, an hour's flying down the coast of the Adriatic. K–King and nine other Liberators from Celone were ordered to Brindisi to collect supplies which were to be dropped that night to the beleaguered partisans in Warsaw.

Bates was one of five Britons seconded to 31 (SAAF) Squadron, who set off for Brindisi in K–King just before midday. Their operation to Warsaw, an astonishing story of courage and resourcefulness, would be the last wartime sortie for the five sergeants and three South African officers aboard.

The briefing for the Warsaw trip was given that afternoon when a self-assured Polish Air Force officer told them airily how easy it would be. The officer, who was among Polish crews based at Brindisi with 1586 Flight, said he had flown to Warsaw the previous night and had experienced no trouble. He said, with a grin: 'Eet vas a peeza cake'.

K-King's SAAF skipper was Lieutenant Bill Norval, whom Bates describes as 'tall, well-built, pompous and rather self-opinionated. He had spent most of the war flying VIPs round South Africa in Ansons and Oxfords and this had given him a sense of importance. Norval was not popular, even with the other two South Africans.'

Second pilot was Second Lieutenant Bob Burgess, a slim, friendly and quiet young accountant from Cape Town. Norval had not yet allowed the uncomplaining Burgess to fly the Liberator, apart from assisting during take-off and landing. The second pilot's previous flying experience had been limited to twin-engine training aircraft.

The third South African was Lieutenant Noel Sleed from Bloemfontein, who was on his second tour. A first class navigator, he was a great pal of Bob Burgess and, like him, quiet and reserved.

Wireless operator/air gunner Stan Payne was a complex character. With his thick slicked back black hair and clipped moustache he looked like a spiv. In fact, he was a loveable rogue. Always hard-up, Payne ran a permanent overdraft with Bates, redeemable each pay day. Bates is still owed £2. Payne, from Wantage, near Oxford, disliked any form of authority and was disinclined to book-out of camp, or attend parades.

Taff Lewis, the mid-upper gunner, came from a village near Barry, South Wales. He was small, thin and wiry, with a mass of light hair. His face normally wore an expression of serious contemplation. He was a few years older than the rest of the crew and had been a British weightlifting champion. He had a disconcerting habit of walking on his hands in the middle of a conversation. A regular airman, he had been a PTI (physical training instructor) before remustering as an air gunner.

The rear gunner was former farm labourer Bill Cross. He was a squat, square-shouldered man with deep-set eyes, who looked a tough nut, but had a placid, friendly nature. He had enlisted in the RAF Regiment before remustering to aircrew and was a rock of reliability. Steve Appleyard, normally a bomb-aimer with another crew, had been brought in that day to man K-King's beam guns.

Twenty-eight heavy bombers began taking off from Brindisi just after 7.00pm, packed with supplies, and with auxiliary fuel tanks fitted for the long journey. They included ten Liberators from 31 (SAAF) Squadron, another ten from 178 Squadron, four Halifaxes from 148, and four more from the Polish 1586 Flight. (Two Liberators were destined to be lost from 31 (SAAF) Squadron and one from 178. Several other aircraft would be forced back because of electrical storms over the Carpathian Mountains, or engine trouble.)

K-King made two changes of course to avoid Lake Balaton in Hungary and Kracow in south-western Poland, where the massed German defences were known to be strong and vigilant. Cruising at 12,000ft, K-King flew too close to Kracow and drew enemy fire, but corkscrewed out of trouble. Failed hydraulics later meant Bill Cross had to wind the rear turret round by hand, and thirty miles from Warsaw Norval was forced to lose altitude to avoid contact with a Junkers Ju88 fighter which had been spotted by one of the gunners. Fighters did not follow the bombers into the flak. They patrolled outside waiting for incoming Allied aircraft, hoping either to shoot them down or cripple them.

Five miles from the target, they throttled back from the cruising speed of 180mph to around 150mph and continued to descend to between 400 and 500ft, before they hit the Warsaw suburbs and came within range of the most ferocious German gunfire. Bates remembers: 'We were really too far from the target to throttle back. I think we should have throttled back and put flaps down about a half or a quarter-of-a-mile from the target.'

As they roared above the river Vistula, Bates, in the nose, looked for the four bridges. Normally on the way to the target he had a map beside him with a torch, its beam masked by half-a-dozen layers of toilet paper. By the time they reached the target the map would be committed to memory. He says:

'I wanted to approach from a certain angle. The four bridges across the Vistula were the main points of reference by which we could find the dropping zone. It was difficult. It's all right going in at 8,000ft. You can see everything, just as it is on the map. When you are so low, you can see a bridge over here and a bridge over there, but you've got no idea what's in between. I gave course corrections to direct the pilot to where I calculated the target should be. The navigator and I decided, in our innocence, to go round Warsaw airfield. With hindsight, we should have come into the city from the north, where the Poles were gathered in some strength.'

Approaching the airfield they saw another bomber coned by the searchlights. Flak poured into the unfortunate aircraft. They spared a moment to wonder if they knew any of the crew in the blazing bomber, whether they had drunk with them in the mess and talked wistfully about home and the end to this damned war. And yet, perversely, they were glad the searchlights had concentrated on those poor bastards instead of themselves.

Then, as Norval skirted the airfield in a clockwise direction, the disabled aircraft plunged into the ground and the searchlights switched unerringly to K-King. They remained glued to the Liberator until it reached the dropping zone at Krasinski Square. They continued to lose height and by now were flying through an almost solid mass of green and red tracer hosepiping at them from all sides. The voices of the first and second pilots crackled over the intercom to report that the port inner engine had been hit and was being feathered. The starboard outer engine began heating up and was throttled right back. It played little further part in the progress of the Liberator, which was now effectively reduced to two engines. Wireless operator Stan Payne was helping Appleyard on the beam guns when his wireless and chair on the flight deck were shot to pieces.

Buildings blazed little more than 300ft below them while bullets tore into the aircraft. Even German riflemen were taking pot-shots at the bomber. The crew knew each time the Liberator had been hit because the wind noise changed. This happened constantly.

Bates was now lying in a pool of hydraulic oil. He recalls: 'There was a lot of smoke and flames, not as much as aircrews talked about on later missions, but they had come in from the other end, over the old town. My feelings at this time were of abject terror. I had never seen anything like this. I couldn't see how we could live through it. There was no way the enemy gunners were going to miss us as far as I was concerned. I could see tracers ahead and all round us.'

Memories of home and a saner world came in fragmented flashbacks, but it was easier to imagine K-King being torn apart by an explosion, a moment of hideous pain, then oblivion. They were afraid of death and mutilation and what seemed a certainty: they would never see their loved ones again. It was now, more than at any other time, that their training and discipline held them together as a team and forced them to carry on. All the time the aircraft was wrapped up in a ball of light from the searchlights, allowing their progress to be followed continually by the German gunners, who were putting up a wall of flak which seemed impossible to penetrate, but the Liberator limped on. Bates again:

'At this time the pilot was doing quite nicely, and I was passing him slight course corrections. There was a lull for a bit while I was trying to get my bearings. It was then he shouted at me:

"Haven't you dropped those supplies?"

"We're not there yet, skipper," I replied. Norval snapped:

"Get rid of them!". I reminded him:

"You have a jettison lever if you need to use it." Norval didn't reply.

'My voice seemed to have risen by a couple of octaves because I was frightened. I wanted to get rid of the stores and get out. I'm sure we all did'.

There was no photoflash fitted to record the drop. They could have dropped the supplies anywhere. But the Poles were desperate for the equipment they were carrying.

The bomb-aimer could not identify Krasinski Square, the primary dropping zone, but called for the flaps to be put down when he believed they were within a street or two of the target. Bates continues: 'As the speed dropped, I was pleased to find that for a few seconds the tracer was passing in front of the aircraft. I jettisoned the supplies, which were carried in twelve huge containers. The pilot opened up the throttles and climbed away, still followed by the searchlights.'

At 7,000ft, the Liberator began to judder and almost immediately went into a stall-turn to starboard and seemed to fall out of the sky. Bates was lifted from the floor and pressed against the ceiling by the G-force. Unable to move, he watched Warsaw coming towards him. He would have felt even more uncomfortable had he known that Norval had already baled out and Bob Burgess, the second pilot, with little experience of flying a Liberator, was fighting with the controls. Burgess heroically pulled the Liberator out of its dive at 500ft and Bates fell back to the floor.

He switched on his intercom to inquire what was happening, but it had become disconnected. He reconnected the intercom plug in time to hear the rear gunner Taff Lewis complaining:

'Basher, shut those bloody bomb doors, there's a wind cutting my bloody feet off.' Bates replied:

'I've shut 'em, Taff,' to which the little Welshman replied sharply:

'No you haven't, you come up here and feel the draught.'

Normally a red light showed if the doors were still open. The light was out, but Bates pushed the lever which closed the bomb doors. There was a sigh of pleasure from Taff Lewis. 'That's better.'

Burgess called navigator Noel Sleed to the flight deck and told him what had happened. Sleed clambered into the nose and said the skipper had gone. Bates, mystified, followed Sleed on to the flight deck, wondering if Bill Norval had been killed. He saw a long roll of tarpaulin pushed to one side and wondered if the pilot's corpse was wrapped up in it.

Then he learned the staggering truth. Burgess had seen Norval juggling with the controls without any response from the plunging Liberator. The pilot, without a word, then grabbed his parachute and made for the bomb-bay doors which he partly opened, using the manual handle. Norval jumped through the partly opened bomb doors into the crazy turbulence of Warsaw from a little under 7,000ft, leaving his second pilot to cope with what seemed to be a certain death dive. The aircraft survived the dive, but it was severely crippled and the chances of fleeing Poland seemed remote, let alone getting back to base.

There was little time to congratulate the new skipper for saving their bacon. Burgess moved into Norval's seat and told Bates to sit beside him, watch the instruments and throttle back if the engines began overheating. Bates remembers: 'It was an odd experience, my brain had gone into overdrive. Everything was clear, I had no trouble making decisions. My mind was as clear as a bell. Ask me a question and you'd get the answer straightaway. I was usually a ditherer, but this was a very exhilarating experience.'

The bomber slowly lurched its way higher above the city. At least the dive had got them out of the searchlights. They were happily clothed in darkness, but K-King was behaving more like K-Keystone Kops.

'The aircraft was flying in a right-hand circle and no amount of fiddling with the trim would alter matters. On the instrument panel, the gyro compass had toppled and

COLLISION OVER WADDINGTON

Right: Jim Verran was one of many young New Zealanders who came to England to be a bomber pilot. (Verran)

Below: Earlier in the war Jim Verran (right) was based at Driffield. He is seen here behind the rear turret of a Whitley bomber with another pilot, Pilot Officer Alan Frampton. (Verran)

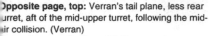

Opposite page, top: Verran's tail plane, less rear turret, aft of the mid-upper turret, following the mid-air collision. (Verran)
Opposite page, bottom: Bill Greenan at a debriefing with his crew a few weeks before they were killed. Greenan, at the left-hand corner of the table, is talking to the bespectacled intelligence officer. (Bill McCrea)

Above left: Wireless operator Alwyn Howarth died when his Lancaster was shot down over Denmark. (Verran)
Above right: The Germans erected this cross over the five men's grave. (Verran)
Below: Jim Verran's burns were treated in the cottage hospital at Vejle. (Verran)

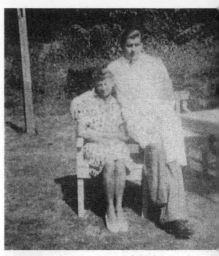

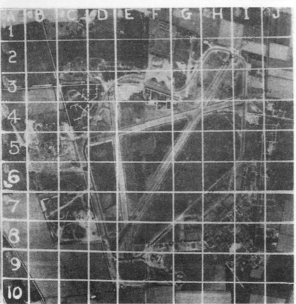

Above left: The Jensen family at Høgsholt, Denmark, who had run from their farmhouse in fright after being awakened by the crashing Lancaster. (Verran)

Above: Dr Carl Svenstrup and his wife. The Danish doctor wanted to smuggle Jim Verran to Sweden, but the pilot's injuries were too severe for the journey. (Verran)

Left: Ambulance driver Hans Stienbrenner and assistant Ejvind Damsgaard drove Jim Verran through German gunfire to the cottage hospital. (Verran)

Left: An aerial view of wartime Waddington. Pilot Jim Verran survived when his Lancaster was in a mid-air collision over the base in March 1943. (Allen)

STRETCHING LUCK TO THE LIMIT
Above: Philip Brett was soon struck by the reality of war after arriving at his operational station, Topcliffe. (Brett)

Above: The wireless operator's transmitter stood above the receiver in the Whitley Mk V. (Brett)
Below: The inside of a Whitley Mk V cockpit. The first pilot sits on the left, next to his second pilot. (Brett)

TOO CLOSE FOR COMFORT
Above left: Sergeant Happy Hanson (left) and Flight Lieutenant Bill Whamond inspe the remains of their Lancaster the morning after their eventful landing at Newton. (Humphrey **Above:** Syerston, 1942. Sharin a joke are, from left: Mac McLelland, Brian Sutton, Happ Hanson, John Cunningham, Jc Humphreys, Nobby Clarke (almost hidden) and Bill Whamond. (Humphreys)

RUNNING A DEADLY GAUNTLET OVER WARSAW
Left: Second pilot George Gra described flames which 'seeme to reach higher than the aircraf (Graves)

Above: Jack Fletcher's regular crew, after their final operation with Y-York.
Back row, left to right: Eades, Adams, Fletcher, Houghton, Seddon. Front row: Butters, Jackson, Butler. (Adams)

Below: A more peaceful setting for some of Jack Fletcher's crew than their experience over Warsaw:
Back row, extreme left: Flight Sergeant 'Snakebite' Butler pretended to be a sloppy gunner.
Back row, fourth from left: Flight Sergeant Bob Jackson, a motor mechanic before the war, kept the engines going during a difficult time.
Back row, third from right: Flight Sergeant Len Eades had the unenviable task of releasing hung-up bombs.
Middle row, second from left: Pilot Officer Eric Seddon manned one of the waist guns.
Middle row, third from left: Warrant Officer Bob Adams: 'We were all very frightened'.
Front row, third from left: Pilot Flight Lieutenant Jack Fletcher descended to 300ft over Warsaw. (Fletcher)

PILOT ABANDONS CREW
Top left: Bomb-aimer Alan Bates had committed to memory the map of the route into Warsaw. (Bates)
Top right: Bob Burgess took over the controls after the pilot baled out over Warsaw. (Bates)
Above left: Bill Cross, the placid rear gunner. (Bates)
Above: Bob Burgess (left) and Noel Sleed after their investiture in Pretoria on 17 August 1945. (Bates)

ESCAPE FROM HAMBURG
Left: 11 Operational Training Unit (OTU), Bassingbourn. From left: Buck Price, Hone Barclay, Red Phillips (a wireless operator friend), Terry Kearns and Morrie Egerton. (Kearns)

Right: 11 OTU, Bassingbourn, in front of barracks. Back row: Hone Barclay, Terry Kearns, Jack Moller. Front row: Buck Price and Morrie Egerton. It was here that they planned how to survive the war. (Kearns)

Right: With Wellington S-Sugar at Warboys, Cambridgeshire, before converting to Lancasters. Terry Kearns, Jack Moller, Morrie Egerton, Curly (ground crew) and Buck Price. (Kearns)

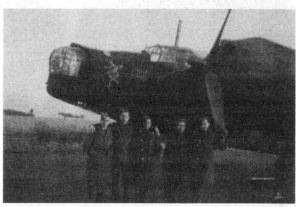

Below: DFMs were presented by King George VI to 75 Squadron's Pilot Officer Alfie Drew, Pilot Officer Hockaday (seen here with his wife), Flight Lieutenant Terry Kearns and Flight Sergeant Hone Barclay. (Kearns)

Date	Hour	Aircraft Type and No.	Pilot	Duty	Remarks (including results of bombing, gunnery, exercises, etc.)	Flying Times	
					Time carried forward :—	108.10	95.10
						Day	Night
2	19.00	Lancaster H 4765	F/o Butterworth	Rear Gunner	Bombing - Krefeld. Failed to Return.		
					Guy Gibson		
					Commanding. No. 106 Squadron.		

I THOUGHT I WAS A GONER

Top: The last page of Alex Kinnear's log book, with the remark 'failed to return', signed b Guy Gibson. (Kinnear)

Above left: Modesty belonged to the past when POWs took up residence at Stalag VIIIB, which provided this forty-seat toilet. (Kinnear)

Above: A Stalag VIIIB watch tower. (Kinnear)

Left: The manacled hands of Alex Kinnear scrape a potato wit a home-made tin spoon. (Kinnear)

Left: Flight engineer Stan Hatt baled out just in time. (Hatt)

Above: At Coningsby, before moving to Syerston. Standing, left to right: Hec Henry, unidentified, Rex Butterworth, John Osmond, Peter Pitchford. On the grass: Alex Kinnear and Doug McCullogh. (Hatt)

Below: Guy Gibson sent letters to the families of aircrews who went missing from his squadron, including this one to Stan Hatt's mother. (Hatt)

No. 106 Squadron,
Royal Air Force,
Syerston, Newark,
Notts.

4th. October 1942.

Dear Mrs Hatt,

I am writing to express my sympathy in the anxiety and suspense which must be yours on receipt of the news that your Son is missing from operations.

He was the Flight Engineer of an aircraft which left here on the 2nd. October 1942 to raid an objective in the Ruhr. Nothing was heard after leaving base, and I regret the aircraft did not return. Opposition in the Ruhr is always of course very heavy, but there is no knowledge of what actually happened. It is possible that the crew were able to bale out, or that the aircraft made a forced-landing and that, although prisoners of war, they are safe. We all hope that this is indeed the case.

Any news concerning your Son will now come from the International Red Cross who will notify the Air Ministry immediately, but should you desire to make enquiries on your own, I am sure a letter to the following address will meet with sympathetic assistance :-

The Wounded, Missing, and Relatives Department,
British Red Cross Society,
11, Belgrave Square,
London.

Your Son originally came to this Squadron as a Fitter from overseas, and when he applied to become a Flight Engineer, I had no hesitation in recommending him. I was very pleased, also, that after the completion of training, he was posted back again as a flying crew. His technical knowledge was outstanding, and he carried out in the air his important duties with complete efficiency. He had already taken part in fourteen raids on enemy territory, and I know that he was very keen on his work. I am most sorry to lose him.

I am enclosing a list of the names and addresses of the next-of-kin of the remainder of the crew as I think, perhaps, you may wish to write to them.

Personal effects will be collected as soon as possible to the Central Depository, Colnbrook, by whom they cannot be released until certain formalities have been complied with. Regarding this, the Committee will communicate with you in due course.

Once again, both personally and on behalf of the Squadron, I offer my very deep sympathy.

Yours very Sincerely,

Guy Gibson

Wing Commander Commanding
No. 106 Squadron, R.A.F.

Mrs. S. Hatt,
33, Thirsk Road,
Mitcham,
Surrey.

THE NIGHT OF THE SNIPE

Left: In the cockpit on a training flight over England, pilot Keith Richardson (left) and flight engineer Reg Breeze, get a two-fingered salute from bomb-aimer Alan Lovett down in the nose. (Lovett)

Below: This picture was taken after VE Day, with a Lancaster looming in the background. Left to right: Huggins, Venables, Trinder, Richardson, Breeze, Lovett (newly promoted to flight sergeant) and Wilson. Canadian Pilot Officer Alf Huggins replaced 'Mo' Young, who had returned to Toronto. (Lovett)

Above: Wesel was probably the most intensively bombed town of its size in Germany. Much of it had been flattened when this picture was taken in 1943; there was little left two years later. (Fazackerley)

LOOPING THE LOOP IN A LANCASTER
Below: Pilot 'Pil' Pilgrim. 'I was suddenly hanging upside down.' (Pilgrim)

Below: Waddington, waiting for the next operation. Back row: two groundcrew, Sgt Gerry Fallon, i/c groundcrew, Short, groundcrew, Williams, Skilton and Kethro. Front row: ATC boy, Pilgrim and Fanning. The Lancaster's bomb doors hang open. (Pilgrim)

Above: Debriefing. From left: Jack Skilton, flight engineer, Roland Kethro, rear gunner, 'Shorty' Short, mid-upper gunner, Jack Williams, bomb-aimer and 'Pil' Pilgrim, pilot. (Pilgrim)
Below: Navigator 'Pop' Benner (back right) maintained a calming influence on the crew. Also pictured are (back left); Eric Toft, Pilgrim's first wireless operator 'borrowed' in 1943 by another crew who did not return. Front: Kethro, Pilgrim and Williams. (Pilgrim)

RICKY DYSON, GM

Above: Rear gunner Ricky Dyson is ready to go. (Dyson) (Ricky Dyson flew with two different crews which figure in the two stories in this chapter).

Above right: This map shows where five Lancasters crashed on the Karlsruhe raid. (Dyson)

Right: Serenity in a churchyard. Back row, from left: Owen Venning and Dennis Bayliss. Front row: Doug Presland and Alan Probert. (Presland)

Lower right: Winter sports for the crew of the doomed Lancaster ME298:B. Flight Sergeant Jack Willcocks, navigator, Sergeant Allan Barratt, rear gunner, Flight Sergeant Bob Lyons, mid-upper gunner, Warrant Officer John Johnstone, bomb-aimer, Flying Officer Dick Oliver, pilot, Sergeant Charlie Gordon, flight engineer and Flight Sergeant William Thomson, wireless operator. (Gordon)

COOK'S TOUR TO DISASTER
Top: Their last trip over Germany ended unexpectedly: 'Red' Scawthorne, 'Swannee' Swan, Gill Pratt, Bill Adams, Tom Collin, Len Banham and Bobby Foulkes. (Collin)
Above: American soldiers explore and guard the Lancaster at the end of the ignominious Cook's Tour across Germany. (Collin)
Left: Tom Collin, pictured receiving his observer's brevet at the end of his training in East London, South Africa. (Collin)

the pointer was slowly going round the dial. The artificial horizon had also toppled and it was describing a graceful phosphorescent loop. It was obvious that if we were not able to fly a straight course we had no chance to reach base and this left us with the options of baling out or heading for Russian territory. We had been told at briefing that we would not be welcomed by the Russians, who discouraged any dropping of supplies to the Poles. They wanted a minimum of resistance, but they did not want a Polish government in-situ when they marched into Warsaw. But we decided this was our best chance.

'All this time we had been flying in right-hand circles and were still very close to Warsaw. The compass was no use to us but, as the moon was almost due east, we decided to tighten the turn until the moon appeared over the starboard wing and then pull out as much as possible until the moon had passed to port. In this manner we gradually crabbed eastward.'

Progress was agonisingly slow, but they were alive, in itself an incredible achievement. The bomber dragged itself into a circle, staggered in a straight line for a few minutes, then stubbornly turned again into a clockwise circle. Burgess was unable to correct its erratic behaviour, they were creeping slowly towards Russia. The new skipper had in his mind the mammoth problems which lay ahead. Even if Russia did allow them on its soil, he had never landed a Liberator by himself. The moment he took over during the dive was the first time he had had full control of a four-engine bomber.

A lone searchlight kept flitting on to the bomber before they cleared Warsaw, but it seemed more inquisitive than predatory, and they soon left its faint wavering beam far behind.

Alan Bates left his second pilot's seat and joined navigator Noel Sleed in the fuselage to manually pump fuel from one tank to another in an effort to stabilise the aircraft. Wireless operator Stan Payne was manning the port beam gun. Bates chatted briefly with Steve Appleyard sitting by the starboard gun. The air was thick with the stench of petrol and Bates was horrified to see the gunner had a pipe in his mouth. Appleyard grinned at his concern. 'It's all right, It isn't lit.'

Bates peered out into the night and was startled to see the sinister shape of a Junkers Ju88, at the same height, keeping pace with them nearly 200yds away. He stared at Appleyard, who sucked contentedly on his empty pipe. 'It's okay,' he said, imperturbably, 'I've been keeping my eye on it for five minutes.' He added, wickedly: 'I'll get Stan to flash it a signal to go away, shall I?'

Bates believed the Ju88 was waiting for another fighter to join him before pressing home an attack. The German pilot would have preferred to attack from underneath but 2,000ft was too low to take the risk. The Germans might also have thought the Liberator was mortally wounded as it crabbed its extraordinarily unpredictable course east. The fighter soon lost interest and veered away into the night.

129

K-King tottered to 5,000ft and suddenly went into another unexpected dive. This time, with two pairs of hands on the controls, they were able to pull it out without too much alarm. After two hours, the bomber stopped crabbing and, to his relief, allowed Burgess to steer a fairly straight course. They thought later that fouled control wires might have caused the crabbing.

As dawn crept over the horizon, they looked for somewhere to land. It had been impossible for Sleed to fix a course when the aircraft was crabbing. He didn't have a map of Russia, but believed they were heading in that direction. Russia was K-King's only hope because they no longer had enough fuel to reach Italy. The port outer and starboard inner engines were working well, the starboard outer was just ticking over. They were flying steadily at 3,000ft.

Bates says: 'Despite what we had heard at briefing, we were not all that nervous about the Russians. We thought, in all innocence, that Russia was our ally, we'd land there, tell them we were British and that would be that. We were very young and rather naive. We should have been terrified.'

Ten hours after they had left Brindisi they spotted what appeared to be a landing strip. They looked out of the port side and saw small crouched cottages encircling a big ugly modern building, which they identified, quite correctly, as the commissariat. The little village appeared deserted, but it was only a little after 4.00am. They were about 400 miles east of Warsaw.

They flew in low, shooting off several red Very cartridges in an attempt to alert the sleeping villagers and get help. No one appeared and the landing strip was a disappointment, too. It was a fighter strip, much too short for the Liberator and obviously no longer used, for a strip of concrete about 2yds wide had been removed from the middle. There were no buildings to be seen, other than the village beyond the field. They decided to land on the grass beside the runway.

'We now had to decide on a wheels–up or wheels–down landing, bearing in mind we had no hydraulic power and consequently, no flaps or brakes.' Burgess decided to try a wheels–down landing and asked everyone if they wanted to bale out, but no one relished the idea. Over the hell of Warsaw they had put their trust in a man who had never previously flown a Liberator. Instinctively, they knew he would get them down safely. Besides, he deserved their moral support.

Noel Sleed and Alan Bates had the job of manually winding down the wheels. In the nose-wheel compartment they held on to each other, put a foot on the wheel and pushed it forward with all their might until it dropped out and locked into position. It was a hazardous operation. A stumble and one of them could have slipped through a gap and out of the aircraft. The other two wheels they wound down from inside the fuselage. Each of them had to be locked down. The port wheel proved difficult. Burgess waggled the wings which was enough to give the wheel a jolt so it could be locked in position.

They made two low runs over the airfield, firing off Very cartridges. Bates attempted the futile task of pumping flaps and believes he had managed five degrees before being overcome by fatigue. He jumped, panting, into the second pilot's seat, ready to cut throttles when Burgess gave the word. Everyone except Burgess and Bates, was braced in crash positions as they flew on to the ground at over 150mph.

Bates says: 'We were travelling much faster than usual owing to the lack of flaps. The landing was good, but I could see that we were heading for a large cartwheel which was standing on its axle. Fortunately the field we had landed in was almost a quagmire and the aircraft came to halt with undignified haste in no more than 200yds.'

As they touched down Bates cut the throttles and held them back. The great wheels struck the waterlogged ground and sank in with a sickening shudder. The Liberator's nose jerked forward into the mire, carving a deep trench until dropping back. Bates cut the engines and switched off the fuel. There were sighs of relief and murmured congratulations to Bob Burgess. It was always a relief to return from a normal bombing operation, but to land safely after one packed with so much drama, each man was gripped with an extraordinary euphoria.

They got out through the bomb doors, stiff and exhausted, with grey, haggard faces, and surveyed the flat desolate landscape over which drifted a waist-high ground mist. It was a freezing cold morning. Later, when the sun came up, it became unbearably hot. They had landed in the Ukraine, near the village of Jemilszinc in the state of Zhitomir.

Burgess, Bates and Sleed were burning their maps, flight plans and navigator's logs when a welcoming party arrived. The other four crew manning the Brownings inside the Liberator, in case of trouble, watched a Red Army major appear on a horse, galloping from the village. He was followed by an ancient open truck of First World War vintage, toiling gallantly along a dirt road. As the rider drew near they saw he was armed with a pistol in a holster and what seemed to be a sten gun slung over his shoulder. The rattling truck contained six Red Army girls, with chubby red faces and enormous bosoms. They wore grey shifts, held in the middle by leather belts.

The major dismounted, glanced at the aircraft, which was peppered all over with bullet holes, removed the sten gun from his shoulder and regarded them with tight-lipped curiosity. He was thick-set, with bandy legs exaggerated by baggy knee breeches. The truck jerked to a halt. Each of the girls aboard was armed with a sten gun.

Burgess shouted: 'British!' then 'English!' and 'Angleski!' before trying 'South African!'. There was no reaction from the Russian until Burgess said, with feeling: 'Bomben sie Deutsch,' and the sten gun came up menacingly. Then, in desperation, Bates cried: 'Rule Britannia!' The major's grim face became wreathed in smiles. 'Aah! Roola Britanya!' he bellowed, shouldering the sten gun and shaking hands. When the others inside the bomber realised the danger had passed, they joined the party. The

Russian girls, jabbering in harsh, coarse voices, were happy to show off their sten guns, demonstrating proudly how they would still fire after being covered in mud.

Breakfast was a revelation. The major sat at the head of a long table in a room at the commissariat. Each of the aircrew received a plate of pickled gherkins. This was followed by two plates in succession, one containing very tasty chips, the other bearing a fried egg. Each man had what appeared to be two tumblers of water in front of him. Bates sipped at one, coughing and spluttering. It was vodka. The major laughed explosively and smiled expansively. 'Niet!' he cried, throwing back the vodka with one great gulp before tossing down the glass of water after it, like a man putting out a fire. Not wishing to lose face, the bomber crew followed suit.

They were taken to villagers' homes to rest. Bates was in a little cottage with one room and a bed. He recalls: 'I was so tired, but could not sleep as the events of the night whirled through my mind and I realised how lucky we had been. There was a family of four sitting in the room watching me tossing and turning. They told me in sign language not to be afraid, but I wasn't frightened, there was just too much to think about to be able to sleep.'

Next day they were taken to one of many towns which are called Novograd (new town). Short of fuel, the Russians mixed 100 octane petrol from the Liberator with paraffin and poured it into the tank of the ancient truck. The aircrew travelled with the major, a driver, and two other soldiers. On the way, enamel mugs were handed round to everyone, including the driver. A few drops were poured into each from a small bottle. Bates believed it to be wood alcohol. The fiery brew was chased down with a tumbler full of water. The decrepit truck made a merry but erratic progress along the rough track to the air base outside Novograd. Here they were entertained by the Russian Air Force, who had an inexhaustible supply of vodka. They toasted Stalin, Churchill and Roosevelt until no one was left standing.

A flight next morning by Dakota to the USAF base at Poltava was diverted to Kiev. Here a flight of seven tiny aeroplanes with open cockpits like Tiger Moths was assembled for them. There was room for the pilot and one passenger. The Russians were keen to show that as ace pilots, they had no equals. They flew at ground level, hopping over hedges at the last second until Stan Payne decided he had seen enough. He got out of his seat and started walking across one wing, holding nonchalantly to the struts. The Russians took his point, climbed to normal height and Payne settled back into the cockpit.

They were accommodated near Poltava at a rest camp full of Russian amputees, later being flown to Moscow, where the Britons were de-seconded from the SAAF and started the long journey home. It took them through several countries, including Egypt where, in Cairo, the two South Africans were sent home on leave. The five Britons returned to England in November 1944, their fighting war at an end. Wrongly described as prisoners-of-war, they became inextricably caught up in bureaucratic red tape. After two weeks at an aircrew rehabilitation centre at Nairn in east Scotland, they were split up. Bates was moved to flying control at an airfield on Dartmoor where the RAF provided target towing for the Royal Navy.

Lloyd Lyne, a bomb-aimer from 178 Squadron, had been shot down while manning the beam guns over Warsaw on the night Bill Norval baled out and became a POW. He met Norval briefly in a hospital near Warsaw. Norval told Lyne he had ordered his crew to bale out. He said nothing about the pilot's duty being to remain at the controls of a stricken aircraft until his crew had escaped.

For their last operation, Bob Burgess received a DSO; Noel Sleed, a DFC, and Alan Bates a DFM. The other four crew members were mentioned in despatches. They each received from Poland the Cross of Valour, the Home Army Cross and the Warsaw Uprising Cross.

15

ESCAPE FROM HAMBURG

Terry Kearns mastered the art of low flying long before he was allowed his first solo flight. His instructor, Flying Officer 'Johnny' Nelson, was so confident in the youngster's natural ability as a pilot that he wanted Kearns to go solo after only three hours' tuition in a Tiger Moth, instead of the minimum six.

Even in 1941, when pilots were desperately needed in England, the flight commander across on the other side of the world in New Zealand at 1 Elementary Flying Training School (EFTS), Taieri, near Dunedin, was sternly unbending. Six hours it must be and not a minute less. There was no place on Flying Officer 'The Pirate' Lambert's flight for any young maverick pilot, who might later be responsible for messing up the war against Germany.

Kearns, a stocky twenty-one year-old farmer's son from Reefton, on the west coast of New Zealand's South Island, had abandoned one dream for another. The burning ambition to become a civil electrical engineer swiftly crumbled after Kearns, in his late teens, had admired First World War pilots buzzing their monoplanes over the rolling mountains and lush green countryside.

Nelson told his eager pupil, 'There's nothing more I can teach you. All you need now is experience. I can give you that all right.' In Nelson's personal flying manual, 'experience' did not mean hours of routine flying and an endless grind of circuits and bumps. Nelson was considered an expert chimney pot skimmer. An extrovert character, he loved low flying, not only for the excitement, but because he believed it should be an important part of every pilot's strategy. Certainly the 'Johnny Nelson experience' was to save the life of Terry Kearns and his crew more than once during bombing operations, particularly on a dramatic summer night two years later after attacking Hamburg.

Kearns and Nelson, only four or five years his senior, practised far away from the prying eyes of the flight commander. Kearns recalls:

'We charged flat out at trees. I had to fly between them. Often we needed to go through gaps where I had to tilt the wings. Johnny whetted my appetite for low flying. He just sat back and let me get on with it. The Tiger Moth had in-line seats and there was a little mirror at the front. I could see him grinning in it. He had a very infectious grin. We had a lot of fun, but he was a perfectionist. He showed me, very clearly, what to do and what not to do. Johnny was a lovely bloke. He was killed in the Pacific.'

Kearns qualified as a Royal New Zealand Air Force pilot at 1 Flying School, Wigram, near Christchurch, before coming to England for more training on Airspeed Oxfords at Cranwell, and blind approach flying at Coningsby. He crewed up at 11 OTU, Bassingbourn, Cambridgeshire, at the end of January, 1942. The formation of wartime bomber crews was always a curiously informal affair. Pilots, navigators, wire-less operators, bomb-aimers and gunners were gathered haphazardly into a room, drinks in their hands, and left to get on with it. About 100 young men, many of them strangers to each other, met at Bassingbourn. Feeling awkward and shy, some of them wondered if they might end up like dance hall wallflowers by pilots who did not care for the look of them.

Some of their potential skippers were nervous, too. Each pilot shuffled slowly round the large room, picking men he thought would blend into an efficient and work-man-like unit. Kearns, an essentially quiet man, who back in New Zealand had enjoyed rugby, deer stalking and swimming, wanted a crew he could trust, fellows he could rely on in a crisis.

At first, there were six of them, all New Zealanders, all sergeants. Later, when it was decided that the twin-engine Wellingtons should not have a second pilot Johnny Gow, from Dunedin, left to form his own crew. He did not survive the war.

Kearns chose John Barclay, from Dunedin, as his navigator. Barclay was known as 'Hone', pronounced 'Honie' – after a famous Maori chief – and he was also a qualified bomb-aimer. Kearns remembers: 'Hone was a grounded pilot, he just couldn't land his Tiger Moth in the time available. When I got to know him better he told me, "I could-n't find the ground. I was either ten feet above it or ten feet below." I said we'd soon fix that. We went up in a Wellington and I told him what to do. He could soon fly as well as me, probably better, but by then he had no ambitions to be a pilot.'

Maurice 'Morrie' Egerton, the wireless operator, from Winton in South Otago was, at twenty-six, the oldest member of the crew. Egerton was married with a baby son who had been born after he had left New Zealand. Little Morris became the crew's mascot. They spent a few days on the Isle of Bute, in the Firth of Clyde, where Egerton had relations. He was the crew's anchor man, mature and a steadying influence because, unlike the others, he had a wife and baby waiting for him back home.

Jack Moller joined the crew as wireless operator, when they were preparing for a posting to the Middle East. The trip to warmer climes was cancelled when they were drawn into the 1,000-bomber raids on Germany. Moller, aged nineteen, who was bois-terous and full of fun, became front gunner/bomb-aimer and spare wireless operator. Although Moller was the official bomb-aimer, Barclay released the bombs. Kearns regarded Moller as more useful in keeping a look-out and making sure the aircraft stayed on a constant line, rather than going in circles during violent evasive action.

Harold 'Buck' Price, the rear gunner, had been brought up on a farm like Kearns, with whom he shared a love of outdoor pursuits. He would not shoot down as many German night fighters with his four Browning machine guns as he had culled deer with a .303 rifle, but he did enough later to be awarded a DFM. He fussed and adjusted his guns with the affection and anxiety of a conscientious parent.

After crewing up they spent a merry weekend getting tanked up on beer in London. It was here in March 1942, they got to know each other well, talked about home, the RAF and girls. They also, most importantly, sowed the seeds of a plan to help them survive the war. As Kearns recalls: 'The basic idea was to see the bloody war through. We talked very seriously about what we needed to know. After that weekend we listened carefully to the instructors. They were aircrew resting from operations and we learned from the tales of their hairy experiences.'

The instructors had come through at least one tour of thirty operations, all of them with bloodcurdling stories to tell, ideas of different strategies, together with situations and battlegrounds to avoid. Kearns and his crew listened to them avidly, believing the veterans held the key to their own survival. By now, a lot of aircrew had been killed and maimed, but Kearns and his crew never shared the widely held philosophy of invincibility – that death only struck down the other fellows. It was a grim fact that some of their pals would never see New Zealand again. They knew they must prepare for every eventuality to increase their chances of going home after the war. Kearns remembers:

'We reckoned there were two ways you were going to get clobbered. One was by guns from the ground, the other was night fighters. Both Buck and I knew that if you were trying to shoot a running target, you had to aim in front of it. The gunners are presupposing that the target is going to stay on the same course, at the same speed and height. Your aeroplane is occupying a piece of sky. The German gun has to be aiming at that piece of sky. Once the shell or bullet is fired it's off and running. The gunner no longer has any control over it. 'Our search plan was to have a ring of eyes covering every part of the sky around our aeroplane. Each bloke had an area of sky to watch. That was his responsibility. Everyone reported to me. If there was an attack from the front and below, looking down you'd see a flash on the ground. The shell might be coming for you, it might not, but we always assumed it was and never carried on the same track. We moved one way or another. We moved up or down, increased or decreased our speed. If that gun had been aimed at us we were not in the place where the gunners had expected us to be. Our solution to the process of staying alive was to get our aeroplane out of that piece of sky as quickly as possible, so we weren't where the opposition expected us to be.

'Fighters have got to see you to shoot at you. If they can see us then, in theory, we can see them, therefore you've got to keep a good look-out. The best place for them to hide from you was in a dark piece of sky. Any sort of movement, even a sensed movement, was reported to me straightaway. Someone might say: "I can't see anything, but I think...". So you move away and say: "Where is it? Up? Down? Below?". "It's up." So you move in underneath it and look up to see whether it is a fighter or not. If it is, you keep watch. If it isn't you gently move away.

'The emergency signal by any of the crew for the sighting of an unexpected night fighter in an attacking position was "Go! go! go!". That meant get the hell out of here as quickly as you can. I'd slam one of the throttles shut, kick the rudder on that side down as far as it would go, turn the wheel upside-down and pull.'

Kearns believed they were often saved by not steering a steady course. Their training and thinking was absorbed not only by bombing enemy targets, but also by staying alive. An aircrew should never be taken by surprise. That was how so many of them were caught. Once, when their team was depleted by one man, they nearly bought it, their strict training sabotaged by his replacement. Buck Price was ill and they were forced to take a rear gunner who was on his first operation. They briefed the new man on their tactics and assumed he understood them. They were crossing Germany with a full bomb-load, en route to Saarbrucken, when wireless operator Morrie Egerton cried: 'Go! go! go!'

As the Wellington swung to port and on to its back and dropped, a stream of cannon shells passed within inches of the aircraft's underbelly. Egerton later reported that the German Junkers Ju88 night fighter had crept up behind them. Price would have seen it long before. They found the new rear gunner, who had seemed calm and lucid over the intercom, cowering in his turret, frightened and covered in vomit.

They discussed 'what if?' situations in formulating new tactics. Each man was encouraged to think up wild ideas. What if a night fighter bursts out of a cloud, its guns blazing? What if they suddenly saw something they had not seen before? These problems were thrashed out over a pint in the sergeants' mess or local pubs, including The Oak in the Norfolk village of Feltwell.

Searchlights posed serious problems, being coned by up to fifteen of them was a frightening experience. In the early days it was good enough for Kearns to increase speed or fling the aircraft into a diving swerve out of the light. But that wasn't good enough to cope with the blanket defences of Hamburg on the night of 26/27 July 1942. It was after that traumatic operation that Kearns devised new tactics to escape the dreaded coning.

They were based at Feltwell with 75 (New Zealand) Squadron in 3 Group. It was the crew's fourteenth operation together. A total 403 bombers set off for Hamburg that night: 181 Wellingtons, 77 Lancasters, 73 Halifaxes, 39 Stirlings and 33 Hampdens. Twenty-nine of them would not return.

Kearns piloted Wellington III, 3396, S-Sugar. He admired the Wimpy for its robustness and reliability. The bomber's emblem, the Saint, with a bomb under his arm, was painted on the nose. The weather was murky, the flight from East Anglia fairly quiet. They flew north of the Frisian Islands in the North Sea, where flak ships lurked, then turned down towards Hamburg. Some crews flying at higher altitude had to deal with icing. Kearns flew at 5,000 to 6,000ft. He comments: 'We reckoned the aeroplane flew better at lower altitude. It was more responsive, performed better and wasn't so damned cold. The squadron always flew around that height.' He also felt safer at the lower height, especially during a trip when most aircraft were flying at 10,000 to 15,000ft.

'We figured the German gunners would not have enough time to set time fuses on their shells for us at the lower height. These went off when they reached the right altitude or at the set time. They might have had time to set proximity fuses, which caused a shell to explode as it neared its target. But if most aeroplanes were above 10,000ft, all the Germans needed to do was fire their shells at that height and they'd have a good chance of hitting somebody. Other shells had impact fuses, which meant they would explode on impact. At 5,000ft, we mainly had to contend with light flak from Oerlikons.

'We were on our fourteenth op and experienced, which meant we went in on the first wave with incendiaries to set fires to mark the target for the main force to bomb. That was the origin of the Pathfinder Force. Less experienced crews carried the bombs. The best crews were sent in at the beginning of the raid to find the target and bomb it. Then the rest came in to stoke up the fire.'

The following October, with 156 Squadron, Kearns and his crew would become the first in the RAF to be awarded their Pathfinder wings.

The sky approaching Hamburg was already a battlefield. Flak was savage, several bombers were in trouble, rocked by shells exploding nearby. Another squirmed helplessly in the incandescent beam of several searchlights, like a terrified fat moth fluttering against an electric light bulb. Flames spurted from the engines of other aircraft continuing bravely to the target area, which was the centre of the city.

'The aiming point for all these raids was the centre of town. Essen, for instance, was slightly different as the Ruhr was so heavily built up and the industrial complex so huge, that in clear conditions you could actually see it. More precise bombing came later. In the early days you never had a cat in hell's chance of getting your bombs on the place that you aimed at. The bomb-sight wasn't accurate and the natives weren't friendly.'

S-Sugar droned over the centre of Hamburg and dropped the incendiaries, which had been packed into nine containers; then the wait for the photoflash, which fell with them, to illuminate the target for the aircraft's camera. They had some thirty seconds to wait before the flash exploded at about 1,000ft for the camera to take one photograph, which would be examined later by experts in England. Before the photoflash had time to go off, the Wellington was caught in an eruption of brilliant light. They had been coned! Kearns recalls:

'It was like being a fish lit up in a glass bowl. There was a solid ring of light all round us. I knew fighters were circling waiting for someone to be caught by the searchlights. They'd move in to shoot you down like a chicken. Everyone concentrates on your aeroplane. There's probably a whole bunch of bombers all around, but you are the one being illuminated. Everyone on the ground is intent that you go no further.

'I rolled the aeroplane around the sky to get out of it, but I couldn't. I oscillated around 5,000 to 6,000ft. I hit the throttles and went faster, then slower. I kept the revs up high so I wouldn't stall the engines, the worst thing I could do. There seemed no way I could escape. They were hosepiping shells and bullets at us, everything they had. The lights stayed on us, it was very unfriendly.'

Kearns used all his innate skills, throwing the Wellington about the sky, but the lights followed, trailing behind them a deadly whiplash of shells and bullets. He slid sideways, but the lights remained attached to the bomber as steadfastly as an inquisitive schoolboy holds a torch at night in a garden, following a scuttling beetle, before stamping on it. Perspiration was running down his forehead and he was breathing hard as again he threw the faithful S–Sugar into a fearful, snarling corkscrewing plunge to port, but the malevolent umbilical cord of lights was still there, setting them up for God knows how many gunners and fighters. His crew hung on, helpless really, except to gasp out a possible escape route or warn of a night fighter, as they searched their quarters of the sky illuminated brilliantly around them. They knew as the seconds passed, their lives were ticking away. Only one well directed shell was needed to blast them all into oblivion. Surely one of the thousands pumped up at them would find its mark?

The steep dives to increase speed had brought them to within yards of the rooftops of Hamburg's south-western suburbs. Behind them 800 fires burned in the city, 523 of them massively, leaving 337 people dead and 1,027 injured. A total 823 homes were in ruins, over 5,000 damaged.

There was not a lot of light, just enough to see ahead. Searchlights briefly brushed the ground behind them, then disappeared to search for easier victims. They had escaped the coning, but were still not out of trouble. At 200ft they hit the searchlight belt around Hamburg. The German operators had been warned about the lone Wellington and concentrated their lights just above ground level. Kearns lost even more height.

'I was as low as I dare go. My old instructor Johnny Nelson had given me the confidence to do this without any qualms. I could see trees and fields. The lights no longer waved about the sky, they were dropped to the ground, attempting to pick us up. That was fine because, although they couldn't see me, they were illuminating all the trees and stuff ahead. The trees appeared as dark patches. I sank down as low as I dared in line with what I could see to keep the light on the other side of the trees. It didn't always work and they picked me up.

'I was keeping reasonably straight, going like hell, doing a little bit of dodging. Guns fired at us, Oerlikon-type stuff. Some were not far off the mark. We saw flashing lights ahead, showing the position of the firing guns. We diverted slightly and hid below the trees. Lights found us and we saw the trees lit up on the other side.'

On each trip, the crew had an escape plan. When they were in trouble the front and rear gunners quickly lined themselves up with anything in the sky, the moon or a star, to mark their exit point. It was difficult in all the excitement to scan the sky, but Hone Barclay, in the tumbled chaos of his navigator's compartment, was clinging tenaciously to his map and compass, working out where they were and a route for home.

Kearns was thinking, 'We'll have to do something about this bloody coning,' when Jack Moller, the front gunner, suddenly yelled: 'Christ! Power lines!'

Kearns gritted his teeth when he saw the electricity pylons from 50 to 100yds away. The wires dipping between them were invisible. For an instant he saw the confident grin of Johnny Nelson reflected on the windscreen as their Tiger Moth puttered between two trees, then he plunged to zero feet. 'I had no chance of going over the wires, there was no time. I had to go as low as I possibly could and wait, judging it accurately. In this situation we were at a disadvantage with a Wimpy, which had a very high tail. I had to get under the wire, then pull the stick back so the tail dipped as I went under and came up again. In those circumstances you don't think about it, you just do it.'

They did it, slipping beneath the wires which would have incinerated them had they been no more than gently kissed by the Wellington's tall tail.

'By now I reckoned our props were very often scraping the ground, at least cutting the grass. The crew were keeping their eyes peeled for anything I had missed.' The bomber twice went over gun emplacements. The first time the German gunner heard them coming and timed his burst as they were yards away. Kearns deliberately put the nose down and Moller returned the fire. The German bullets did not follow them across the field. Two searchlights wavered ahead. Kearns turned towards them:

'We were bloody angry. We saw them swinging around to try and find us. We went off course a bit and kept low behind a copse. I aimed for the lights ahead. We pulled up over the top of the trees. I said: "Okay Jack, they're just ahead of you. Are you ready?" Jack said: "Yeah!". As we went over, I whipped into the beam and put the nose down. Jack fired and the searchlight exploded. The light went out and disintegrated. We fired at several searchlights on the way out of Hamburg.'

Kearns dived beneath another set of power cables before Hamburg and its ferocious defences receded behind them. They had been travelling at about 180mph, normal cruising speed, but frighteningly fast for night hedge-hopping, with unknown obstacles lying ahead. They were used to beating up the Norfolk countryside at church steeple height, no more than an occasional angry fist waved after them, but not with a host of gunners doing their best to tear them to pieces. The threat of annihilation had added an edge to the flying, sharpened the pilot's reflexes, and caused them all to keep a tightly squeezed sphincter. Kearns recalls:

'It didn't bother me too much, except that we couldn't see too well. It never occurred to me that we wouldn't get through. There was no way that I was going to walk home. What pleased me is that we worked as a unit. The whole principle of our plan was for anyone to call out as soon as they saw anything. I always knew from his voice who it was. I'd probably have seen it at the same time, but it confirmed my sighting, reinforcing the urgency. Quite often I just looked and thought "can I do it or can't I?". The answer was always "yes I can". It had to be. Our escape from Hamburg lasted for about ten minutes. It seemed longer; it really was horrendous. Thank God, the countryside was so flat. After we had got through the flak belt it was dead easy.'

But not that easy. Kearns had pulled up to nearly 200ft to keep clear of any unexpected obstacles. Barclay, busy with his maps and calculators, reported over the intercom that they were between 50 and 100 miles south-west of Hamburg. There were few landmarks for him to give a more accurate position.

Their speed continued at 180mph and after a brief consultation with the crew Kearns decided they were safer not going any higher. He believed they could escape without being picked up by the Germans. Then Kearns and Moller saw the glint of a river ahead. Barclay asked, 'Is there anything particular you can tell me about it?'. Kearns replied: 'Yes, there's a bloody great island in the middle of it,' to which Barclay cried, 'Christ! Turn!'.

While they had been talking, Kearns had allowed the nose to drop and as he came to turn he realised that he had to lift the bomber otherwise a wing would dip in the water.

'I lifted the Wimpy, pulled it around and skidded in a 90-degree turn to the side of the long island. As we turned and went up the river, all hell was let loose. Bullets streamed towards us from half-a-dozen light flak guns. Jack returned fire from his front turret and Buck from the rear. I don't know how they missed us. If we'd stayed on the same course we'd have been right in the middle of them and they'd have had us. As it was, we just managed to pick it up. Luckily Hone had an idea where we were. We were just south of Wilhemshaven or Emden. Once we got out of it, we carried on for another twenty minutes or half-an-hour at this height, climbed to 2,000 or 3,000ft and then just came home.'

It was after 4.00am when they landed. They had been airborne seven hours. Back at Feltwell, Kearns wrote in his logbook: 'Seven searchlights destroyed and one machine gun nest'.

After fourteen operations, all their plans for survival had so far worked, except how to escape the searchlight coning. They knew they had to try something to confuse the Germans. Kearns had been thinking. Next day he asked his crew: 'How brave are you blokes?'. They shrugged, chuckled, and asked if it was worse than being shot full of holes. Kearns warned them: 'It'll be awful bloody rough'.

His plan, if they were coned again, was to turn the aircraft over and kick on hard top rudder so it dropped sideways like a stone. Once it had fallen, he would kick the nose over and they would be down and away. 'We tried it out that day in daylight and found it was frightening, but decided to do it in an emergency to see if it worked. Blow me, next night we were sent to Hamburg again and we were coned. This was at the time of the 1,000-bomber raids. Many more aircrews had been briefed for this trip from other squadrons, but bad weather grounded most of them.'

Heavy cloud prevented any bombers from leaving 1, 4 and 5 Group bases that night. Only 256 aircraft took off, 165 from 3 Group, together with 91 belonging to operational training units. These included 161 Wellingtons, 71 Stirlings and 24 Whitleys. The weather got worse on the flight to Germany and the OTU aircraft were recalled, although three pressed on and bombed Hamburg.

'The weather was appalling, with low cloud and rain, although clearing over the target. One of our crews aborted just after take-off. When he landed back at Feltwell, he was told the other groups had been scrubbed (cancelled), but 3 Group was not recalled. I was coned on the way to the target. I started weaving a bit as usual and they were following us, so as I said "Stand by!" I kicked on hard top rudder. The Wellington slid down sideways, like a sharp knife slipping through warm butter. When I kicked on opposite rudder and eased the stick forward a bit, the nose came down, and we went away. It was staggering. As we appeared to turn they tried to follow us, and we dropped out of the bottom of the cone, losing 2,000 to 3,000ft. They had no idea where we were. They searched all round the sky. It had worked. We climbed back up again and carried on.

'It was amazing the confidence it gave us after that to know that if we were caught again in a searchlight cone, we could slip out of it before becoming a target for flak or fighters.'

Bomber casualties were heavy that night: sixteen Wellingtons and nine Stirlings were lost from 3 Group. Four OTU Wellingtons did not return and a Whitley crashed in the sea.

Kearns completed 90 operations, including thirty-one with Lancasters in 617 Squadron. In recommending a DSO for Kearns, the station commander at Woodhall Spa, Group Captain M.G. Philpott, wrote on 12 July 1944:

'The unsurpassed gallantry and devotion to duty which this officer has so long and so enthusiastically displayed has had a most profound effect upon the morale and fighting spirit of his squadron. His cheerfulness, great courage and determination have enabled him to create a crew whose efficiency could not be exceeded in the Royal Air Force of today. His efforts have resulted in much damage to the enemy and his conduct and leadership throughout his operational career have been an inspiration to all and are worthy of the highest praise...'

Kearns was also awarded a DFM a month after the two Hamburg trips, and later a DFC. Hone Barclay received a DFC and a DFM. Morrie Egerton, Jack Moller and Buck Price were each awarded a DFM.

16

'I Thought I was a Goner'

A force of 188 bombers left England on the night of 2 October 1942 to bomb the industrial town of Krefeld in the Ruhr Valley. It comprised of 95 Wellingtons, 39 Halifaxes, 31 Lancasters and 23 Stirlings. Seven aircraft were lost, including Lancaster W4768, skippered by Pilot Officer Rex Butterworth from 106 Squadron, based at Syerston in Nottinghamshire.

On the previous day this bomber had flown with the squadron to Syerston from Coningsby, to make way for an army of Irish navvies employed to lay concrete runways. Butterworth chose to pilot his car, a Ford Eight, instead of a Lancaster to the Nottinghamshire base, missing an occasion in which he would have revelled.

The squadron commander was Wing Commander Guy Gibson who, the following May, would lead the stunning Dambuster raids. Gibson allowed his crews one burn-up of the Lincolnshire airfield before they left but many got carried away, making up to eight passes, coming in at 50ft from all angles over the station. Butterworth's rear gunner, Sergeant Alex Kinnear, flew with Gibson that day. He recalls: 'Gibson was hopping mad. He had an open line through to Syerston. As the pilots arrived there, he had them put under station arrest.'

Less than five hours later the squadron was airborne again, heading for Wismar, north-east of Hamburg. Because the airfield at Syerston was built on a hill, this sometimes caused problems. The aircraft charging down the runway in front of Butterworth's Lancaster that night could not drag itself off the ground, and plunged into the valley.

Kinnear says: 'We saw the smoke as we took off. We were nearly 300ft up when the fire engines arrived. It wasn't a good start, a bit frightening really, especially over a strange 'drome. We said "poor devils", although I learned years afterwards that no one had been killed.'

Butterworth's Lancaster was halfway across the North Sea when wireless operator Sergeant Peter Pitchford believed he had picked up a squadron recall. There was a crack in the insulator and the aerial was banging against metal, interrupting messages on the radio. The crew who had carried out an NFT (night flying test) on Butterworth's aircraft during the flight from Coningsby had not picked up the fault. 'I'm getting the recall sign,' called Pitchford, 'but I can't make out the rest of the message.' Butterworth turned for home.

In fact only one bomber had been called back, with a glycol leak, which could have led to an overheating engine. The crew of W4768 faced the wrath of Gibson in the Syerston debriefing room, where he virtually accused them of cowardice. It wasn't the first time Gibson had taken this attitude. Butterworth had earlier aborted a trip on the airfield at Coningsby when a navigation detonator exploded, filling the cockpit with smoke. On that occasion Gibson screeched to a halt beside them in a Jeep and angrily exclaimed: 'You've got four good engines, you'll bloody well go and bomb Germany'. They went twenty minutes after the Main Force, flying alone to the Ruhr. The crew resented Gibson's attitude as Kinnear recalls:

'We were a good crew and trusted one another to do our jobs. Gibson had had a maximum effort on that night with thirteen aircraft. That was a show off on our first night at Syerston. The other squadron, No 61, only sent half that number. Gibson's squadron was top in 5 Group for the tonnage of bombs dropped and third in the whole of Bomber Command. He wouldn't be happy until he headed that command, too. But there was a war on and you can't knock a man for that. We weren't losing any more aircraft and crews. Some lads thought he was a gong hunter, but I thought that was unfair.'

The high-spirited Butterworth, at twenty-two only a year younger than his squadron commander, clashed many times with Gibson who believed the pilot was too easy going, too often in trouble and, perhaps, not treating the war as seriously as he should. Yet there may have been other reasons why Gibson resented the young pilot officer. Butterworth was a burly giant of 6ft 5in whom Gibson, stocky – but almost a foot shorter – always had to look up to. And Butterworth, although not a show-off, was never short of money. He was the son of a rich woollen cloth mill owner in Holmfirth, Yorkshire.

Despite Gibson's reservations, Butterworth was a fine pilot, a stickler for safety, with a carefully nurtured working relationship with his ground crew, anxious to keep his kite in first class order. Not unreasonably, when he was not flying, the extrovert Butterworth, who was also a bachelor, liked to enjoy himself. Gibson, however, did not always approve of the way the pilot chose to let his hair down.

There was the memorable night when Butterworth, very drunk, stationed himself, grinning, outside the WAAF quarters, pretending to be the duty officer, while looking for talent. One light summer evening, after another glorious booze-up at a Coningsby pub, twenty young men crammed into Butterworth's Ford Eight, clinging to the roof, bonnet and spare wheel, singing and giggling in high spirits, for the short, hazardous trip back to camp along an almost deserted country lane. Butterworth, surrounded by bodies and unable to see, was incompetently navigated by several tipsy passengers and crashed, with gales of laughter, causing slight damage to the base's barrier gate. He was on a charge for each incident, but left Gibson's office with a jaunty shrug after severe reprimands. He didn't give a damn about Gibson, or the rank difference.

After several nights without an operation from Coningsby, Gibson decided there was too much boozing going on, declaring that the alcohol content in his aircrews' blood stream was getting too high. He arranged for the squadron, including its officers, to have two days logging in woodland about four miles away, near Woodhall Spa. Rear gunner Alex Kinnear remembers: 'Trees were crashing down all over the place. It was more dangerous than being on ops, but it was good sport. Gibson also arranged for Woodhall Spa swimming pool to be opened specially for us. We blew up a couple of dinghies. Chaps were getting into them and being tossed out. That was the good part of Gibson after the hard work of the logging. It's not everybody who would have thought of that, but he did.'

Many of the squadron aircrew, including Alex Kinnear, had not unpacked before leaving for the next operation, the day after arriving at Syerston. At briefing, they were instructed to bomb Krefeld, just south of Düsseldorf. The targets included railway marshalling yards and the industrial heart of the town. Kinnear says: 'We had looked forward to getting to Syerston because it was near Nottingham, which had a reputation for having a lot more women than men. We didn't have time to leave the camp before going to Krefeld. Still, we thought, there would be plenty of time to visit Nottingham later on.'

Take-off was at 7.00pm. It was the crew's sixteenth operation together. Casualties were high in Bomber Command and after surviving fifteen trips, including several to the Ruhr, they considered themselves a good team. They were in good spirits that night because next morning they were due to go on leave.

Pilot Officer Johnny Osmond was a competent navigator. About 5ft 9in tall, he was slim, dark-haired, married and serious, looking forward to starting a family and watching the children grow up. He never left anything to chance and was always checking their in-flight position.

Sergeant Stan Hatt, twenty-seven, the flight engineer, had been a ground crew corporal engineer in the Middle East before volunteering for aircrew.

Wireless operator Sergeant Peter Pitchford was a fresh-faced, husky young draughtsman from Gloucester. He loved music. His small bedroom in the Coningsby mess had been crammed with jazz records. He was courting a Gloucester girl named Iris May.

Many crews had at least one loner. Sergeant Bob Marsh, the stocky bomb-aimer, did not even eat in the mess with his crewmates. Kinnear recalls: 'We never got to know him. We felt he was keeping us at arm's length all the time.'

Mid-upper gunner Hec Henry had worked his passage from Australia to England on a cargo boat in the thirties. He had been a rigger before becoming a gunner. Much older than the others, in his mid-thirties, he was married to an English nurse. Henry was much admired for his ability to roll a cigarette deftly with one hand.

Rear gunner Alex Kinnear, twenty-three, born in Preston, left school at fourteen and attended evening classes at technical college for five years, while working a 50-hour week in Queen's Mill, Preston. There, in the din of the loom arms crashing against the shuttles, he learned to lip-read.

At the age of twenty, the stocky, blue-eyed Kinnear had been weaving manager at a textile mill in Athlone. It was on the windswept green fields of a farm outside this town in Southern Ireland that he learned to be a good shot, knocking over rabbits with a twelve-bore rifle.

The sky was hazy over Krefeld, making the Pathfinders' task a difficult one. Butterworth encountered heavy flak after crossing the Dutch coast and penetrating Germany, but no worse than other trips to the heavily defended Ruhr Valley. Kinnear was freezing in the rear turret. Outside there was eighteen degrees of frost. The only parts of his body exposed were his eyes, and sometimes even his eyeballs seemed to have frozen in their sockets. He wore a canvas suit that was fitted with primitive heating. 'There were wires up your arms and legs and across your body. Sometimes you had short-circuits in the system. One trip I had shorting and burning. I felt blisters coming on my legs and turned the heating off, but ten minutes later I was freezing to death and had to turn it on again. It was on and off all the time. I don't know why I didn't suffer from frostbite.'

To give the rear turret extra fire-power, two rails on either side of the fuselage fed bullets for the four Browning machine-guns, providing each one with about 2,600 rounds. Flak did not become a problem until the Lancaster droned towards the target area at 14,000ft. Suddenly, on the outskirts of Krefeld, they were caught in the dazzling beam of a radar-controlled master searchlight. Another half-dozen searchlights homed in on the bomber until it was lit up like a Christmas tree. A voice over the intercom murmured nervously 'Oh God, they've got us cold!'. Kinnear remembers: 'It was serious. We'd had the odd searchlight pick us up, but not a controlled effort like this. They were all locked on to us as we were on our run-in, flying nice and steady, ready to bomb on the Pathfinders' markers.'

The stricken bomber was so close to the coloured markers, Butterworth decided to press on, rather than try to dive away from the searchlights and come round again. Then the German flak began pumping up at the bomber, pinned helplessly to the sky by a deluge of bright light. Shells exploded all round them as Butterworth concentrated on keeping the aircraft steady, relying on the instructions of bomb-aimer Bob Marsh in the nose. The searchlights followed them, unwavering.

Kinnear and Hec Henry, tense and helpless, could only scan the sky for fighters. They saw none. Kinnear says: 'Normally, you never fired at an enemy fighter unless he began attacking you, because you didn't want to draw attention to yourself and give him the advantage.'

There was no time to dive away from the searchlights. At about 9.00pm, seconds after Marsh had cried out 'Bombs gone!', with the Lancaster still flying level, waiting for the automatic camera to operate, the German gunners found their target. A shell smashed into the cockpit and Butterworth's aggrieved voice registered loudly over the intercom: 'Christ, they've hit me in the leg'.

Hec Henry saw flames and thick smoke pouring out of both starboard engines. He waited tensely for instructions. The next voice to be heard was that of flight engineer, Stan Hatt. 'I've tried the extinguishers,' he said. They were as effective as urinating into an erupting volcano because both engines were burning out of control. There was little time for speculation – when the fires got into the wing fuel tanks, the bomber would explode.

Butterworth came through again. 'There's no chance with this, boys. It's every man for himself now. Bale out.' The bomber was still flying straight and level. Kinnear believed Butterworth had switched to automatic pilot and was preparing to get out. In the rear turret, lit eerily by the surging flames from the engines, Kinnear felt more cut off from the world than usual. He tried to work quickly, but even in three pairs of gloves, his fingers were cold and clumsy, and the simple tasks he had to complete before extricating himself from the turret became monumental.

He started opening the rear doors, realised the guns were on the beam and thought, 'God, I haven't centralised them'. His thoughts assembled themselves into priorities.

'I had to centralise the guns, lock the turret into position, slide open the doors and come back into the fuselage. If I hadn't locked the turret the slipstream would have swung me round all over the place.

'Luckily, the turret was still working automatically. I locked it then slid open the doors. Then I tried to disconnect myself from the intercom, oxygen and electrics. Each one was a metal bayonet socket. Trouble was I'd never trained for this. Normally you didn't disconnect until you were back at base, taking off your gloves to do so.

'The intercom was easy enough, then I felt really isolated, not knowing what was happening in the rest of the plane. I wrestled and struggled with the other leads, but couldn't move them. I gave up, leaned back in my seat and thought I was a goner. I could see the smoke and flames from the engines.'

The thought struck him that he might be the last man in the crippled Lancaster. The others had probably all baled out. He had not spoken of his difficulties over the intercom. No one would come looking for him. Even now, as he peered out, the flak was still chasing the blazing bomber. Kinnear, a Methodist, overcome by black despair, cried out, 'Oh Lord, get me out of this'. He sat up again, pushed the leads and twisted them and they came out straightaway. 'It was a miracle,' says Kinnear.

A rear gunner needed to be a contortionist to get out of his turret. Kinnear came out backwards. He slid back on the rough rear spar, twisted round and put his feet on the lid of the Elsan toilet. It was an unwritten rule that, for the benefit of rear gunners, the Elsan lid should be left down. As he stepped on to the fuselage floor, Kinnear saw Hec Henry standing by the open starboard door watching the flames leaping from the two engines.

The rear gunner grabbed his parachute from beside the toilet, quickly clipped it on and joined Henry. Flames surged past the door. Henry, noted for a dry sense of humour, said calmly: 'My God, you've taken your time, haven't you?'. He gazed into the flames. 'There's no sense us jumping down into that lot.' He pointed at the burning mass of Krefeld. 'We may as well bide our time, we've got bags of height.'

A direct hit on the front of the aircraft changed their minds. The bomber almost stood on its tail. Henry leaped out without another word and Kinnear followed him, holding the parachute release handle, gasping at the fierce heat from the blazing engines. 'We were at about 12,000ft. As I came down, I was swaying and this, together with the tension made me vomit. Suddenly I saw the ground coming up and landed in a ploughed field.'

Gathering up the parachute, Kinnear saw an elderly German walking towards him. They were probably as nervous as each other. The German wore a yellow armband emblazoned with a black swastika, and carried a rifle. Henry had landed in the next field and started shouting: 'Alex! Alex!' to which Kinnear yelled back, 'Shut up, you silly bugger, I've been captured!'.

The German's first words were 'Kamerad? Kamerad?'. Kinnear shrugged uncomprehendingly and limped dolefully across the field. One of his flying boots had been yanked off in the aircraft's slipstream. The German pointed at the gunner's stockinged foot and said, 'Kaput? Kaput?'. Again, Kinnear shrugged, wondering what would happen to him, deciding against snatching the man's rifle. He might have stood a chance in Belgium or France, but not in the heart of Germany.

He was led into a country cottage where the man made a telephone call. Kinnear saw a young, frightened woman who had been crying and two small large-eyed children who stared fearfully at him. Kinnear slid a bar of chocolate to them across a table.

Two huge armed policeman bundled Kinnear into the back of their car. About three miles from the cottage, they saw a body lying in the road. It was the wireless operator, Peter Pitchford, badly wounded in the lower stomach and groin, still attached, unconscious, to his parachute. The Germans bundled him roughly into the car.

They drove through the burning town to a police station with all its windows blown out, where Pitchford asked for water. He didn't recognise Kinnear and grabbed the leg of a policeman who spitefully kicked the wounded airman. Kinnear protested, 'For God's sake'. He was given water and moistened the lips of Pitchford, who was screaming in agony. Kinnear says: 'He died next day. He was not given any medical attention. They had just been bombed, they weren't going to be too kind.'

Kinnear was driven to the Luftwaffe airfield where he was allowed to use a toilet. While a guard waited outside, he calmly shredded several documents, including his identity card and dropped them into the cistern. There had not been time to put them away in his new quarters. The others were all captured within an hour. Hec Henry stumbled into a gun pit and Bob Marsh landed on the roof of a house in Krefeld. He slid to the ground and was attacked by civilians, collecting a few bruises before being rescued by policemen.

Seconds before the last shell struck, engineer Stan Hatt's legs were dangling through the front escape hatch. One flying boot was whipped away in the slipstream as he put his head between his knees, ready to roll out. He recalls the time, 9.10pm. Hatt remembers nothing more until waking up badly hurt in a patch of stinging nettles in a wood at 10.30pm. His head was cut, probably from striking the escape hatch. He was in too much pain to move and, after cursing the Germans for spoiling his leave, smoked a cigarette and went to sleep.

At dawn he staggered to a road and was picked up by a lorry driver who handed him over to police in Krefeld. He was given a cup of ersatz coffee and a slice of rye bread and honey, before being taken by armed guard on a tram through the bombed town to a Luftwaffe camp. Weeks later Hatt was X-rayed at Stalag Luft III at Sagan, south-east of Berlin, where it was discovered he had a compression fracture of the second and third lumbar vertebrae and two broken ribs. They were never strapped up or plastered, but gradually healed after sleeping on a straw paliasse on bare boards.

Rex Butterworth and navigator Johnny Osmond were probably killed by the last shell to burst in the cockpit. Their bodies were found later. Pitchford very likely caught the full blast of the shell as he was going through the escape hatch in the nose.

In the squadron commander's office at Syerston, Wing Commander Gibson sighed and signed the seven logbooks belonging to the missing aircrew. Neatly written above his signature were the words: 'Bombing Krefeld. Failed to return.' Seven telegrams would go out that day to the men's families, followed by seven letters written by Gibson.

Next day the four survivors from Lancaster W4768 met after being let out of their separate cells. A feldwebel (sergeant) who spoke good English told them, 'We're not supposed to let you mix, so if you hear us shout "officer", dive back into your cells'.

They were taken by train to the interrogation centre at Oberursel outside Frankfurt where they were put into solitary confinement. Three weeks later Kinnear was put on an unheated train for the interminable journey to Poland. The train stopped occasionally for the prisoners to go to the toilet. Kinnear recalls how 'the guards stood in a circle and you just did what you wanted beside the track. There was no luxury of toilet paper. Some found grass or dock leaves. It was foul and degrading.'

Stalag VIIIB at Lansdorf, Silesia, held 30,000 prisoners, 800 of them RAF, with 100 in each of the eight crowded barrack blocks. These numbers would soon rise to 1,000 as more RAF aircrews were shot down and captured. They slept in bunk beds alive with fleas and bugs. Each wooden building contained ten tables and one stove with half a bucket of coal to last a month.

In the ablutions, cold water dribbled into sinks like cattle troughs and it was impossible to wash properly under the primitive showers. Water was rationed in the summer. The toilets were communal forty-seaters.

Kinnear discovered the ingenuity of his fellow prisoners. Cups and cutlery were made out of tin cans saved from Red Cross parcels. Fan heaters, geared up to a pulley wheel, all made of tin, and fuelled from a single stick, quickly boiled billycans of water.

The sandy soil was not helpful to men planning to tunnel to freedom, but they tried. Shortly before Kinnear arrived the Germans filled one tunnel with excreta. No one was desperate enough to go that way again. Too many people knew about the second tunnel and the Germans had their stooges. A table covered by a blanket was carried from a barrack into the compound. A prisoner clung beneath the table, scraped sand from a trapdoor, crawled along the short tunnel and continued scraping towards the wire fence, as his mates pretended to sell goods from the table above. The tunneller filled bags with earth which he hung under the table to be dispersed later. The Germans let them go so far before swooping.

Cigarettes were used for bartering. The number of cigarettes a man held was the difference between being rich and being a pauper. The Britons got by with their occasional packets of 200. The richest among the POWs were the French-Canadians who received parcels of 1,000 cigarettes, and could outbid anyone.

Kinnear received a letter from the Inland Revenue in 1943, telling him how much it intended extracting from his RAF pay which was building up in England. Poland was no tax haven. He didn't reply. By the time he was released, in April 1945, a substantial nest egg was waiting for him, and he had been promoted to warrant officer.

Conditions became more harsh when the RAF POWs had their hands tied up for twelve hours a day. It was a tit-for-tat measure taken after Germans had been captured and tied up, in breach of the Geneva Convention. The ropes led to prisoners developing poor circulation and chilblains and they were replaced by shackles. Anyone caught with loosened shackles was stood against a wall until 8.00pm, when the airmen were normally released. The shackles were easily opened with a sardine can key. Lookouts reported approaching Germans from the main compound gate or the barracks door. The word got through 'Jerry up!' and the shackles were snapped back together.

An electronic whizz made a valveless wireless set, using silver foil from inside cigarette tins. His aerial was a very fine wire running through the eaves of the barracks. It was never found. On 6 June 1944, D-Day, the prisoners had full details of the invasion by 2.00pm.

Food was awful, often weak soup made from sour vegetables grown outside the camp, fertilised by raw sewage removed from pits below the communal toilets. They each received daily, one-tenth of a loaf of black bread, usually so old and stale, green mould had to be scraped from it. Their meagre diet was topped up by infrequent Red Cross food parcels, often withheld from them as a punishment.

Occasionally there were opportunities to bait the Germans. Guards in smart uniforms marched along a roadway which ran beside the camp, singing the Horst-Wessel Lied. The RAF lads decided to give them moral support. About 200 of them marched inside the wire, singing Colonel Bogey, drowning the voices of the thirty guards forcing them, three days later, to change their route through the camp.

At 6.30am one icy morning in February 1945 the prisoners were told they were moving out at 8.00am. The men heard the rumble of Russian guns from the east as they marched through knee-deep snow towards Germany. Kinnear was in a group of 4,000 prisoners. They spent their first bitterly cold night in a stone quarry, out of the freezing wind. Kinnear slept soundly, but had left off his boots and took over an hour to get them back on his feet next morning. He didn't remove them for the next forty-three days, the time it took to march about 800 miles to Ziegenheim, south-east of Kassel. Nights were spent in the open or in barns. Food was scarce. Once Kinnear found and killed a hen and, with others, sucked the eggs out of its stomach. Only 1,000 remained of the original 4,000. Some had died, others were in hospital. Kinnear was thankful he had kept fit by walking round the compound every day at Lansdorf, even in the cruel depths of winter.

Once an American plane strafed the middle of the new camp. About fifty men, mainly Serbs, were killed. It was the morning of Good Friday when the guards disappeared from the towers and Kinnear joined two other prisoners walking into a village. Their stomachs rumbled hungrily when they saw an American Jeep unloading loaves of freshly baked white bread. A suspicious lieutenant questioned them closely. Kinnear said he was from Lancashire, described the countryside, and added, for good measure, 'You guys dropped one of your aircraft on the school at Freckleton, killed a lot of kids and you built them a community centre'. The lieutenant stared at Kinnear, then snapped an order: 'Give these boys everything they want'.

The rear gunner, who regarded himself as placid and unsentimental, could not prevent tears of joy streaming down his face when he saw the white cliffs of Dover from the American Dakota which landed him at Leighton Buzzard.

Alex Kinnear went to Gloucester to meet Peter Pitchford's family. He also met the wireless operator's attractive girlfriend, Iris May. They fell in love, were married in December 1945 and settled in Gloucestershire.

17

THE NIGHT OF THE SNIPE

Alan Lovett will never know if he would have survived the war had he qualified as a pilot. More certain is that his limited experience in tiny training aircraft was enough to save the lives of himself and his six crew mates in a Lancaster during a horrifying incident over Belgium on a cold, desperate night in March 1945.

But before that in 1943, Mesa, a small town near Phoenix, Arizona, seemed light years away from the grinding war in Europe. A long way too, from the damp, smog and shuffling traffic of Leytonstone in east London where Lovett had been born and raised. It was in cramped but proud London suburbs such as this where defiant civilians had regularly raised two fingers at Hitler's rampaging bombers in 1940 during the Battle of Britain, and said prayers for our dwindling fighter pilots, before flocking stoically into underground shelters.

Lovett made many discoveries at Falcon Field airfield in Mesa, where he started training as a pilot in May 1943. There was plenty of food and sunshine, with oranges growing in well tended groves. There was no rationing, wailing sirens, blackout, bombing, nor streets full of smouldering, pulverised houses. The distant war was intently followed in newspapers and on the wireless, almost as if it were an epic novel serialised day by day. American towns like Mesa, where many British aircrews trained, were brought closer to the conflict when families invited into their homes young boys in blue with strange, sometimes incomprehensible, accents.

The station at Mesa was run by the RAF and had American civilian instructors. Lovett gained solo flying experience on the Harvard monoplane and the PT17A Stearman biplane and after completing the initial course, went impulsively with two friends on a memorable week's leave to Hollywood, a glitzy fantasy town which has led to the downfall of many young men more worldly wise than Lovett. He made the mistake of falling in love with the wrong woman, neglecting his training and being removed from the pilots' course, which only had a few weeks to run.

Lovett was twenty-two, angry and ashamed by his stupidity, for he knew he had the ability to become a bomber pilot. Yet few young men training for war remained angry for long. Learning to kill is an absorbing and single-minded occupation. He went quickly to Canada where his anger was more easily turned against the Germans. He qualified as a bomb-aimer at Rivers, Manitoba, never dreaming that he would get the opportunity to fly again.

The end of the war was less than two months away on 23 March 1945, but no one knew that on 106 Squadron at Metheringham, Lincolnshire, where it was business as usual. Lovett says: 'We were told not to think too much about the future. They knew so many of us would still be killed, however near to the end of the conflict we might be.'

Late in the afternoon Lancaster crews were briefed to bomb Wesel that night. Among them was Sergeant Alan Lovett, bomb-aimer in T-Tommy, skippered by Flying Officer Keith Richardson, aged twenty-three, who had been born in Argentina, where his father was involved in railway construction, before the family moved to the less exciting environs of Luton.

Richardson had also trained in the USA, at Terrell, near Dallas. He was a man who knew his job well, even though this would be only his fifth operation. The pilot was always clear and precise in his instructions to the crew and never hesitated when faced with a difficult decision. Although he was friendly with them, off-duty Richardson preferred to seek out a quiet corner of the officers' mess. He trusted his crew, and they respected him as a good, responsible pilot. It was a bitingly cold night and Lovett had lent the pilot his warm and expensive Belgian cycle racing sweater.

The crew were a mixed bag, who blended into a successful team. Bomb-aimer Alan Lovett, now twenty-three, enjoyed the comradeship he found in the RAF. Before joining up in August 1942 he had worked as a junior draughtsman at a Tottenham factory building giant Horsa gliders. A keen athlete and racing cyclist, Lovett would still be coaching and competing, holding British records for the over-70s in long jump, triple jump, hurdles and pentathlon fifty years later.

Sergeant Maurice 'Mo' Young, twenty-two, the navigator, had gone straight from school in Toronto to aircrew training in the Royal Canadian Air Force. He didn't socialise much with the rest of the crew, preferring to stay in the sergeants' mess drinking and yarning with his Canadian pals. Unusually for a young man, he preferred shorts to beer, with a singular fondness for gin of which he sometimes drank too much. The crew knew, however, that their navigator would not let them down. However much stale booze splashed about inside him during a raid Young remained astonishingly cool and alert.

T-Tommy's wireless operator was Sergeant Alexander 'Sandy' Wilson, whose parents would not let him become an RAF apprentice at sixteen, but instead allowed him to join the Air Training Corps (ATC) and stay on a friend's 200-acre dairy farm during holidays from Cumnock Academy. The hard work and long hours on the farm helped this engaging Scot, with his dry sense of humour, to settle more easily into service life far from his Auchinleck, Ayrshire, home a few years later. An eye defect prevented him from being accepted on a pilots' course. At thirty-six, Flight engineer Reg Breeze had already worked as a wartime voluntary fireman and as a salesman before joining the RAF. The others often turned to the older man when needing to make the all-important decision about where they should spend a night off. Breeze, from Fulham, London, usually chose their favourite pub, The Albion, in Lincoln, less imposing than The Saracen's Head, where the officers gathered, but comfortable and friendly enough for their needs. When Joe Loss brought his orchestra to Lincoln's Drill Hall, the promise of good music for dancing, and girls, was an even greater attraction.

Sergeant Dick 'Tommy' Trinder, came from South Cerney, Gloucestershire. The mid-upper gunner met his wife-to-be Beryl at a mess dance and, like Wilson, became a headmaster after the war. Trinder continued his interest in flying by taking up gliding, but was killed in a flying accident in 1970.

Sergeant Jack Venables, aged twenty, the rear gunner, from Dagenham, Essex, was the quiet bloke of the crew. Lovett was best man in 1946 when Venables married Anne, who had been manageress of the station NAAFI.

On the morning of 23 March 1945, 106 Squadron aircrews gathered outside the flight offices for a group photograph. Much to their chagrin, Lovett and Wilson, as two of the squadron's shortest men, were instructed to sit in front of the others on the grass for a lighthearted start to the day.

The pilot and flight engineer of T-Tommy took the Lancaster up for air tests after it had been serviced. Apart from the pilot, its crew had only completed three operations, but none of them had been pushovers since their first sortie to the Wintershall synthetic oil refinery at Lutzkendorf. The others were to Bohlen and Hamburg. A total of thirty-one Lancasters had been lost on these three raids.

Their fourth trip was to be to Wesel, a small town on the Rhine north of Duisberg. Wesel was probably the most intensively bombed town of its size in Germany, with 97 per cent of its centre being flattened. The rubble of Wesel had become strategically important to the Allies for German troops based here were preventing the British Army from crossing the Rhine. Field Marshal Montgomery himself had asked for the support of Bomber Command to blast a way through for his men. The knowledge that Monty had actually requested their help put a proud spring into the step of the aircrews when they left the briefing room at Metheringham. In their eyes, Monty was almost as big a hero as Winston Churchill.

They took off at about 7.30pm, part of a force of 195 Lancasters and 23 Mosquitoes of 5 and 8 Groups. Earlier that day, 80 Lancasters from 3 Group had raided Wesel. This, the final raid of the war on the unfortunate German town, would be the coup de grâce.

Following the rule book, Lovett stood in the cockpit behind the pilot until the wheels had been retracted. The Lancaster had climbed almost to 1,000ft before he stepped down into the nose. Rear gunners rightly claimed they were most vulnerable to enemy attack, yet the bomb-aimer's lot was not always a happy one, especially when a

German fighter released a burst of cannon fire which raked the bomber's unprotected belly. Lovett lay prone on the thin metal floor. The spreadeagled bomb-aimer presented a target unseen by the gunners, but comprehensively exposed to their shells and bullets. Some fastidious bomb-aimers, with passionate girlfriends awaiting their return, carefully put their tin helmet beneath their genitals before a bombing run, believing that a man's balls were more important to save than his brain. Lovett was not one of them.

Air Ministry regulations did not offer suggestions for aircrews wishing to protect their genitalia on operations. The brasshats believed it was enough during training to show innocent young men a gruesome film of what could happen to their privates, infected by syphilis and gonorrhoea, after sleeping with loose women. It had not occurred to Air Ministry boffins that a protector, similar to the cricketer's box, would be a useful investment for keeping up the spirits of aircrews for whom a night with a good, or even a bad, woman was adequate compensation for risking life, limb and wedding tackle for his country.

Lovett carefully, lovingly, inspected his bomb-sight, the computer mechanism and bomb selector switches and other equipment necessary to direct the bombs accurately to their target. The fifteen 1,000lb bombs, fused to explode on impact, were selected to leave the bomb-bay in a set sequence to cause least disturbance to the balance of the aircraft. Lovett knew the terminal velocity (the forward movement of the bombs after they were released), and the angle of them dropping from 12,000ft, and set his bomb-sight accordingly. The wind velocity would be released to the Main Force by the Pathfinders about five minutes before they reached the target. Scores of bomb-aimers would then hastily adjust their sights to make sure bombs were not blown off course.

They were roaring towards Orford Ness when Lovett cocked the two .303 Browning machine-guns in the front turret. He would never need to fire the guns in action. The bombers passed in a steady stream over the east coast and headed for Holland. Lovett comments: 'We didn't all want to be bundled up together. Each airfield had its times worked out. Time was of the essence.'

It was not easy to marshal scores of aircraft through the night, making sure they went over the target one after the other, unleashing an almost constant destructive storm of bombs. Some bombers did stray off course, but it was important to remain within the stream. A lone bomber was easier prey for night fighters or flak. Collisions were a problem too, though some crews might complete an operation without seeing another bomber. It was galling to lose bombers in this way.

Lovett recalls: 'It was a quiet journey to the target and there was little flak over Wesel. There was no sign of any fighters. The actual raid was extremely easy. We were to bomb at 12,000ft.'

As T-Tommy drew near to the target Lovett took charge, the pilot reacting to the bomb-aimer's instructions. Ahead lay the outskirts of the devastated town of Wesel, the remaining population cringing into whatever shelter they could find. None of the war weary civilians, nor the wall of German troops could be seen by the bombers far above. The bomb-aimers could see only the blazing markers dropped by the Pathfinders. They drew nearer to the target. This moment belonged to Lovett. 'Left, left, steady, left, left, steady.' He watched the aiming point move beautifully towards the graticule. As it touched, Lovett pressed the tit (button). 'Bombs gone!' he cried, checking that no lights remained on his equipment to tell him that any bombs had been hung up, before closing the bomb-bay doors.

'That night it was not just another raid. We'd been told Monty couldn't carry on the advance without our help. In our small way we were writing history, being part of a definite push against the Germans. We banked to the south-east, then south-west over the Rhine to head into Belgium when safe to do so, descending to 3,000ft. By now, the Germans had been pushed back to the Rhine and we did not anticipate any problems on the way home.'

Belgium slept uneasily below as Sandy Wilson, his intercom switched off, waiting for the half-hourly check with Metheringham, discovered that the frequency to base had failed, although he could still receive Morse and broadcasts from civilian radio stations. He later learned that a valve had failed in his T/R 1155/1156 radio transmitter/receiver.

They had been briefed to fly home at 3,000ft. Had they been allowed to remain at their bombing height they would probably have had an untroubled return to Metheringham. Trouble was not on their minds as the bomber was cruising comfortably over Belgium, near Charleroi, until a 'missile' hurtled through the cockpit windscreen. The pilot was knocked unconscious and the Lancaster went into a steep dive. Lovett was checking his instruments when the voice of flight engineer Reg Breeze snapped urgently over the intercom: 'Come up here quick, Alan. Keith's been hit. He's unconscious.'

Lovett had seen neither flak nor fighter and he leaped, mystified, into the cockpit. He found Breeze, his face taut, hauling on a blood smeared control column and Keith Richardson slumped in his seat. A high-flying bird, a snipe, had burst through the windscreen and smashed, in a pulpy mass spiked with shards of perspex, into the face of the pilot, ricocheting on to the metal casing of the Gee box. A German fighter gunner would have been proud of such marksmanship. Warm blood from the injured pilot blew on to Lovett as he reached over Richardson's shoulder and, with Breeze, hauled the Lancaster back to level flight.

'Christ!' muttered Trinder in disbelief, climbing down from his turret to survey the carnage, 'it's a bloody bird!'. Wilson thought they had been hit by a shell when he heard the loud bang, shivering as a biting wind poured into the fuselage. He turned on his intercom, then found Trinder behind him anxiously searching for the spare parachute. He had accidentally pulled the ripcord and opened his own 'chute. Wilson handed

Trinder the spare then helped the gunner half carry and half drag the injured pilot to the bed, behind the main spar, where they tried to clean up Richardson's badly lacerated face.

Wilson remembers how the bird's remains were passed round for inspection. Surprisingly, the head and beak were intact. Richardson says, 'There was no panic in my last seconds of consciousness, I just accepted what had happened and that I was going to die'.

Lovett, the only other member of the crew with flying experience, slipped into the pilot's seat, perfunctorily wiping away some of the blood. He screwed up his eyes against the ferocious icy blast screaming through the 10in hole in the windscreen and gazed in dismay at the complex array of flickering lights, and banks of instruments and switches. England suddenly seemed as far away as the moon. The Harvard and Stearman training aircraft in which he had happily pottered about in the comfortably pampered warmth of a sunny sky above Arizona were Dinky toys compared to the great, growling Lancaster, now patiently awaiting his instructions.

'I automatically got into the pilot's seat because I knew I was the only one with experience and Reg had asked me to take over. There was nothing gallant about it. I had no thoughts whatsoever at first other than getting into the seat and stopping us hitting the ground. I must have gone through a phase of nervousness, but there was an awful lot to occupy my mind. I cannot explain how devastating and impossible it was to see ahead as the hole in the screen was in direct line and level with my face.'

It was difficult to think at first, to form a plan, to take charge in a cockpit which had somehow been transformed into a madhouse. The bomber switchbacked gently towards England as Lovett tried to put himself through an impossible instantaneous conversion course from tiny trainer to heavy bomber. At first, Lovett did not worry about flying, but he was scared about what had happened to the pilot and the extent of his injuries. Then he realised it was now his responsibility whether they all lived or died. A plan evolved. It was obvious the skipper needed urgent treatment. His life might depend on how quickly the medics could get to him. Clearly, Metheringham was too far away. Lovett reckoned they were about half-an-hour from Manston, Kent, the nearest emergency airfield. He continues:

'Until I got the feel of the controls I was a bit like a learner driver starting up a car and proceeding down the road in a series of unnerving kangaroo hops. The first thing I thought was "how do I work this ruddy radio?", then I asked Mo Young give me a new course for Manston. It occurred to me that we might not make it, but I had to put that thought aside. It was then I called up the crew, told them what had happened and that I was flying the Lancaster. They knew I had flying experience. They also knew that I had never flown anything bigger than an AT6A Harvard. I told them Keith was lying behind me unconscious.

'Halfway to Manston I began to get the hang of it and was able to steer and hold a level course. It wasn't easy at first. The hole in the windscreen made it a good deal more difficult. No one said they were scared. If they were, they kept very quiet about it. Jack, the rear gunner, did announce that his innards were taking a pounding, but he didn't leave the turret. He still had to do his duty. He never knew, even though we were comparatively safe over France in those days, whether a German night fighter might pick us up.'

Lovett squinted into the battering ram of freezing air which poured into the cockpit, clawing and pummelling his face. He tried to seal the hole with the first aid pack. The blast subsided gloriously, but only for a second, before the pack was sucked out into the darkness. There was no way to seal or patch up the hole. The wind wrenched off Lovett's flying goggles and flung them far back into the gloom of the fuselage. His task would have been difficult enough if Richardson had suddenly, quixotically, given him the controls of the Lancaster for circuits and bumps one sunny morning at Metheringham, but this absurd situation was not even covered by the Link Trainer. He could not look directly at the windscreen and relied on the instruments and assistance from the flight engineer whose name, Breeze, suddenly seemed singularly inappropriate. Reg Breeze stood helpfully to his right, away from the funnelled hurricane of air, continuing to offer words of encouragement.

As they droned nearer to Manston, Lovett thought of the procedure when a pilot approaches an airfield for a landing. He remembered landing solo wasn't too difficult with a monoplane. However, despite his imagination working in overdrive, it was not easy to equate landing a Harvard with a four-engine Lancaster. He had last flown a trainer in November 1943, a lifetime ago. He tried boosting his own morale by telling himself they would make it. None of them wanted to die because of a damned bird. Shot down by a bird, for God's sake. How would that look in their obituaries spread out in the local newspapers?

As they approached the English coast, Lovett called flying control at Manston, identified himself and explained his problems. He told them he preferred to land wheels up, if his crew agreed to bale out. Lovett said he would attempt a wheels up landing because, almost certainly, he would be unable to make a smooth touchdown on the runway at Manston. If the nose was too low they might turn over, catch fire and be trapped in the wreckage. There was the risk that nerves or bad luck might prevent him from touching down at all, just skimming across the airfield into the nearest building or hedge. A wheels-up landing would write off the propellers and the floor of the fuselage. There might be a fire, as the aircraft hurtled along the ground, but Lovett decided this way would give them a better chance of survival. He realised two other men should remain aboard the aircraft. The injured pilot would have to be strapped to the bed. It would be madness to push him through an escape hatch clipped to a parachute. He needed Breeze to help him land the bomber.

The crew, without exception, said they did not want to bale out and Manston warned him against landing with the wheels up. They could offer no further advice to an unqualified pilot attempting to touchdown, even though he could not see the airfield or runway lights through the broken windscreen. It became clear to Lovett it would be fiendishly difficult for him to land with the wheels down. Again he contacted Manston, asking for guidance. As he did so, Wilson routinely wound in the trailing wireless aerial.

Lovett made two circuits of the airfield at 1,000ft. 'It was damned difficult when I went round and started to nose down because I couldn't see properly. My eyes were full of water. Manston couldn't really help except warn me that our circuits were taking us over the sea.'

In a dramatic movie, Lovett would have circled the airfield, getting in the right position for the approach, keeping the bomber level, slowly descending for its main wheels to kiss the runway at the right spot at the same time at exactly 90mph, gently touching the brakes prior to turning on to the perimeter. This was a far cry from reality. Lovett again:

'We had sufficient fuel. I intended to continue circling at about 110mph until I'd memorised the area below to provide me with sufficient confidence to go in, feeling I'd make it as well as humanly possible, considering my vision was so seriously impaired. I went round a third time and Sandy came over the intercom to say in a worried voice that Keith was conscious and prepared to take them down.

'Sandy said: "Although Keith can't see very well, he can see as well as you under the circumstances. Keith thinks it would be for the best, considering his experience."'

Richardson remembers: 'I had been wakened by Tommy Trinder calling for a spare parachute and later realised Alan was having problems when we arrived at Manston. The navigator was reading out heights and speeds and I could tell that the circuits were erratic. What Alan had done was absolutely magnificent. He had flown straight and level to Manston, despite the howling gale coming through the windscreen.'

Richardson's anguished face was a mask of blood as he was helped into the pilot's seat and felt for the controls. Lovett stood on the right side of his skipper as a guide, glad at last to escape the rush of cold air and wipe his eyes free of tears. Breeze stood by in readiness to operate flaps, ailerons and throttles when necessary.

Lovett says: 'We had often said that Keith could land the Lanc with his eyes shut and that's exactly what he did. He flew the aircraft without really seeing the world outside.'

Richardson again: 'I couldn't see when I got back into my seat. I had to rely on people telling me what the heading was. It was surprising how easy it was, as if I could see all the instruments. When I was on the circuit I saw a blurred light. It was a searchlight and very useful, too.'

The pilot instinctively took control, coaxing the bomber twice round the airfield. Lovett and Breeze talked Richardson down, supplying a steady stream of information, altitude, speed and position then, as they entered the final phase: 'Left a bit! Hold it! Hold it! Steady!' The wheels came down as they approached the runway, and Wilson shot a red Very flare above them.

As they turned for the runway the others took up crash positions. In the rear turret, Jack Venables turned the turret to the port side and slightly loosened his sliding doors, ready for a quick getaway. Then he hung on and waited.

Lovett: 'Reg put down the flaps a degree on the final leg of the circuit. We were three-quarters of the way along the runway when Reg cut the throttles. Our landing speed, which should have been 90mph, was nearer 65. The aircraft stalled and we literally dropped in with a tremendous bang from about 30ft, tail wheel first and crawled along the runway to a stop.'

Venables recalls: 'It was a bit hairy. I was bounced about two or three times. When we stopped I got out pretty quickly.' Lovett and Breeze were thrown to the floor. They got up and saw an ambulance waiting under the port wing, with a fire engine nearby. The time was 12.50am.

The shock and stress was too much for Richardson who collapsed. His crew watched anxiously through a glass wall of the sick quarters at Manston as their skipper's face was cleaned up. The surgeon's first task was to slice up Lovett's prized sweater to reach the pilot's lacerated flesh. Afterwards, Richardson was flown to the RAF hospital at Halton, Buckinghamshire. He went on to serve thirty-six years in the RAF, rising to the rank of wing commander. He is now virtually blind in his right eye.

The abrupt landing at Manston punctured the bomber's tyres, damaged its fins and rudders, but it was repaired and flew again.

The task of writing a report about the incident was given to Lovett. Perhaps he understated the part he had played in the write-up which he handed to his squadron commander, Wing Commander Levis. In January 1946, months after Richardson had collected his DFC from the King at Buckingham Palace, Lovett was called into the adjutant's office at Metheringham, wondering if he was about to get a wigging for some forgotten misdemeanour. Instead, he was handed a small bronze oak leaf and a certificate, dated 1 January 1946, which had been received in the post. Belatedly, Lovett had been mentioned in despatches for the night he, a failed pilot, had brought the Lancaster and its crew safely home. Reg Breeze's important role on that return journey to Manston went unrewarded.

All bombers which took part in the last attack on Wesel returned safely to their bases. Only T-Tommy had come under sniper's fire at 3,000ft.

18

LOOPING THE LOOP
IN A LANCASTER

On the morning of 8 April 1943, the crew of Lancaster ED433 returned cheerfully to Waddington after a routine fighter affiliation sortie with a Spitfire, to be told they were on ops that night. They could not have known their morning's work in avoiding the exuberant pursuit by an RAF fighter aircraft over Lincolnshire would be of considerably less assistance to them above Germany, hours later, than their young pilot's earlier dogged work at ground level, on the station's Link Trainer.

The Lancaster, of 44 (Rhodesia) Squadron, had been armed with a camera gun which could be used later to assess whether the twisting, turning and diving bomber had escaped unscathed from the Spitfire. The pilot, twenty-one year-old Flying Officer Lawrence 'Pil' Pilgrim believed that, theoretically, it was almost impossible to be shot down by a German fighter which had guns fixed on its wings, if the bomber crew had a good pilot and two good wide awake gunners. 'They always had to get their nose in front of you because obviously, like clay pigeon shooting, you've got to aim just in front of the aircraft, otherwise you'd miss it. Therefore the steeper the dive, the steeper the turn you can put the Lanc into, the steeper the turn the fighter has got to make.'

His theory was well-supported by a lot of pilots, some of them only after they had been badly shot up by a fighter. There were plenty of pilots like Pilgrim who insisted on training for every possibility. There were also those unable to resist the lure of the bar instead of taking a bomber up and testing old and new theories of keeping out of trouble. This did not mean a large proportion of pilots and their crews were an indolent lot, rather that they grasped every opportunity to distance themselves from the pain and nastiness of war.

Pilgrim enjoyed exercises on the Link Trainer, considered a chore by many pilots. He believed they were vitally important, as most of the operational flying was done at night. The Link was a device which allowed blind flying to be taught and practised on the ground. It had an enclosed cockpit, equipped with all the normal controls and instruments of an aeroplane. Pilgrim doggedly worked out tests, to add interest to run-of-the-mill exercises. He put himself at, say, 20,000ft, then found the aerodrome and landed, using only the SABS (Stabilised Automatic Bomb Sight) system.

Pilgrim also practised exercises with the gyros toppled, using only the basic instruments of turn and bank indicator, airspeed indicator and altimeter. 'It was probably these exercises which enabled me to cope on the Duisberg raid,' he comments.

Pilgrim was slim, blue-eyed, with fair hair already starting to recede, standing about 5ft 7in, weighing a trim 10st 3lb. He was fit, earnest, but very laid back. Nothing made him raise his voice, lose his temper, or self-control. He was also a man who recognised there were definite advantages in flying by the book, survival being one of them. Discipline and training were rated very highly by Pilgrim, who was born and brought up in Islington, east London. An articled clerk to an accountant before joining up in February 1941, Pilgrim was a hard worker with ambitions which did not include dying for his country, so he trained resolutely to be a survivor.

His ability to detach himself from the war when he was not flying helped him develop an easy going manner, which lent even greater resolve to his already iron clad nerves rather than weakening them. He didn't take chances, but had a young man's clear-headed ability to make split second decisions.

As far as he was concerned, he had an important job which was to get into an aeroplane and accurately bomb the enemy. When Pilgrim came back to the airfield, the war was over until he was told he was on operations again. He never allowed the war to worry him between ops.

The pilot could only be provoked if any of his crew were guilty of not doing a first class job on a raid. Early on their tour, bomb-aimer Jack Williams released the bombs too early on a target. Pilgrim believed they had another minute to run and told him so. Williams replied that the flak was getting close and he thought he'd better get rid of the bombs. Pilgrim said that was not on and gave him a wigging over the intercom. The pilot's home truths had an effect. He was to later head the squadron list for aiming point photographs – which meant his bombs hit the targets more accurately than any other aircrew.

Everyone had his own way of passing the long hours before taking off on a bombing operation. Some tried to absorb themselves in books or newspapers. Others listened to records or the wireless, played cards or wrote letters home, then worried whether to drop them into a post box or leave them on their bed with a hastily scribbled request for last messages to be sent on if they didn't come back from a raid.

Pilgrim once lent a wireless operator friend five shillings just before a trip. The pal returned safely that night and was talking in his room with Pilgrim when he suddenly said, 'Ah, I won't need that again,' and screwed up a note which admitted that he owed the pilot five shillings.

Pilgrim was more positive than that. He never considered the possibility of not coming back and saw no reason to waste valuable time and energy preparing for his own demise before each operation. Such a grisly and negative attitude, he thought, opened up all kinds of emotional weaknesses, blunted a man's resolve and thinking, leaving tiny gaps in his concentration through which mistakes could slip, turning a problem into a crisis, a successful aircrew into a dead one.

He enjoyed a good lunch in the mess that day before finding a comfortable chair and going to sleep. Thoroughly rested, an hour or two later, Pilgrim stretched, ambled outside and, fully relaxed, scrounged a lift in a van to the Lancaster at dispersal, and made sure the gunners had spent some time going over the bomber to check that it was in first class condition.

The gunners were contrasting types. Roland 'Keth' Kethro had the berth in the rear turret. A very dapper, God's gift to women type, he had a thin Ronald Colman moustache and a mass of wavy hair brushed back. His appeal to women was enthusiastically reciprocated. Pilgrim was to become best man at Kethro's wedding at the end of the war.

'Shorty' Short in the mid-upper turret was a bit of a loner, a Geordie, who spent a lot of his free time on camp, only occasionally going out with Pilgrim and the others into Lincoln for a pub crawl to The Crown and The Falcon. The pilot believed the gunner had a bit of an inferiority complex and found it difficult to mix socially with an officer. Indeed, not all officers even contemplated drinking with anyone who was non-commissioned, even if they regularly spent hours shut up in a bomber facing death together.

Pilgrim's crew – all flight sergeants – were his mates. They might have eaten and slept in different messes, but on nights off they went out as a group, at least five of them did. Wireless operator Jerry Fanning was even more of a loner than Short. He was an efficient operator, but rarely mixed socially with the crew and was something of a mystery man. The others knew nothing of his background, except that he was British.

The only non-Briton aboard was Canadian mining engineer 'Pop' Benner, the Lancaster's navigator. A craggy-faced man of thirty-five, he could be called nothing else but 'Pop'. Almost old enough to be the others' father, they respected his maturity and calming influence. Pop would eventually marry a WAAF. Of Pop, Pilgrim recalls: 'I believe he was probably the bravest of all the crew because there was no doubt that sometimes during our tour he did get nervous, perhaps because of his age. He probably appreciated the stupidity of it all more than the rest of us.'

Benner constantly refused to leave the sanctuary of his navigator's position during an op to inspect the violent world outside the Lancaster and look down into a burning target. Leaving his position spelled danger and possible annihilation. He had the curiously naive belief that when he had pulled the black curtains across his cramped office, he was safe, nothing could harm him – his ticket back to base was assured.

It was only on their thirtieth and last operation together as a crew, to Mannheim, at the end of their tour, when the others determined that Pop should join them at one of the windows. They pulled open his curtain and almost dragged the protesting navigator out to see the burning city. He peered down, saw the spreading mass of flames and small bursts of flak, gasped a horrified 'Christ!' and scuttled back behind his curtain.

Jack Skilton was flight engineer and an ex-Halton brat (apprentice). London-born, he had been in the RAF since before the war, shortly after leaving school. Of a similar height to Pilgrim, he was slightly heavier with his fondness for good food edging him towards tubbiness. He had a great feeling for the ridiculousness of a situation, and held little respect for rank.

Bomb-aimer Jack Williams was a handsome blond who, like Kethro, never had any trouble in finding a girlfriend.

They all had a good sense of humour. It would have been difficult for anyone to fight a war without humour, which could be used in large dollops to dilute apprehension, even fear. When they were flying the humour was put away and they became deadly serious.

Half-an-hour before take-off the crew were dropped off by bus at dispersal and went through the normal intensive checks after walking round the Lancaster, making sure everything was in order. They checked for tyre creep, that the ailerons and elevators were free-moving and in the right direction and the pitot head cover had been removed. The pitot head led to the airspeed indicator in the cockpit. If the cover was not removed the pilot could only guess at his air speed. If a car breaks down, it can be stopped, the bonnet lifted and the engine inspected. If a Lancaster's engine stopped during a flight over Germany, the flight engineer couldn't walk across a wing and fix it, therefore the pre-flight checks were vital.

The night was closing in when the squadron's Lancasters lifted off. By the time they had crossed the coast near Southwold, linked up with nearly 400 other bombers, reached the North Sea and climbed to 20,000ft, their off-duty mates back at Waddington would have got through a satisfying amount of beer. They thought about that, fleetingly, enviously, and then concentrated on staying alive.

There was flak about over Germany, but nothing unusual. Lancaster ED433 would not tangle with a fighter on this trip, but the aircrew took no chances. Pilgrim talked to his crew every few minutes, making sure they were alert and sweeping the sky. Occasionally he warned both gunners that he was about to bank very steeply, so they could see underneath the aircraft. 'Do a sweep under the aircraft Shorty and Keth, I'm now banking to the left... I'm now banking right.' He always called his crew by their nicknames.

'Officially it was wrong and I admit it was rather peculiar. Most of the squadron commanders and station commanders were pre-war officers. Officers were God and the airmen just serfs, cannon fodder. The commanders could not understand how you could have discipline by calling your gunners Willy or Skilly or whatever. But I did. I had no trouble with my bods. They knew that when we were out on a pub crawl, it was just a fun night, but once we'd got into the aeroplane, whatever I said, they did without question.'

Pilgrim's mind ranged busily ahead over the cloud-shrouded hills and valleys, where thousands of disillusioned and frightened German civilians, cowered in cellars and bunkers. Soon they would reach their target of Duisberg in the Ruhr, where they would have to bomb into a forecast 10/10ths cloud, onto target indicators dropped by the Pathfinders. He preferred to bomb in moonlight. There was a greater danger from fighters, flak and searchlights, but he liked to see where he was going. It was a fifty-fifty situation. Cloud cover made the bombers safer from enemy fighters and searchlights, but increased the chance of them colliding with one of their own aeroplanes.

Fifteen miles short of Duisberg they didn't see the other bomber, clawing through the thick cloud, no more than 200yds ahead of them. They were suddenly enveloped by a huge blinding white flash as the leading Lancaster, with a full bomb and fuel load, received a direct hit and blew apart, instantly reducing its young seven-man crew to fried droplets of meat and bone.

The incident registered in Pilgrim's brain, no more than that. The moment swiftly passed, the stark image of death wiped deliberately from the minds of the pilot and his crew. There was no time to mourn for their incinerated comrades. Mourning interfered with concentration, which needed to be unwavering and needle sharp. Pilgrim says:

'Aeroplanes were frequently lost like this. Sad, but it was one of those things. Nothing seemed extraordinary about it. In that fraction of a second there was no reason to think the incident would involve us at all, there had been no great turbulence from the exploding Lancaster.

'I realised something was wrong when I no longer had control of the aircraft. I had lost all my instruments which were controlled by the gyros, which had toppled, including the artificial horizon. I was left with the basic pressure instruments: the turn and bank indicator, the air speed indicator and an altimeter.'

The aircraft had slid inexorably into the vacuum caused by the exploding Lancaster, turning over without the crew being aware of what was happening. 'I was suddenly hanging upside-down from my straps and Skilly, my flight engineer, who had been standing up watching the instruments, was floundering about on the ceiling. The Lancaster was flying on its back. It was almost instantaneous, as if we'd been picked up by a giant hand and turned over.'

A wavering cry came over the intercom from Kethro, isolated in his rear turret 69ft behind the nose: 'Get rid of the sodding bombs!' Pilgrim, gritting his teeth as he wrestled with the controls, snapped: 'Don't be a bloody fool Keth, they're on the roof.' It is possible Kethro did not know the bomber had turned over, although he would have been subjected to terrific G-forces as his turret was whipped round.

Sitting behind Pilgrim, hidden by the magic folds of his black curtain, navigator Pop Benner, whose precious instruments, maps and charts had all cascaded off his table on to the floor, murmured unruffled encouragement into the intercom, 'Steady boy, steady'. Navigator and wireless operator clung to their screwed-down tables. The startled bomb-aimer was thrown about violently in the nose, wondering what was happening.

Thirty tons of inverted Lancaster, including a 4,000lb Cookie, together with twelve cans of incendiaries, ammunition for the Browning machine guns and a seven-man crew, began to dive at high speed, the four Rolls-Royce Merlin engines blaring. Pilgrim gritted his teeth.

'I was relaxed. This was no time to get worried. Whatever is happening to you, however horrendous it appears, getting het up and into a state doesn't help at all. It just makes the position worse. As soon as I was upside-down and realised I had got to pull the stick back to come down in half-a-loop, I knew I'd got to knock my speed off. I didn't want to come down with full power. I had to get the aeroplane back into a flying position so I could control it. As far as I was concerned, I had no real worries because I had plenty to do.'

It took Pilgrim a little longer to sort out his flying position with the instruments that were still working. He was unable to look at the image of the little aeroplane on the artificial horizon, getting it level, but which was no longer working.

'The speed was a bit haywire. You look at the altimeter and if that's going down like the clappers, you know that you're in a dive. If it's going up, you know you're climbing. It does take a little longer to sort out your flying position with only those instruments than if you've got the little aeroplane to balance yourself in.

'At that time, and even immediately afterwards, there was no great trauma or any heart pumping as far as I was concerned. I think that was mainly because of the position I was in having only those three instruments. I had worked on this situation a number of times with the Link Trainer.

'I was amazed that everyone stayed with me. No one panicked. There was a shout to get rid of the bombs, but just imagine the speed with which the rear gunner was whipped round, then having nothing to do except sit there worrying about what the hell was going on. At least I knew what was happening.'

Pilgrim rapped out an order to his engineer as the Lancaster screamed through 18,000ft at nearly 300mph. 'Close the throttles Skilly, quick!' But the pilot had overlooked the impossibility of the engineer carrying out such a task. Skilton was still squirming helplessly on the Lancaster's metal ceiling.

Bombers passed in undisturbed streams overhead. If they had seen the solitary Lancaster below, fighting for its life, there was nothing any of them could have done to help, except offer a brief prayer, be thankful it was another aircrew's problem and mutter a terminal 'poor bastards!'.

Pilgrim, strapped into his seat, adapted quickly to the upside-down controls. He began pulling back on the control column to carry out a half-loop, painfully aware as he did so that such a manoeuvre under power and with a full bomb load ran the risk of over-stressing the airframe to such an extent they would probably have to bale out. But he had not reckoned on the incredible strength built into the Avro Lancaster.

As soon as the bomber bottomed out of the loop, Skilton hit the deck, reached for the throttles and reduced power, but by then Pilgrim had regained control and they were climbing rapidly towards a full loop. Pilgrim called for the extra power demanded by their changed circumstances, but this was difficult because Skilton was on his way back to the roof. Fortunately, the engineer managed to hang on to the throttles, Pilgrim got the power he needed and the Lancaster ponderously returned to an even keel at 6,000ft, having executed one-and-a-half loops.

The pilot quickly checked to make sure everyone was in one piece, speaking to them in turn. 'Are you okay? Are you serviceable?' Everyone was except the gunners, whose ammunition had fallen from the trays and was scattered all over the floor. Pilgrim says:

'Understandably, at night with a limited instrument panel, our recovery to some-thing approaching normal flight was preceded by a few unsteady turns, dives and climbs. Eventually we settled down and I took stock, prior to deciding our next course of action.

'Although these events had taken but a minute or two, to me it had seemed like an eternity. It was a bit hairy. Fortunately, I had been actively engaged throughout, but my crew had been forced to observe helplessly and to this day I am both surprised and relieved that they didn't bale out at the first opportunity.

'We had come down at a hell of a rate. The needle of the speedometer had gone twice round the clock. I estimated that we'd touched 350mph, a speed unheard of in those days for a bomber. We were obviously damaged, although I didn't know to what extent. The options were to turn immediately for home or continue. I chose the latter course. A solo transit home was a dubious proposition at the best of times. In a damaged aircraft that was unable to take evading action, it would be suicide.

'In any case my gunners were unable to fire since the contents of the ammunition trays – and for that matter the Elsan toilet – were distributed throughout the fuselage. We stank like polecats. To make matters worse, the navigator's charts and instruments had disappeared, so he was unable to calculate any new route home.'

The Lancaster's engines coughed a bit as they pressed on towards Duisberg. The aeroplane did not respond as readily to the controls. Instead of tripping along with the spirited gait of a sprightly young maiden, she was behaving more like an arthritic old woman, sluggish, crabby and unsure of herself. She became even more difficult with the bomb doors open and, at slower speed, displayed a disconcerting readiness to stall.

There may have been the odd sigh of relief, but the crew quickly settled to their tasks as they rapidly came upon the target. The navigator, unable to find all his instru-ments, had to make do with a pencil and a chart.

They were still at 6,000ft. There had been no time to regain height. There was a chance they might be hit by bombers overhead. After what they had just experienced, it was a risk they were prepared to take. There were no problems from flak or fighters on the bomb run but the Lancaster, not surprisingly, was flying uncertainly and the bombing was not as accurate as they would have normally expected. The cookie was released first, followed by the incendiaries, timed to go off and set fire to the debris. Pilgrim remembers: 'We bombed below the cloud cover and were the only crew to see the target that night. It was a bad height to be, we were vulnerable to the ack-ack guns and stood a good chance of being bombed from above, but we were so damned relieved to be flying level that we didn't think too much about that.'

As they headed for home they worried that the wings might drop off after the fearful stress they had endured, but as each minute took them nearer to Waddington and the bomber remained intact, their confidence grew and they thought, fingers crossed, that they would make it. Pilgrim eased the tortured, stumbling Lancaster very gradually up to 16,000ft at 100 to 200ft a minute, instead of the normal 400.

'We didn't run into any great ack-ack or fighters. If we'd been attacked by fighters I wouldn't have been worried, but I might have been a bit doubtful whether the aircraft could have stood up to a lot of corkscrewing. I came back at about 160mph, 30 or 40kts slower than I would have normally.

'I didn't have a very good landing. It was a safe one, but not the nice smooth landing I liked. It proved to be quite difficult, although as we came in I thought that as we'd got this far it would be a normal landing. Of course, when I levelled out and cut the throttles the Lanc just fell out of the sky. It was only a couple of feet from the ground. It didn't matter very much, but you do bounce a bit. We weren't very sweet smelling when we got out, but we were alive.'

The crews of nineteen other bombers who did not return that night were less lucky.

Pilgrim and his navigator Pop Benner were each awarded the DFC for the parts they played on the night their bomber looped the loop. The Lancaster, the tops of its wings very badly rippled, was withdrawn from service for repair. It completed a few more operations before being lost on 3 October 1943, over Kassel.

19

REAR GUNNER'S TWO AMAZING ESCAPES

26 November 1944. It had been a filthy day. Winter was on the march, bringing to south Lincolnshire a dreary mixture of cold and damp that sneaked into the bones and dragged at the spirits. Rear gunner Sergeant Ricky Dyson, twenty-six, had missed two trips with his regular crew because of a badly sprained ankle and had been picked as a spare bod to fly with Flight Sergeant Doug Presland, replacing the normal gunner, Sergeant Porky Taylor, who was recovering from a head wound sustained during a raid on Duisberg.

They were in 189 Squadron, which had joined 49 Squadron at Fulbeck on 2 November, only a fortnight after being formed at Bardney. Dyson found that broad-shouldered Presland, twenty-two, from Woodford Green, Essex, was a genial, confident pilot with a cheerful crew who quickly made the slightly-built Dyson welcome.

Windsor-born Dyson had been a junior salesman in a Maidenhead furniture shop before the war and joined the RAF in December, 1935, at the age of seventeen. To his disappointment, he failed a wireless operator's course the following year at Cranwell and reverted to aircraftsman second class/general duties, the lowest form of human life in the RAF. Despite this setback, Dyson was a lucky man. Stationed in France with 59 Squadron, he survived his first brush with death at the time of Dunkirk. Retreating from Arras, his column was strafed by German aircraft with bombs and machine-gun fire. Dyson was unhurt.

While stationed at Manston, Kent, a direct hit from a German bomb killed everyone inside an air-raid shelter. Five yards away, Dyson was thrown across his billet by the blast, sustaining minor cuts from broken glass.

In the autumn of 1943, Dyson responded eagerly to an Air Ministry recruitment drive as aircrew losses mounted and he qualified as an air gunner at Stormy Down in South Wales. He joined Presland's crew on the night it was part of a force of 270 Lancasters and eight Mosquitoes from 5 Group, briefed to attack Munich. It was Presland's seventh operation, Dyson's ninth.

The airfield was overcast when they climbed into Lancaster PB745, Q-Queenie, at dispersal. When they took off at 11.53pm, the weather had closed in and the bomber was soon swallowed up by a thick layer of low cloud. The pilot steered on a course for Beachy Head, Sussex. Dyson peered out of his turret but could see nothing. He heard

Bayliss the engineer, over the intercom, calmly calling out the air speed as they gained height to about 1,000ft. Then fate took over.

Presland recalls: 'I thought we had hit something, or something had hit us underneath as we were climbing. There was a definite scraping noise. Another bomber did crash nearby that night. I told the crew to brace themselves for a crash.'

The bomber made a climbing turn and Dyson squinted anxiously into the blackness. Alarmed to see trees and hedges whizzing past 100ft below, he was about to cry out a warning to the pilot when the Lancaster smashed, with a dull thud, into the side of a hill. They had been airborne eleven minutes.

The thirty-ton Lancaster rampaged across a lane and a field, smashing through hedges, with a mad crunching, shrieking and gouging, shuddering from nose to tail. A series of loud bangs was followed by a blinding flash which lit up the countryside. An awesome explosion ripped the bomber apart, then silence.

Dyson was struck briefly unconscious. He came to and discovered the rear turret was attached to a piece of fuselage which had been hurled 50yds clear of the main wreckage. A fire roared behind him. The heat was intense, and the turret doors had jammed. He swiftly got out of his boiling and cumbersome yellow Taylor flying suit, took an axe from its clamps on the turret wall and tried to smash the clear vision panel. The turret was so cramped he could only chip at the heavy duty perspex, but the flames drawing nearer drove him to greater efforts, as he became afraid of suffocating before he could escape.

He made a small opening and crawled agonisingly through, over the four buckled Browning machine-guns and fell clumsily to the ground. He landed on his back, scrambled to his feet and ran petrified into the darkness as fire began consuming the rear turret.

The pilot, Doug Presland, his seat disintegrated, had been thrown half out of the aircraft, his open parachute billowing around him in the wind. As Presland lay there, gathering his senses, the aircraft in flames, he heard a shout from the injured mid-upper gunner, Sergeant Jock Fender. Presland called back, 'I'll come and help!'. He tried to get up but couldn't move. Looking down at his legs he yelled. 'Sorry Jock, I can't make it!' Presland's left leg had been torn off at the knee. The bloody stump shone gruesomely in the flames. The rest of his leg was lying somewhere in the blazing aircraft. His right leg and left wrist were broken, and he was suffering from third degree burns.

Dyson's frantic gallop across the field ended when he plunged headlong into a hedge. He looked back, gaping at an unbelievable sight. The whole field seemed to be covered with burning wreckage. A series of explosions sent showers of debris rocketing into the sky. He realised, with horror, that somewhere in that inferno was the rest of the crew. The Lancaster had been fully laden with fuel for the return journey to Munich and carried a mixed load, including high explosives, cluster bombs and incendiaries.

No one heard his involuntary cry of anguish as he raced back to the main part of the burning wreckage. As he got nearer he heard groans and cries for help. He found some of the crew sprawled on the ground and dashed from one to another, trying to comfort them until the rescue services arrived.

The pilot was trapped in the wall of the burning fuselage, which had been part of the main cockpit, now crushed to waist height. Feeling no pain, he was in danger of being roasted alive. Dyson scrambled in beside him as exploding bombs, fuel tanks, ammunition, incendiaries and oxygen cylinders rent the night sky. Flaming debris continued to shoot high into the air as he pulled a piece of burning metal out of Presland's body. The heat began to suck air from the gunner's lungs as he fought to move blazing wreckage off the pilot, and dragged him out of the aircraft and into the field, where he thought his skipper would be safe. Yet nowhere within hundreds of yards of the bomber was safe, as shrapnel from fragmented bomb cases and exploding ammunition whizzed and whistled through the air in all directions.

The rear gunner pulled the bomb-aimer, little dark-haired Irishman, Sergeant Billy McClune, from the wreckage, then turned to the navigator, twenty-one year-old Sergeant Alan Probert, 15yds away. His clothes were on fire and Dyson beat out the flames with his bare hands. It was all for nothing. An incendiary bomb had burned through Probert's clothing and into his stomach. He died later that night. Probert, from Merseyside, had spoken fluent German and occasionally enjoyed scaring the rest of the crew with his best Luftwaffe fighter pilot impressions over the intercom.

Three other members of the crew also died from appalling injuries: bomb-aimer Billy McClune, the handsome Canadian wireless operator Sergeant Owen Venning, and Sergeant Dennis Bayliss, the flight engineer from Birmingham. Dyson ran desperately through the blazing wreckage, shocked and panic-stricken, shouting for help. Some bodies were engulfed in flames. He tried to put out the flames with his hands, but when he succeeded, it was to find the man was already dead from other injuries.

Jock Fender, the mid-upper gunner, was trapped crushed and unconscious in his turret. His back and legs were rammed hard against the twisted metal. His head was embedded in the electrical junction box in the roof. Dyson, by now suffering from badly burned hands, ignored the gnawing pain and tried in vain to release him. As he dragged at the battered turret rescue vehicles arrived, but they halted 200yds away until the explosions subsided. Fender was later cut free by firemen, still alive, but with a fractured skull and both femurs broken by the butts of the Browning machine guns. Fender's turret, like Dyson's, had been thrown clear of the main wreckage. It wasn't until days later that Dyson realised how lucky he was to escape serious injury.

'This terrible scene, with the pungent and awful smell of burning flesh, cordite and petrol, together with the pall of acrid smoke, is still unforgettable and remains a constant reminder of my own miraculous escape and survival. I have never been able to obliterate the horror of that night from my mind.'

Presland, weak from loss of blood, saw American soldiers helping at the scene, and got one of them to put a tourniquet on the stump of his left leg.

The field in which Q-Queenie had crashed was in farming country on the Lincolnshire and Leicestershire border, between the small villages of Saltby and Croxton Kerrial. Customers at The Nag's Head and The Peacock still talk about the crash for which there has not been an official explanation.

The three survivors were taken to hospital. Presland showed great courage in the ambulance. He managed to crack jokes, especially about the welfare of his moustache, but he was distressed about the fate of other members of his crew. With them was Dennis Bayliss, who had blood on his face. Presland remembers, 'Ricky and I argued about his condition. I was sure Dennis was dead, but Ricky kept saying he was only unconscious. I'm sure he did this to save my feelings.'

Tough and fit, despite his injury, Presland persuaded the nursing staff to take him to the camp cinema three weeks after the crash. Following his discharge from the RAF, Presland became a teacher.

Fender spent a long time in hospital where his skull was fitted with a metal plate. He married the Rauceby Hospital ward sister who helped look after him.

Dyson received a fortnight of treatment for burns to his face and hands, then was sent home on leave. Three weeks later, he returned to 189 Squadron at Fulbeck and resumed duties with his regular crew, skippered by Flying Officer Desmond 'Ned' Kelly, an Australian, supporting Allied troops in France by day and by night, hitting targets in the heart of Germany.

It was not until the war in Europe was over that Dyson knew he had been awarded the George Medal for bravery. The citation reads: 'Sergeant Dyson showed outstanding gallantry by his persistent efforts to help his comrades and undoubtedly saved the life of his pilot.'

Ned Kelly, from Queensland, was at the controls of Lancaster PB840, K-King, on the night of 2 February 1945, when nineteen bombers from 189 Squadron were part of the force of 250 Lancasters and eleven Mosquitoes of 5 Group to attack railway yards and factories at the industrial city of Karlsruhe, capital of Baden. Take-off was twice delayed because of bad weather. Kelly, twenty-one, freckle-faced, with a finely tuned sense of humour looked down at Fulbeck for the last time. Of Kelly, Dyson says 'Your first impression of Ned was that he was someone you could trust and confide in'.

Flying Officer Roger Webb, twenty-eight, a Canadian, had replaced their regular navigator, Flight Sergeant John Turkentine, who was suffering from an ear infection. Turkentine would be killed on a subsequent operation.

Sergeant Jack Howarth, twenty-seven, the balding flight engineer, was reliable, steady and good at his job. His wife Mary was expecting their first child. Wireless operator Warrant Officer Jimmy Grubb, twenty-two, a New Zealander, short and stocky, was married to a girl from Nottingham.

Flight Sergeant Tony James, twenty-one, the good looking bomb-aimer, came from Dover. An ex-Sunday School teacher, he enjoyed nature, poetry, dancing and girls. Flight Sergeant Frank Fox, twenty-one, was deputising for the regular mid-upper gunner, Sergeant Frank Cowlishaw, twenty, who had a bad cold and sinus problems. Fox had a girlfriend he met after a forced landing at Bottesford, Nottinghamshire. His brother Clifford, a twenty-two year-old wireless operator/air gunner with 635 Squadron, had been killed on an operation against Nuremberg the previous March.

Dyson, on his fourteenth bombing trip, had mixed feelings about the rear turret.

'As far as enemy action was concerned, you were in a very vulnerable position. Most fighter attacks came from the rear where we were sitting. My job was to spot enemy aircraft and instruct the skipper to corkscrew out of the line of fire until it was safe to carry on. When you dive, the enemy fighter goes over the top of you, then he has to turn and you're turning and climbing. If he comes at you again, you dive. The G-force is terrific at the moment of turning at the bottom of the dive. The rear gunner is facing the rear, hanging on to his machine guns. The whole idea is to evolve a manoeuvre whereby he is going beneath or over the top of you, at an angle where he can't fire at you.

'Yes, we were vulnerable; on the other hand, a rear gunner sat on a platform held by a few bolts. The turret often broke off after an impact with the ground. That saved my life when we crashed into the hill.'

Even so, casualties among rear gunners were high and the Air Ministry asked the Irvine Parachute Company, of Letchworth, Hertfordshire, to design a special harness for rear gunners and adapt a parachute which they could sit on like a cushion. Rear gunners had died after their turret jammed, leaving them unable to reach their parachutes stored in the fuselage behind the turret doors.

Before an op Dyson's feelings were a strange mixture of exhilaration when he knew where the target was, and sheer funk of not knowing whether he would be back to sleep in the same bed he had climbed into the night before.

'This feeling of fear lasted after you'd had your briefing and probably during the meal you had before going to the flights. Once you went to the flights, where the aircraft was standing, you chatted among yourselves, smoking endless cigarettes, until it was time to board the aircraft. There was a terrible sinking feeling in your stomach before doing your inspections and, whatever the weather, I sweated in my warm flying suit, but once you were aboard there were things to do and, in a moment, the fear seemed to disappear.'

They left Fulbeck at 8.00pm. The weather was much worse than the met officers' forecast and Kelly's aircraft experienced severe icing and electrical storms over France. Enemy fighters were busy that night, for Bomber Command had despatched over 1,051 aircraft to attack Wiesbaden, Wanne-Eickel and Karlsruhe.

When they reached the target area at between 17,000 and 18,000ft, K-King was uncomfortably sandwiched between two layers of cloud – black stuff below, obscuring the target, and above, formations of altostratus through which the moon shone, making them a sitting target for German fighters.

They bombed on coloured sky markers, which together with chandelier flares, glowed through the cloud. Bomb-aimer James reported routinely 'Bombs gone, skipper'. The aircraft lifted and they made a climbing turn to starboard, away from the target area. Both gunners rotated their turrets, searching the sky for fighters.

Suddenly, a looming black mass blocked Dyson's vision in the rear turret. There was a blinding white flash, which lit up the sky, followed by a devastating explosion. A blast of searing heat surged through the fuselage and he saw the Browning machine-guns turning white hot and twisting into a bizarre knot. The turret disintegrated and he was shot upwards like a human cannonball into the cold night air. It was a moment of total unreality. The gunner felt his head and neck being brutally rammed into his stomach, while his legs were thrust upwards. It was if a giant hand was trying to cram him into a small container. He thought, 'So this is what it's like to die,' before blacking out. He came-to whirling around like a twig in the violent shock waves of the explosion. He thanked God for his new parachute, then he was somersaulting earthwards. Dyson, in a fearful panic, reached for his parachute pack which, thankfully, was dragging behind him.

'I felt for the D-ring release on my harness and pulled until the ring and wire attachment came free in my hand. I prayed that the pack itself was not burned or in some way damaged, and for an awful moment thought it was not going to open. Then there was a terrific jerk, I looked up and with great relief saw the huge canopy burst open above me. My brain was now clear and I was soon in an upright position with my hands grasping the parachute guide lines with which I was able to steer. It was at that moment that the full horror of what had happened came over me.'

He saw in the sky what appeared to be a huge rectangular box-like inferno, burning debris being flung from it in a turbulent cascade of flames and sparks, resembling a great Catherine wheel. Dyson realised it was K-King, probably carrying the bodies of some of his friends.

Dyson discovered much later that his aircraft had been struck by another Lancaster. What he had seen was the two Lancasters, shorn of their wings, locked in a grotesque embrace as they plunged earthwards. K-King crashed between the villages of Unterowisheim and Oberowisheim. The bulk of the other Lancaster, ME298:B, came down closer to Unterowisheim, but wreckage from the two aircraft was spread over a wide area.

Two other men survived the mid-air collision. They were the navigator Flight Sergeant Jack Willcocks, and nineteen-year-old flight engineer Charlie Gordon, both aboard Lancaster ME298:B, which was piloted by Australian Flying Officer Dick Oliver. Oliver's aircraft had been hit by flak over Karlsruhe and later corkscrewed to avoid a fighter. The blazing port inner engine would not feather and the pilot, who had lost contact with the rear gunner, gave the order to bale out.

Gordon helped the bomb-aimer, Warrant Officer John 'Bluey' Johnstone, to open the nose hatch. Johnstone indicated to Gordon and Willcocks to go. The young engineer went first, followed by Willcocks, both believing the pilot and bomb-aimer would follow. Gordon, a Scot, remembers: 'They didn't leave and that will always be a matter of painful conjecture. A short time after baling out, I was aware of aircraft noise, explosions and a long period of eerie silence before landing in a pine tree near the small village of Lanshausen.'

Sergeant Gordon and Willcocks, from 463 (RAAF) Squadron at Waddington, were both captured, the engineer after a cold, wet and wretched week living off potatoes and turnips.

Four other Lancasters were either in collision or shot down in that area the same night. Out of thirty-five aircrew only five survived, three of them rear gunners. The raid was not considered a success because heavy cloud over the target between 3,000 and 6,000ft prevented accurate bombing.

After the exploding and burning mass of the two Lancasters had disappeared into the cloud below, Dyson's despair for his friends turned towards self-preservation. While watching the blazing bombers he had been blown towards the target area. He pulled quickly on the parachute guide lines, praying he could avoid being caught in the probing beam of a searchlight. He gazed down at the burning city of Karlsruhe.

'It was like looking down on a carpet of gold with the chandelier flares suspended above, illuminating rivers of red from bursting incendiaries. The green sky markers winked intermittently with yellow and black smoke billowing skywards. I saw streams of multicoloured tracer shells bursting from the anti-aircraft guns and a series of explosions as sticks of high explosive bombs burst, sending red and yellow flames high into the air. With the searchlights stabbing the sky, it was an awesome spectacle. I had seen it many times before from the rear turret of a Lancaster bomber returning to England.'

Dyson suddenly realised his feet were frozen. He looked down, wiggled his toes and discovered his flying boots and socks had been sucked off as the bomber exploded. Worried thoughts crowded in on him. Was he injured? Had his face been burned? Were his legs and feet all right apart from being cold? He tasted blood, but felt gingerly around his face and could find no gaping wound. He dropped through broken cloud, becoming more aware of the rate of his descent and, despite the horror of the explosion, a curious sensation of exhilaration as he swayed and floated towards the ground.

The target area was now only visible as a diffused red glow and he glimpsed woods and snow-covered fields below. Dyson pulled on the guide lines to steer himself away from the woods and a cluster of buildings, praying for a safe landing. He was actually enjoying the descent when the earth rushed towards him and he landed with a bump in a frozen ploughed field. He tried to relax as he touched the ground, allowing his legs and body to go limp as he rolled over in the snow. He was dragged a few yards as the silk canopy collapsed, then waited a moment to catch his breath. He banged the release button for the harness to fall away and realised to his great joy that he was alive and had landed without breaking any bones. His watch had disappeared, but he believed it was about 1.00am. He quickly gathered up the parachute canopy and stumbled to a nearby spinney. He tore off strips of silk to bind up his bruised and freezing feet and buried the rest of the parachute beneath a pile of leaves and snow.

'I felt scared, cold, miserable and very much alone. I wondered about the rest of the crew and thanked God for my survival. I had again escaped death through incredible good fortune. I owed a great debt of gratitude to the WAAF who had packed my parachute, and to the Air Ministry order which instructed rear gunners to wear the seat-type parachute. So many in the past had perished because there was no time to collect their parachute from its storage inside the aircraft fuselage.'

Dyson's only injuries were slight burns to his hands and face, a scorched head of hair, and a few cuts and bruises. He was worried about his feet and wondered if he might scrounge some shoes before the German countryside woke up for its breakfast. He removed his yellow Taylor flying suit, very useful for being spotted by rescue aircraft after ditching in the sea, but the gunner would stand out like a beacon to Germans in the snow. He missed the warmth of the suit and reluctantly buried it under another blanket of leaves. Dyson checked to make sure he still had his escape pack with compass, silk map of the area, chocolate and foreign money, and wondered vaguely how far he was from the French border.

Dyson became increasingly concerned about his feet and the danger of frostbite and decided to abandon the shelter of the spinney to go in search of some shoes while it was still dark. Without the flying suit, the cold began eating into him and he became badly affected by delayed shock, blundering into ditches and hedges, falling over roots and stones. He wandered, shivering and disorientated, across a field, up to his knees in mud. Hearing in the distance dogs barking and whistles blowing, he assumed they were search parties looking for survivors of the crash.

It was a cold, grey dawn, and an exhausted Dyson just wanted to find somewhere to curl up and sleep. He saw a small barn in a farmyard. He stumbled into it, quietly closed the door, and began searching for something he could put on his torn and frozen feet. A minute later, the door burst open and Dyson met his first German, a soldier armed with a rifle and fixed bayonet which was pointed at him.

He was taken to a cottage and pushed into the kitchen, where there were two old women, looking as frightened as Dyson felt. Another soldier appeared and thrust him roughly against a wall. The two women seemed to be discussing his appearance. The heat of the kitchen was overpowering. He was dazed and weak, saturated, muddy and streaked with blood. Dyson made signs that he wanted to vomit and one of the women brought him a small slipper bath. She also gave him some socks and a pair of old shoes, which were far too big, but Dyson could have hugged her. She then gave him cubes of sugar flavoured with cinnamon, which warmed him and settled his stomach. After a brief interrogation by an officer who spoke very little English, he was hustled into a truck and driven to jail in the village of Ubstadt where he was questioned again before being locked into a damp underground cell without heat or light.

Later he was taken by lorry to the town of Bruchsal where he met Flight Sergeant Les Cromarty DFM, also of 189 Squadron, the rear gunner and only survivor of Lancaster PB743, which had crashed near Weingarten. He had also been blown from his turret. Fourteen Lancasters were lost on the Karlsruhe operation, four from 189 Squadron. All aircrews killed nearby that night, and who were buried in different villages, were later exhumed and interred in the British War Cemetery at Durnsbach, near Bad Tolz in Bavaria.

Dyson and Cromarty were put in separate cells and given a meal of black bread, sausage and rosewood tea. Then, to their amazement, they were both wrapped in paper bandages and liberally splashed with red ink, suggesting they were nursing serious wounds. They were tied on an open lorry and driven round Bruchsal and outlying villages, exhibited as the 'British Terror Bombers'. It was a terrifying experience to be hit by garbage and spat upon by people whom they had bombed the night before. After leaving the cottage where he was captured, Dyson had seen the corpses of American airmen, hanging by their necks from lamp-posts, and the two rear gunners believed they were going to their own execution.

Instead, they were taken to the cellar of another village jail. The walls dripped with water and they slept miserably on the floor, each wrapped in a single blanket. For three days they survived on a daily ration of one glass of water and boiled potatoes. Dyson complained about the state of his feet and, to his delight, was given a pair of suede, fur-lined flying boots. Then he saw the names inside them. One had belonged to his flight engineer, Jack Howarth, the other to Frank Fox, the mid-upper gunner.

For ten days, Dyson endured solitary confinement and frequent interrogation at Dulag Luft, Oberursel. Then came a long, hard journey south, on foot and in crowded, filthy railway cattle trucks across the shattered landscape of Germany until he reached Stalag VIIA at Moosburg, near Munich, on 15 April. American tanks rumbled into the camp fourteen days later. Dyson had shed three of his ten stones during an ordeal lasting more than twelve weeks. He arrived back in England on 11 May.

20

COOK'S TOUR TO DISASTER

A single Lancaster from 617 Squadron rumbled down the main runway at Woodhall Spa, scattering a few squawking rooks as it picked up speed. Few at the airbase saw the aircraft leave. None would see it return.

The bomber took off, its four Merlin engines on full power, and banked to the south-east before it began to climb. It was mid-morning on 16 May 1945. The war in Europe had been over eight days. For some, the peace was just as exciting, with none of the hassle.

The pilot of Lancaster PD139, YZ-W, was American Lieutenant Bill Adams who had been seconded to the RAF. Tall, broad, ruggedly handsome, a notorious ladies' man, with a smouldering smile, he was known to some in the officers' mess as the Errol Flynn of 617 Squadron. Adams took a deep breath and grinned to himself. He would be going home soon. Until then he could still have a good time. Why not? After a long war a chap needed to kick up his heels.

He seemed an unlikely pilot for the crack 617 Squadron. A milkman back in Boston, Massachusetts, he used to brag about the advantages of speed and reliability that America's electric floats had over plodding horses and carts still being used in some parts of Britain. Another eccentricity which set him apart from most pilots was his dis-interest in beer. He preferred to sit chatting with a pint of milk in his hand. He did share one preoccupation of aircrews. He was very fond of girls. He spent a good deal more time with his girlfriends than with his crew.

Adams was a fine pilot nonetheless, but at East Kirkby, on 630 Squadron, much to the horror of his crew, whose thirst for excitement had not matched their skipper's, he volunteered them to join 617 Squadron. After the successful dam busting raid in May 1943, Bomber Command believed 617 Squadron could handle all the dirty and danger-ous jobs. They were given a lot of them.

In addition to the normal seven-man crew on that fine May morning in 1945, the Lancaster carried three passengers, ground crew from Woodhall Spa – airmen who, at the height of the bombing, had often gone without sleep to keep their aircraft in the air. Without its dedicated groundcrews, Bomber Command would have ceased to function during the war.

As a special thank you for their efforts, hundreds of ground crews, both men and women, were flown across Germany to see the devastation inflicted by their bombers. These unarmed trips became known as Cook's Tours.

Adams looked down at the green rumpled eiderdown that was Lincolnshire's sprawling countryside and reflected on their very agreeable change of fortune. All bombing operations had come to an abrupt end and he wondered how they had managed to survive the war. Non-operational trips like this amounted to little more than a lighthearted Sunday afternoon putter in a motor boat round the bay. Adams was not complaining. He was fed up being another man's target. Life had suddenly become something he could rely upon. He'd had some hairy moments and considerable luck had helped him live through them. Often a split second, or an inch or two this way or that, decided who lived or died. A lot of his pals who had run out of luck were buried in foreign graveyards, poor bastards.

The Lancaster continued to climb gently as the pilot thought of the lucky moments. They included being shot down over Germany in the early days of the war when he was based at East Kirkby. He'd lost some of his crew, but not his nerve. Adams impetuously joined a crowd next day, which included grim-faced members of the SS, looking at the wreck of his aircraft. He was helped to escape from Germany, through France, Spain and across the Pyrenees, passing through the hands of several courageous partisan groups, whose members risked torture and execution by the Germans, until he made it safely back to East Kirkby.

The pilot's flight engineer, Flight Sergeant 'Swannee' Swann, short and cheerful, and eagerly looking forward to demob, was absorbed with his dials and warning lights.

Flight Sergeant Gill Pratt, the wireless operator, having survived a string of perilous bombing raids, would later die tragically from a brain tumour after the war at RAF Topcliffe, Yorkshire. The tumour developed after a fall down a flight of stairs.

The mid-upper turret had been removed from this special operations Lancaster. The bomber had been modified so it could carry the deep penetration 22,000lb Grand Slam bomb. Mid-upper gunner Flight Sergeant Fred Banham, a Rhodesian, sat on the rest bed. The rear gunner, with nothing to shoot at, was there to enjoy the ride and act as a loquacious guide to the passengers. Slim north Londoner Flight Sergeant 'Red' Scawthorne enjoyed the view from the rear turret. The freezing cold at 20,000-odd feet was but a shuddering memory. Scawthorne described his vulnerability to attack, stuck precariously on the tail.

There was no need for Scawthorne to exaggerate how lonely his turret had been as the Lancaster now flew across an empty sky. A very short time ago it had swarmed with predatory German fighters and been punctured by storms of flak. The loneliness was obvious to each of the visitors as they squeezed in turn into the rear turret, sat silently behind the Browning machine-guns and used their imagination.

Navigator Flying Officer Tom Collin, 29, from Levenshulme, Manchester, a veteran of 49 wartime operations, had already given his skipper a direct route to Hamburg. There was no need for a dog leg to confuse the enemy. The enemy had gone home or into prison camps, while many of its strutting high-ranking officers with fat Swiss bank accounts and the right connections, were being smuggled to comfortable new lives in South America. Consequently, there was no need for the Lancaster to climb very high – this was, after all, a sightseeing trip. The closer the Lancaster flew to the ground, the better the view.

Next to the pilot, the navigator was the most important member of an aircrew. They all depended on him to get them to the target on time and then safely home, as quickly as possible. If the bomber ran out of fuel or was badly shot up, it was his job to set course for the nearest friendly airfield. Collin had been an industrial photographer in Civvy Street, enjoying cycling and Scouting. A short, stocky bustling man of 5ft 4in, he worked busily and meticulously at his navigator's table. On the side of the fuselage was an air speed indicator and an altimeter. On his left stood the Gee box, which picked up two crossed bearings from different air bases. They enabled him to plot their position very accurately. He considered himself a bloody good navigator whose efficiency had help keep them out of trouble.

On Collin's right stood the bulky Loran H2S radar which had the obvious advantage of carrying pictures on its screen, giving the shape of the coastline or that of a densely packed town. Collin had used it with great success at night, mine-laying from 50ft in the Skagerrak straits, south of Norway.

There was a lot of equipment: charts, maps and his flight plan, carefully worked out earlier that morning, spread neatly over the table, with dividers, protractor, course and speed calculators, India rubber and pencils, all carefully fastened down with bits of string in case the bomber needed to suddenly dive away from an attacking fighter. No navigator wanted to spend time grovelling on the floor of the fuselage in near dark for pencil and dividers. Time was precious. Lost seconds could lose lives. They had encountered their last aggressive fighter, but Collin had not yet been persuaded to untie his instruments.

'I never felt any uneasiness going on ops. I just accepted that if I got the chop I got the chop and that was it. You're resigned to it and had to detach yourself from death, danger and terrible injury. Baling out was a lesser evil, but I didn't think about that, either. On this cross-country Cook's Tour, I thought I had made it. We all did.'

As usual, Collin had been the last to board the aeroplane that morning. It was one of his habits and he still hated tempting fate. He also always made sure he emptied his bowels before an op. Such fastidiousness nearly caused him untold grief at East Kirkby one night as he sat on the wooden seat, casually lighting his pipe. He dropped the match between his thighs into the pan, set fire to the paper and rose with a mighty yell as flames licked at his backside and balls.

His rituals were strung together like charms on a bracelet, although some were rejected after they had been found to be flawed. A friendly Land Army girl gave him one of her green pullovers for ops, but both times he wore it the bomber was badly shot up by fighters, so on future trips it was left behind in the mess.

Collin always wore one sock inside-out. He didn't know why. Perhaps one night they returned from a gruelling trip and he discovered that, accidentally, he had put one on the wrong way round. A lucky sock should not be ignored. Aircrews needed all the luck they could find, and Collin needed his inside-out sock, even on this pedestrian Cook's Tour.

The bomber casually crossed the North Sea and lumbered brazenly over the Dutch coast, near Ijmuiden at no more than 3,000ft. He had more time to think that morning without sudden death waiting in the next cloud. He thought with great fondness of the 7hp Austin Ruby, EGP41, back at Woodhall Spa. He had bought the car at a give-away price of £15 from an insurance agent who admired the work he was doing as a bomber's navigator. He made a handsome profit on the hard-working Ruby after the war when he sold it to a man in Lincoln for an astonishing £120.

Collin was enterprising enough to be able to stretch his aircrew's petrol allowance. At an Air Ministry building in Woburn Place, London, he discovered that he could obtain petrol without anyone stamping his logbook. At Stickney, near East Kirkby, there was a garage where farmers used to leave plenty of free petrol coupons for the aircrews. And Collin was not the only car driver at Woodhall Spa who was aware that 100 octane fuel used in Lancasters could be mixed satisfactorily with red hydraulic oil and used in a small car, without damaging the engine. Seven of them, including the bulky 6ft 2in pilot, had several times squeezed into the little four-seater for the drive to a dance in Horncastle.

Collin also had time to think about the pals who had not made it to the end of the war. Confined to bed in Boston, Lincolnshire, with German measles, his first crew had flown on their second operation on 21 May 1944 to Duisberg with a spare navigator, after kidding him that his blotches looked like real swastikas. When Collin returned to base at East Kirkby, twelve miles north of Boston, he went straight to the crew room to find them. He was told they had been shot down on their return over Holland. There were no survivors. Although the odds were heavily stacked against an aircrew surviving the war, Collin was stunned to hear that all his crew had bought it while he lay comfortably in a hospital bed. After flying for a while with another pilot he joined Bill Adams.

Lancaster PD139, YZ-W, descended slowly to 1,000ft. Germany was stretched out below, a cowering conquered beast, which had long ago lost its taste for war. No one spoke as the crew gazed in awe at a country they had only seen burning at night, never by day, and never so close. For their passengers it was their first sight of Germany in war or peace.

After so many years of grinding war, it was difficult not to experience the vice-like tightness within the stomach, the dry mouth, the chilling knowledge that each breath might be your last, while swirling, disconnected thoughts reached desperately out across land and sea to family and friends. Adrenaline still pumped urgent messages to the brain compelling each member of the crew to perform his given task smoothly and without question, while minutes of numbing uncertainty stretched into hours.

Even now their eyes automatically searched the ground for signs of flak being pumped up at them, and peered into the blue spring sky for lurking German fighters, eager to turn them into pulp to join thousands of RAF aircrews already in their graves. There were no fighters, no flak. It seemed too good to be true. They found themselves imagining the flak and the fighters all round them, preparing to react with loud cries to the skipper to corkscrew to safety or snatch up their Browning machine-guns to fire at a pouncing Bf110 or FW190.

The sky remained tantalisingly empty, just them and the Lancaster which had brought them safely through at least fifteen ops. It was a curious feeling, almost like disappointment, but that would be madness after all they had been through.

During ops Collin had been cocooned behind curtains in his little navigator's office, which had no window. Now all he could see through a smudged fuselage window was a bleak and battered landscape, which appeared to have been abandoned by mankind. No large town had escaped the wrath of the Allies. The larger the town, the greater the destruction. Although it had been a case of 'them or us' none of these young men found much pleasure in seeing what they had done. The destruction was on such a vast scale.

Recalling Wesel, Collin says, 'It was a town on high ground. It had been razed to the ground, an amazing sight. The ground forces had shelled it, with the RAF bombing at night and the Americans during the day. German troops had been here in some numbers. It was them we had been bombing.'

Nothing appeared to be moving anywhere. How could Germany ever recover from this? One of the three ground crew staring open-mouthed through the windows, a flight sergeant, was half-way through a letter to his son. He read out a bit to the navigator: 'We have just flown over a scene which is the result of man's greed and degradation'. Collin shrugged, unable to think of an apt comment.

Even Collin's best friend, Flight Lieutenant Robert Foulkes, was unable to find words to adequately describe his feelings as they approached the obliterated city of Hamburg which, on the horizon, looked like a monstrous crushed graveyard. Foulkes, the bomb-aimer, a refined young man, stood out from the rest of the crew. An antique dealer from Exeter, his passion for long case and bracket clocks compelled him to spend a good deal of his off-duty time peering in the windows of old houses, and scouring Lincolnshire's antique shops for bargains.

He and Collin shared a turret room above the front door at the officers' mess which occupied the Petwood Hotel in Woodhall Spa, nearly three miles from the airfield. A fine old writing desk stood in the corner of the room. It had been carried back triumphantly in Foulkes' Morris 8 Tourer after a successful hunt through Woodhall Spa with Collin.

Foulkes' greatest fear was that Simon, a large dirty white poodle, might cock his leg against the valuable desk. Simon had been left in their safe keeping by Wing Commander Leonard Cheshire VC, former commander of 617 Squadron, who had been posted from Woodhall Spa in July 1944, after his one-hundedth operational trip. During the day Simon ran wild in the town, deflowering as many on-heat bitches as he could find, before returning to the mess to sleep soundly on the best sofa. More easily supervised were the goldfish which Cheshire had entrusted to Kitty, one of the mess waitresses.

No one knew what caused the streak of madness which prompted Bill Adams to fly in low tight circles around the Rathaus (town hall) which stood gloomily among the ruins of Hamburg, destroyed by Bomber Command. Perhaps it was immense relief at the end of the war, and growing jubilation that he would soon be returning to his home and family in the States. Adams suddenly murmured over the intercom, 'I'm going to have a mosey around'.

Collin remembers: 'Bill was not an impulsive man. He was normally an absolute stickler for rules and regulations. But he threw them all out of the window that day. I remember seeing the big tall end of a building still standing amidst the rubble. A pre-war advertisement was painted on it – "Rinso". They would have needed a good deal of Rinso to clean up this shattered city.'

They didn't see another aircraft, being piloted sedately and much higher across the rubble of Hamburg. But its pilot saw them, flying so low that the Lancaster almost merged into its own shadow. The pilot above them was a group captain, who was so angered by Adams's antics that he reported the incident when he returned to Coningsby, having identified the bomber as the only special duty Lancaster flying over Hamburg that day. It was one thing to have dropped thousands of tons of bombs to destroy a German city in wartime. It most certainly was not the act of an officer and a gentleman to rub the Germans' bloody noses into the mire right after their surrender.

Adams's frolicsome mood had not been totally spent. Brunswick passed without incident, then half-way to Hannover, Adams noticed the bent figures of several dozen women working in the fields near the village of Oberg. He found their upturned bottoms irresistible. He switched on the intercom and said, with a sinister edge to his voice, 'I'm going to give those Krauts such a scare it'll really put the shits up them'.

Bobby Foulkes had left the bomb-aimer's position in the nose and was sitting on a spar. He looked across at Collin, his face sagging with apprehension, and said 'Oh my God, what's he going to do now?'. Good and bad moments of the war flashed through the mind of Collin. The future which that morning had seemed so bright and promising was surely about to end in the most terrible anti-climax.

The great Lancaster dived to 20ft and roared over the terrified German women who dropped to the ground in heaps of floundering clothes. 'Sorry chaps,' growled Adams apologetically, pulling up for a steep turn, 'I wasn't properly lined up. I'll go round again.'

Collin had lived through nearly fifty operations and numerous passing encounters with death. He regarded himself as one of the war's lucky survivors. Life was good and at last the future beckoned with a smile. They no longer had to take chances. But now, on a Cook's Tour, his bloody pilot was gleefully and deliberately prising open the jaws of death.

The Lancaster roared over the fields towards the scattering women – lower, lower and lower. Adams's crew gazed out of the windows in stunned disbelief. Collin saw a number of long trenches and thought they might have been planting potatoes. The women's mouths were open, their horrified screams obliterated by the Lancaster's roaring engines.

If the aircraft had been absolutely level they might have got away with it, suffering no more than a mild dose of the jitters, before flying on to Hannover. By this time the pilot's skylarking might have been spent as he looked forward to a good lunch and a night out with the latest girlfriend. But the starboard wing was too low.

The bomber hit the ground with an earsplitting crash, crumpling the propellers and smashing both starboard engines, which immediately caught fire. Adams's big, powerful hands hauled on the control column with all his might trying to lift the fatally wounded Lancaster, its port engines roaring, 100ft over a small copse, but he was unable to regain any kind of control. The aircraft crashed into the next field. It slithered and crunched along on its broken belly, raising a bigger storm of dust than a herd of stampeding buffaloes.

Shocked, the aircrew clung to anything that was not sliding around. The even more shocked ground crew were considerably bounced about, confirming their recent regret at leaving the safety of Woodhall Spa for the insanity of a Cook's Tour. They would not thank the crew for the spectacle which had been laid on for them. The philosophical flight sergeant reminded himself to add a venomous postscript to his son's letter.

The main dinghy burst out of its compartment in the starboard wing with a violent detonation, inflated itself and hung towards the ground like a grotesque orange carbuncle. The navigator's maps, charts and flight plan, slithered to the floor while everything else on the table jiggled from a dozen pieces of string. Collin recalls the confusion:

'It was a mad scramble to get out. There was a very real danger that the aircraft might explode in a ball of flames. Men dived through every escape hatch they could find. I suddenly found my foot was trapped fast underneath my seat. Seconds passed as I tugged, wondering whether to leave my shoe, before I managed to wiggle my foot free, half expecting the aeroplane to catch fire with me inside. Death by incineration on a Cook's Tour would have been a shocking waste of a life. I jumped through an escape hatch on the port side. We all got out safely, then found both fires had fortunately been put out by the earth that had sprayed over the aircraft.'

They stood in a ragged self-conscious group staring at the wrecked Lancaster with a feeling of foolishness and relief as American Jeeps bounced towards them at high speed across the field. The Yanks were dumbfounded to find a fellow-countryman had been at the controls of the crumpled Lancaster.

Bomb-aimer Robert Foulkes, who minutes earlier had been convinced he was going to die, probably summed up what everyone was thinking about their pilot. 'Stupid, bloody sod!' Afterwards, Bill Adams, scratching his head, was to exclaim without a great deal of conviction, or raising a single laugh, 'Goddammit! I've always liked chopping the tops off German corn with the props, but how was I to know the bloody crop was backward this year?'

In the back of the crashed aircraft were cardboard boxes packed with eggs which had not yet been removed after an aborted mission of mercy to starving refugees. They had been turned into what was potentially the world's largest omelette. The smashed eggs were claimed as legitimate salvage by the Americans who immediately put a guard on the Lancaster to prevent hungry Germans sneaking into the wrecked bomber.

The Americans later kicked two German families out of their cottages in Oberg so the Lancaster aircrew could move in for the night. Their passengers were accommodated elsewhere in the village. Collin remembers:

'Steam from the cattle below reached us through the cracks in the floorboards as we slept. We were driven to Celle, a former Luftwaffe base, next day to pick up a Dakota for Brussels. The driver slowed down as we approached Belsen. Prisoners, no more than bundles of rags, shuffled by on either side of us. At Celle there was a terrific assortment of beautiful cars which had belonged to German aircrews.

'Another Dakota took us from Brussels to Hendon where we were handed over as distressed aircrew and spent the night there. We had a medical and were each given a medicine bottle full of brandy and ten bob (50p) to spend in the mess, before a Lancaster was brought in next day from Woodhall Spa to fly us back to base.'

Bill Adams was unaware that he had been reported for misbehaving over Hamburg. He told the court of inquiry that he had experienced trouble with the controls, but his explanation was not accepted. Adams was posted to Waddington where he was presented with a DFC before flying back home to Boston. He later became a professor of economics at a university in Quebec. Remembered by his wartime pals for sparkling good humour and robust health, Adams was only thirty-four when he died of cancer in 1956.

Tom Collin settled in Grantham, Lincolnshire, within easy reach of Woodhall Spa and East Kirkby. Collin, who had vowed never to go up in an aeroplane again, returned to his job of industrial photographer, flying all over the world. He made sure that on each assignment one sock was always worn inside out.

BIBLIOGRAPHY

M. Middlebrook and C. Everitt, *The Bomber Commander War Diaries, An Operational Reference Book, 1939–1945* (Viking, 1985)

E. C. Weal, J. A. Weal and R. F. Barker, *Combat Aircraft of World War Two* (Arms & Armour Press, 1977)

Jane's Fighting Aircraft of World War II (Studio Editions, 1992)

M. Middlebrook, *The Peenemünde Raid, The Night of 17–18 August 1943* (Allen Lane, 1982)

B. B. Halpenny, *Action Stations 2: Military Airfields of Lincolnshire and the East Midlands*, second edition (Patrick Stephens Ltd, 1991)

R. G. Low & F. E. Harper, *83 Squadron 1917–1969* (R. G. Low, 1992)

INDEX